Hélène Adeline Guerber

Legends of the Rhine

Hélène Adeline Guerber

Legends of the Rhine

ISBN/EAN: 9783337155612

Printed in Europe, USA, Canada, Australia, Japan

Cover: Foto ©Thomas Meinert / pixelio.de

More available books at **www.hansebooks.com**

LEGENDS OF THE RHINE

BY

H. A. GUERBER

AUTHOR OF "MYTHS OF GREECE AND ROME," "MYTHS OF NORTHERN LANDS," "CONTES ET LÉGENDES," "MÄRCHEN AND ERZÄHLUNGEN," ETC., ETC.

NEW YORK

A. S. BARNES & CO.

1895

CONTENTS.

LIST OF ILLUSTRATIONS.

THE RHINE SONG.

THE Rhine! That little word will be
For aye a spell of power to me,
And conjure up, in care's despite,
A thousand visions of delight:
The Rhine! Oh! where beneath the sun
Doth our fair river's rival run?
Where dawns the day upon a stream
Can in such changeful beauty shine
Outstripping Fancy's wildest dream,
Like our green, glancing, glorious Rhine.

Born where blooms the Alpine rose,
Cradled in the Bodensee,
Forth the infant river flows,
Leaping on in childish glee.
Coming to a riper age,
He crowns his rocky cup with wine,
And makes a gallant pilgrimage
To many a ruined tower and shrine.
Strong, and swift, and wild, and brave,
On he speeds with crested wave;
And spurning aught like check or stay,
Fights and foams along his way
O'er crag and shoal until his flood
Boils like manhood's hasty blood.

—*Lays and Legends of the Rhine.—Planché.*

PREFACE.

THIS book is intended as a contribution to the study of Folklore, and as a Legendary Guide to the Rhine. The Tales have been gathered from many sources, and while *all* the Rhine traditions are not recorded here, the principal ones have been given.

As Teutonic Mythology has been outlined in "Myths of Northern Lands," it has not been included in this volume. The real "Nibelungenlied" and the "Heldensagen" have also been omitted because they form part of the author's work on the "Legends of the Middle Ages."

While countless German authorities have been consulted with great care, the author feels particularly indebted to Mr. Karl Simrock, the German Folk-lorist and Poet of the Rhine, who has versified many of these picturesque tales.

The interest of a Rhine pilgrimage is more than doubled by a knowledge, however superficial, of the legends connected with the principal towns, churches, and castles along its banks, so it is hoped that tourists, old and young, will find room in pocket or satchel for this collection.

The book is sent out into the world with a sincere hope that it may enhance the pleasure of travelers and enable stay-at-homes to glean some idea of the legendary charms of this matchless river.

INTRODUCTION.

THE Rhine takes its source in the St. Gothard mountain in Switzerland, nearly eight thousand feet above the sea, and after an impetuous rush through rocky passes and dark forests, lingers, as if to gain new strength, in the peaceful bosom of Lake Constance.

The mighty river, still in its youth, is only tarrying, however. It has not forgotten its mission, and soon resumes its course, plunging down headlong over the rocky wall at Schaffhausen, hurrying past village and town, boldly leaping all the stumbling blocks which strew its path, and bounding on without a moment's pause.

On the way, many an Alpine stream, foaming in its haste, comes to give a new impetus to its tide. Then, at Basel, the Rhine takes a sudden bend northward, leaves Switzerland, and wends its sinuous way through the German Fatherland. Now hastening, now seeming to rest in some quiet bay, it flows on, until, swollen by the waters of many tributaries, it enters Holland and slowly and majestically rolls its heavy waters toward the sea.

Like many other streams of its magnitude, the Rhine divides near its mouth, separates like the fingers of a hand, and drains off its waters through five principal channels. The most northerly of these branches joins the Yssel and empties into the Zuyder Zee, which was formed by a terrible inundation in the thirteenth century. A canal called the Kromme Rhein, the Waal, which unites with the Maas, and the Lek, draw off the remainder of its waters, which are finally lost in the North Sea, after a journey of about eight hundred miles, accomplished in two hundred and twenty-seven hours.

Varied as the scenery along its banks are the numerous legends connected with every point of interest. These traditions, which form a large part of the German Folk-lore, sung by poets of various times and nations, preserved in many volumes of ancient and modern lore, have been carefully collected, and will here be narrated in their natural sequence as we go up the mighty river.

LEGENDS OF THE RHINE.

STAVOREN.

The Sunken City.

WHERE the waves of the Zuyder Zee now roll, there was once, according to tradition, a blooming and prosperous tract of land, and on the very spot where fishermen now anchor their boats to cast their nets, there rose a beautiful city, carefully protected from the ever-encroaching sea by massive dikes.

The inhabitants of Stavoren, for such was the name of this town, were very wealthy indeed; so wealthy in fact that they paved their banqueting halls with shining ducats. But, in spite of their prosperity, they were selfish, hard-hearted, and neglectful of the poor.

The richest among them was a maiden lady, who had counting houses, farms, palaces, and fleets, but whose sole thought, night and day, was how she might further increase her possessions. With this purpose in view, she once summoned the captain of her largest vessel, bade him sail away and return within a year's time, with a cargo of the most precious and best of all earthly substances. In vain the captain questioned her to know exactly what she wished; she merely repeated her order with peremptory emphasis, and haughtily dismissed him.

Forced to set sail at a venture, the captain left Stavoren, but, not knowing in what direction to steer his course, he consulted officers and crew. As each man had a different opinion concerning the most precious and best of all earthly substances, however, they only increased his perplexity. After much reflection, and the smoking of many a pipe, the Dutch captain concluded that nothing could be more precious than wheat, the staff of life. He purchased a cargo of the finest grain at Dantzic, and returned joyfully to Stavoren, where he arrived long before the year was ended. The lady, in the meanwhile, had duly informed all her friends that her vessel had gone in search of a cargo of the best and most precious of all earthly things, and as she would not even confide to her most intimate friend what that might be, public curiosity was fully aroused.

But when her captain suddenly appeared before her, and informed her that he had brought a cargo of wheat, her complacency vanished. She flew into a terrible rage, and ordered that every kernel should immediately be cast into the sea. In vain the captain expostulated, and entreated that, since she did not want the wheat, it should be given to the poor; she reiterated her commands, declaring she would come down to the port in person, to make sure they were properly executed. Sadly retracing his steps to the vessel, the captain met several beggars, told them a cargo of wheat was about to be thrown away, and by the time the lady reached the dock, the poor had assembled there from all parts of the city, in hopes of securing the despised grain.

In spite of their imploring cries, however, the haughty lady made the sailors cast all the wheat into the sea, while the captain, powerless to hinder this sinful waste, looked on in impotent rage. The last kernel had vanished beneath the turbid waters, when he turned to his august mistress and cried: "As surely as there is a God above us, you will be punished for this sin, and the time may come when you, the wealthiest lady in Stavoren, will long for a few handfuls of this despised and squandered wheat."

The lady listened to these words in contemptuous silence, slowly drew a costly ring from her white hand, cast it into the sea, and coolly declared that, when she saw it again, she might perchance credit his words, and believe it possible that *she* should come to want.

That self-same evening, in preparing a fresh fish for dinner, the cook found the costly ring, which he immediately sent to his proud mistress. She became very pale indeed when she recognized it. A few moments later, bearers of ill-tidings came rushing in, to report in quick succession the ruin of her counting houses, the destruction of her fleet, the burning of her palaces, and the devastation of her farms. In the course of a few hours she found herself shorn of all her wealth, for her own dwelling burned down to the ground during the night, and she barely escaped with her life.

Now that her money was gone, the rich of Stavoren refused to recognize her, and the poor, who had met with nothing but contempt and ill-treatment at her hands, allowed her to die of hunger and cold in a miserable shed. This sudden downfall, and the signal punishment of the haughty lady, did not produce any effect at all upon the other rich people of Stavoren, who continued to enjoy life as before, and to neglect their fellow-creatures; so a second warning was vouchsafed them. Little by little they heard that the port was becoming impracticable, owing to the rapid increase of a sand-bar, which soon rose above the waters, hindering all further commerce. This sand-bank was soon covered with luxuriant verdure. The people, gazing upon it, called it "The Lady's Sand," and declared the vegetation upon it had sprouted from the great quantity of wheat cast into the sea.

But, in spite of its rapid growth, this wheat bore no fruit, and while the rich cared but little for the cessation of all traffic, the poor suffered more sorely still, for now they were even deprived of the small pay they had received for their work of loading and unloading vessels. The second warning had also fallen upon deaf ears and been exhibited before unseeing eyes, yet Providence granted the rich another reprieve, and vouchsafed them a third and last warning.

A little leak was discovered in the dike, through which the sea, filtering into the city reservoir, rendered its waters unpalatable. Laughingly the rich people vowed they would drink champagne, since water could not be obtained, but when the thirsty poor crowded around their gates, imploring a sup of beer, they rudely dismissed them, declaring it would be well were they actually to die of thirst, as they said they should.

This last heartless refusal filled the measure of their iniquities. That self-same night, when the last reveler had sunk into a profound sleep, the sea noiselessly finished the work of destruction, broke down the dikes, and, bursting over Stavoren, submerged the whole town.

Over the spot where it once stood the waves now ripple in the sunlight, or are thrashed into foam by the cold winds sweeping down from the north. Boatmen, rowing out from the dilapidated little fishing town which alone now bears the name of the ancient city, sometimes rest upon their oars, when the waters are smooth and clear, to point out, far beneath them, the palaces, turrets, and ramparts of Stavoren.

The streets, once so populous (thirty thousand inhabitants are reported to have perished during this inundation), are deserted, the market-place empty. No sound is heard save when an inquisitive pike or herring, swimming though the tall belfries, accidentally strikes one of the bells with its flopping tail, and sets it slowly vibrating in the depths of the sea, where it seems to be mournfully tolling the knell of the sunken city.*

* See Note in Appendix.

HAGUE.

The Beggar's Curse.

The Countess of Henneberg, a wise and thrifty woman, was always busy from morning until night. Thanks to her exertions and strict economy, her house was the wealthiest and the best regulated in all the land, and her servants and dependents lacked nothing. In exchange for her care, the countess exacted from them all a close account of their time, and kept them in a state of constant activity.

After portioning out the daily tasks and carefully inspecting her household, she always resorted to the great hall, where all her maids sat spinning, and here, while watching and directing their labors, her own wheel hummed unceasingly.

One morning the aged porter entered the spinning room, and approaching his mistress, respectfully informed her that a poor woman craved a hearing.

"Again, Jan!" exclaimed the countess in displeasure. "How many times must I tell you that I will not encourage begging? Why does not the woman work? Does she expect to eat her bread in idleness? Wait, I shall dismiss her myself!" she suddenly added, as she rose from her seat, and checked her whirling wheel. Giving a sharp glance around the room, and issuing a distinct command to waste no precious time in idle conversation, the countess left the room and hurried along the echoing hall to the great door, where the poor woman anxiously awaited her.

"Nothing to eat!" exclaimed the countess, glancing contemptuously at the poor woman, standing before her with a bundle of clean but threadbare garments on either arm, and slowly repeating her last words. "You must work, my good woman. Only those who earn their bread by the sweat of their brow have any right to eat."

"But, noble lady, I cannot work; the children are so

small they need all my care," cried the poor woman, parting the rags and showing the pale, pinched faces of two puny, new-born babes. "And last week, only last week, gracious lady, my poor husband was drowned."

"What!" cried the countess, who, at the sight of the babies, had started back in dismay. "Two children, twins! What business have you, a beggar, to have children?"

"Gracious lady!" cried the poor woman, "the Lord sent me these children, and now I cannot bear to hear them cry. Help me, lady, help me."

"My good woman," said the countess reprovingly, and without paying any heed to her appeal, "the Lord surely had nothing to do with those children. Do you suppose He would send two children at once to a poor woman like you, who have not the means to feed even one? No, no, the Lord has more sense. The Evil One must have sent you those."

"The Evil One, lady!" cried the indignant mother, clasping her babies closer still. "It was the Lord sent them, and I trust he will one day send you as many as there are days in the year. Then, lady, when you hear them cry you will understand perhaps what a mother feels."

With tears coursing down her pale face, the woman turned and slowly left the castle, while the countess, feeling she had wasted too many precious moments in listening to her complaints, hastened back to her wheel. At the sound of her step, accompanied by the jingle of the keys she always wore at her girdle, the merry maids immediately stopped their innocent chatter, and when the countess entered the room the shining heads were all diligently bending over the flying wheels, whose hum filled the great hall.

But no matter how fast the lady drove her own wheel, it seemed to echo the words which kept ringing in her ear: "May the Lord send you as many children as there are days in the year." Day after day, week after week, month after month, the prophecy haunted her, and her servants shook their heads, as she daily became more querulous and exacting.

But a day came at last when all the spinning wheels in the great hall stood motionless, when the stools before them remained unoccupied, and when, instead of a busy hum, wailing cries echoed throughout the castle. In answer to the beggar woman's prayer, the Lord had sent three hundred and sixty-five infants at one birth to the hard-hearted countess. In vain she wept and wrung her hands, the babes were hers and she could not disown them. But, terrified at the thought of the new duties imposed upon her, driven almost frantic by the children's cries, and especially appalled at the vision of the havoc which so many busy hands and feet would make in her orderly household, the noble Countess of Henneberg fell back upon her pillows and breathed her last.

The three hundred and sixty-five children were strong and healthy, so Count Henneberg decreed they should be carried to the church and duly baptized; but as the exertion required to supply them with individual names would have been too great, he decided that all the boys should bear the name of John and all the girls that of Elizabeth.

This christening, the largest on record, was performed wholesale, and the basin used for the ceremony has ever since been exhibited as a curiosity, in one of the principal churches of Hague.

The Henneberg children faithfully kept their baptismal vow, led pure and blameless lives, and their virtues soon endeared them to all their people.

Periodically they went in solemn procession to visit the countess' grave, which can still be seen about one mile outside of the city of Hague; and as they marched along, their three hundred and sixty-five voices joined in a pious litany for the rest of their high-born mother's soul.

FRIESLAND.

The Christening of a King.

RADBOD was King of the Frisians when the first missionaries, braving every danger, boldly penetrated into his wild and barren country, to preach Christianity, and bring good tidings to the heathen.

Such was the persuasive eloquence of these pious men, that they finally prevailed upon Radbod himself to receive baptism, without which, they solemnly averred, he would never be able to enter the kingdom of heaven.

Their glowing descriptions of Christ's baptism in the Jordan fired the king's imagination to such an extent, that he declared he too would be baptized in a river, and selected for that purpose the mighty Rhine, which bounded his kingdom on the south. Accompanied by bishop and priest, and attended by many valiant warriors who were to receive the sacrament at the same time, King Radbod marched down to the Rhine.

The waves were rippling round his feet, and the bishop's hand was already raised, when a last doubt invaded the royal mind.

"Stay thy hand, oh, bishop!" he cried. "Before I am baptized I would fain ask one more question. Tell me, bishop, tell me, where are all my ancestors, who fought so bravely, ruled so wisely, and nobly died on the field of battle? Tell me, bishop, where are they?"

"Oh, king," answered the bishop gravely, "thy ancestors were heathens; as heathens they lived, and as heathens they died. Without baptism they could not enter the kingdom of heaven."

"Bishop, you have already told me that!" exclaimed Radbod impatiently, his royal eyebrows contracting in displeasure. "But tell me, if not in heaven, where are they?"

"In hell," solemnly answered the bishop. "Thy forefathers, being heathens, have gone to hell!"

"To hell!" vociferated King Radbod, springing out of the water, and seizing the great sword he had flung down upon the grass. "To hell! You villain! Dastardly priest! How dare you say my ancestors have gone to hell? They were brave and noble men, they lived honorably, and died without fear. I would rather—yes, by their god, the great Woden, I swear—I would ten thousand times rather join those heroes in their hell, than be with you in your heaven of priests!"

And turning his back scornfully upon the astonished bishop, Radbod brandished his sword above his head and bade his brave warriors follow him back into the wild forests, there to continue worshiping, in peace, the rude gods of their worthy ancestors.*

GERTRUIDENBERG.

Story of St. Gertrude.

On the left bank of the Waal, not very far from its mouth, is a slight elevation of land, known as the Gertruidenberg, which owes its name to the following tradition:

A brave and loyal Netherland knight fell deeply in love with a maiden, so good, and pure, and lovely, that the grateful poor, in addressing her, always prefixed the title of saint to her baptismal name of Gertrude. The maiden could not but acknowledge her suitor was handsome, brave, and worthy of being loved, but still her heart remained unmoved by all his passionate entreaties. Convinced that she could never return his love, and resolved to put an end to his misery, she finally announced her determination to enter a convent, and there spend the rest of her life in the service of the Lord.

* See "Myths of Northern Lands."

When at last the irrevocable vows had all been taken, and the convent doors had opened wide to receive her; when the white coif and black veil had covered her shapely head, the poor knight, deprived of her sweet society, found life utterly unendurable, and decided to leave the land where every sight and sound constantly reminded him of his lost love and bitter disappointment.

The castles and broad acres he had vainly laid at her feet, the wealth he had hoarded for her to scatter with lavish hands, all his rich inheritance, he gave to her convent; reserving nothing for himself except his noble steed and oft-tried armor. Then, in the gray light of early dawn, he slowly rode toward the convent, cast a despairing glance up at the latticed casement, and breathed his last farewell.

A moment later, startled by the prick of his master's spurs, the noble steed started off with a bound, and soon bore the heart-broken knight far out of sight of his ancestral home and of the old convent walls. All day long he rode straight onward, sunk in mournful meditation, and only when night began to fall did he raise his head and begin to look about him for shelter and food. But, although he peered anxiously about through the gathering gloom, he could not discern the trace of any path or dwelling upon the bleak moorland. Hour after hour he wandered on, hoping to find a place where his weary, stumbling steed might rest, when suddenly a dimly outlined figure appeared before him, and the midnight silence was broken by a voice saying:

"Pause, oh, knight; do not despair! I know your sorrow and would fain allay it. If you will only pledge me your soul—wealth, honor, prosperity, and all the joys of your lost youth shall fall to your lot."

The low, insinuating tones, the tempting offer, the terrible condition attached to it, and a faint odor of sulphur and brimstone diffused over the moorland, enabled the knight to recognize his interlocutor in spite of the pitchy darkness.

Disappointed lovers have often professed to be utterly indifferent whether his Satanic Majesty take possession of them or not; and this feeling, which is said to be quite common in our enlightened age, was already in the fashion in early times, and prompted the despondent knight to answer:

"'Tis a bargain, Satan. Give me wealth and honor, grant me success in arms, and my soul is yours."

"Good!" exclaimed the figure shrouded in darkness. "Name the number of years you would live, sign this pledge, and all shall be as you wish."

A year, in youth and love, seems almost endless. The knight, who was still very young, and whose love was utterly hopeless, quickly concluded that seven years would allow him time enough to taste to the dregs the few joys which remained for him, and to grow quite weary of life.

"Seven years and no more! Seven years will suffice!" he cried, as he signed the pledge with his life-blood and sealed it with his armorial ring.

He was about to depart, when the Evil One cried:

"Remember, oh, knight, when the seven years are over, and the twelfth hour of the last night has come, I shall await you here, on the lonely moorland, to claim your soul."

"The word of a knight is inviolable, even when given to such as you!" proudly answered the knight. "In seven years, at midnight, I shall be here, but until then I am free."

A moment later, the sound of his horse's galloping hoofs died away, the sulphurous odor vanished, and the lonely moorland lay still, cold, and deserted.

From court to court the knight now wandered, scattering with lavish generosity the wealth which Satan provided without stint, and wherever he went, his astounding deeds of valor won him the warmest praise. No matter how brave his opponent, he was always victor in the fight, and taught the proudest heads to bow at his lady's name.

In jousts, pageants, and tournaments the years passed by all too quickly, and, as the seventh neared its end, the knight was troubled in spirit. The longing to see his beloved once more before he met his self-imposed doom finally brought him back to the Netherlands, and guided his steps to the banks of the mighty river. The sight of the familiar convent walls brought hot tears to his eyes, and made his heart beat fast with anxiety. What if that roof no longer sheltered Gertrude? What if another now occupied the tiny cell and gazed out of the latticed window?

These thoughts caused him so much emotion that it was only with the utmost difficulty that he managed to make the portress understand him.

What was not his joy and relief, therefore, when he heard that Gertrude was still there, the light and hope of the convent, and the guardian angel of all the poor.

Admitted into her presence, the gentle tones of her beloved voice ringing in his ear, and her sweet eyes fixed in pity upon him, the unfortunate knight fell upon his knees, and penitently confessed the story of his midnight encounter, of the seven years of aimless, wandering life, and his longing to behold her once more ere he went to meet his fate.

"And now, beloved, farewell!" he cried, as he staggered to his feet to leave her presence. "At midnight, on the lonely moorland, I must meet my doom. Farewell!"

Gertrude, who with dilated eyes and pallid cheeks had listened to his tale, sprang forward and cried:

"Stop, sir knight! Before you leave me you must drink this," and the little hands trembled as she poured some wine into a cup and handed it to him. "Drink! With the blessing of my holy patron St. John, and under the safeguard of my love, it will surely enable you to return." *

The knight took the cup from her hand, and, mournfully gazing into her beautiful eyes, exclaimed:

* See Note 2 in Appendix.

"I drink to you, O Gertrude! The only prayer I am worthy to utter is, 'God bless you.'"

A moment later he had gone to keep his midnight tryst. Darkness rested upon the moorland, and his charger slowly stumbled on. The fatal hour had come. Satan, who in spite of his numerous other failings has never yet been known to miss an appointment, appeared before him as suddenly as on the previous occasion, but instead of pouncing upon him, cried in evident terror:

"Pause, oh, knight; I beseech you, pause! I will give you back your promise, and will restore your pledge also, if you will only stay where you are. She whom you love, she to whom you last drank, has contended successfully for your soul. Before such prayers as hers even my might is powerless. You are free, sir knight. Farewell!"

With a howl of baffled rage the fiend then vanished, leaving the knight alone on the gloomy moorland. Slowly and thoughtfully he wended his way back to the old convent, and there, in the quiet parlor, he registered a solemn vow to spend the remainder of his life in the service of the saint who had answered his beloved's prayer.

It was thus a gentle maiden guided the steps of an erring knight, away from the path of sin and into the narrow way of peace. In commemoration of this deed, her name has been given to the eminence where her convent once stood, which is still called the Gertruidenberg.

KEVLAAR.

The Pilgrimage to Kevlaar.

I.

THE mother stood at the window;
Her son lay in bed, alas!
"Will you not get up, dear William,
To see the procession pass?"

"Oh, mother, I am so ailing,
I neither can hear nor see ;
I think of my poor dead Gretchen,
And my heart grows faint in me."

"Get up, we will go to Kevlaar !
Your book and rosary take ;
The Mother of God will heal you,
And cure your heart of its ache."

The Church's banners are waving,
They are chanting a hymn divine ;
'Tis at Cöllen is that procession,
At Cöllen upon the Rhine.

With the throng the mother follows ;
Her son she leads ; and now
They both of them sing in the chorus,
"Ever honored, O Mary, be thou !"

II.

The Mother of God at Kevlaar,
Is dressed in her richest array ;
She has many a cure on hand there,
Many sick folk come to her to-day.

And her, for their votive offerings,
The suffering sick folk greet
With limbs that in wax are molded,
Many waxen hands and feet.

And whoso a wax hand offers,
His hand is healed of its sore ;
And whoso a wax foot offers,
His foot it will pain him no more.

To Kevlaar went many on crutches
Who now on the tight rope bound,
And many play now on the fiddle
Had there not one finger sound.

The mother she took a wax taper,
And of it a heart she makes :
"Give that to the Mother of Jesus,
She will cure thee of all thy aches."

With a sigh her son took the wax heart,
He went to the shrine with a sigh ;
His words from his heart trickle sadly,
As trickle the tears from his eye.

" Thou blessed above all that are blessed,
Thou Virgin unspotted, divine,
Thou Queen of the Heavens, before thee
I lay all my anguish and pine.

" I lived with my mother at Cöllen ;
At Cöllen, in the town that is there,
The town that has hundreds many
Of chapels and churches fair.

" And Gretchen she lived there near us,
But now she is dead, well-a-day !
O Mary ! a wax heart I bring thee,
Heal thou my heart's wound, I pray !

" Heal thou my heart of its anguish,
And early and late, I vow,
With its whole strength to pray and to sing, too,
Ever honored, O Mary, be thou ! "

III.

The suffering son and his mother
In their little bed-chamber slept ;
Then the Mother of God came softly,
And close to the sleepers crept.

She bent down over the sick one,
And softly her hand did lay
On his heart, with a smile so tender,
And presently vanished away.

The mother sees all in her dreaming,
And other things too she mark'd ;
Then from her slumber she wakened,
So loudly the town dogs bark'd.

There lay her son, to his full length
Stretched out, and he was dead ; *
And the light on his pale cheek flitted,
Of the morning's dawning red.

* See Note 3 in Appendix.

She folded her hands together,
She felt as she knew not how.
And softly she sang and devoutly,
"Ever honored, O Mary, be thou!"

—*Poem by Heine, translated by Bowring.*

CLEVES.

The Swan Knight.

THE next places of legendary interest along the Rhine are the small town of Nymwegen and the Duchy of Cleves, concerning which almost similar traditions have come down to us. The legend of Cleves, the subject of many poems and of one immortal opera, is as follows:

Elsa, the only daughter and sole heiress of the Duke of Luneburg and Brabant, had been intrusted to the care of Frederick of Telramund, one of her father's most powerful vassals. But instead of giving the orphan maiden the protection her loneliness required, this man tried to force her to marry him that he might obtain possession of her estates.

In vain the lovely Elsa declared she did not love him, in vain she appealed to his chivalry, he ruthlessly thrust her into a damp prison, close by the rushing river, there to languish in solitude until she was ready to do his will. A desperate appeal to Henry I. the Fowler only elicited an imperial decree that the matter should be settled in the lists between Frederick of Telramund and a champion of Elsa's choice. Elsa's heart sank when she heard this decision, for she knew full well that no knight of the neighborhood, however brave, would dare accept the challenge of one who had never yet suffered defeat or given quarter. Her apprehensions were only too well founded, for day after day, the herald vainly sought someone to battle for her rights.

Forsaken by all, the orphan maiden now turned to the

Helper of the helpless. Night and day she knelt in her narrow cell, imploring aid, and in her anguish she smote her breast with the rosary clasped in her little hands, until the tiny bell attached to it gave forth a low, tinkling sound. These silvery tones, so faint and soft they could scarcely be heard above the roar of the waters rushing past the tower, floated out through the narrow window into the open air, and were caught up by the winds of heaven and rapidly whirled away. And as they traveled farther and farther, they increased in power and volume, until it seemed as if all the bells on earth had united to ring forth one grand, deafening peal.

These loud and importunate tones penetrated even into the far distant temple on Montsalvat, where King Parsifal and his train of dauntless knights kept constant watch over the Holy Grail. Anxiously, therefore, the king hastened into the inner sanctuary, where the vase diffused its rosy light, hoping to read on its luminous edge the will of Heaven.

"Send Lohengrin to defend his future bride, but let her trust him and never seek to know his origin!" These were the mysterious words which met the aged king's eye, and which he immediately reported to his son. The brave young Lohengrin, trained to receive the commands of the Holy Grail with implicit faith, donned his armor, spoke his farewells, and then and there prepared to mount his waiting steed.

Suddenly a melody, such as had never yet been heard on land or sea, fell upon his ear. Soft, low, and sweet, it rose and fell and rose again, as a snowy swan came floating toward him, drawing a little skiff in its wake. Nearer and nearer came the stately swan, clearer and sweeter rose the mystic strain, until both came to a pause, close by the shore where the knight stood as if entranced.

Without a moment's hesitation Lohengrin sprang into the fairy skiff, and the swan, resuming its melody, soon bore him out of sight. The day appointed for the tournament had dawned, the last preparations had been made; but, among all the brave knights assembled to witness the pageant, not one dared to offer himself as champion for the lovely maiden, who clung to her prison bars, tearfully repeating, for the last time, her agonized prayer: "Send Thou the deliverer, O Lord!" All at once her sobs were checked, for the far-away sound of music fell comfortingly upon her ear. Bending forward eagerly, she soon descried a spotless swan floating gently down the stream, skillfully guiding a little boat, in which a radiant knight, attired in full armor, lay fast asleep on a glittering shield. Just as the swan passed beneath the window where Elsa stood, the knight awoke, and his first conscious glance rested upon her tear-stained face.

"Weep no more, oh, maiden!" he cried, springing to his feet. "Fear nought! I have come to defend thee!"

As the skiff passed on down the river, the prison door opened, and Frederick of Telramund appeared to lead Elsa to the lists. And as the herald began, for the third and last time, to summon a champion to present himself and maintain the rights of the noble young duchess, a smile of insolent triumph curled his cruel lips. The last flourish of the trumpets died away and Frederick of Telramund was about to address Elsa, when a ringing voice proclaimed: "Here am I, the Swan Knight, ready to do battle for the duchess' rights, and win her cause or die!"

A murmur of involuntary admiration burst from the crowd of spectators, as they simultaneously turned toward the Rhine, and there beheld a handsome knight, standing erect in a tiny skiff drawn by a swan. Spellbound they watched him spring lightly ashore and dismiss the swan, which floated down the river and out of sight, to the tune of its own beautiful, dreamy song.

Then, for a moment, Lohengrin knelt at Elsa's feet, registering a solemn vow to save her, and vaulting upon a waiting steed, drew down his visor and took his place in the lists. The noble knights and ladies trembled with fear when they beheld the terrible onslaught of Frederick of Telramund, whose stature was that of a giant, but their fear was changed into admiration, when they saw the dexterity with which the unknown knight parried or evaded his crashing blows.

In breathless silence they watched the conflict; nought was heard but the clank of steel, the heavy breathing of the combatants, and the tramp of their horses' feet, while clouds of dust almost concealed them from the spectators' eyes. Suddenly a terrible blow was heard, the gigantic frame of Frederick of Telramund was seen to sway for a moment in the saddle ere it fell and rolled in the dust! In a second Lohengrin had dismounted and stood with one foot on his rival's breast, summoning him to surrender. Triumphant cries, and jubilant trumpets proclaimed the victory, and cheer after cheer rang through the summer air, as Lohengrin knelt before Elsa once more. The multitude's exultant cries were so loud and prolonged, that they almost drowned Elsa's sweet voice, as she bade her champion rise and name his own reward.

But, although unheeded by the enthusiastic assembly, not one of the low-spoken tones had been lost by Lohengrin, who passionately replied:

"Tempt me not, oh, noble lady! Here at your feet, where I fain would linger forever, I cannot but confess how ardently I love you, and how sweet is the hope I cherish some day to claim your hand."

The pretty flush on Elsa's soft cheeks deepened perceptibly at these words, and the long lashes drooped over her beautiful eyes as she timidly held out her hand and softly whispered:

"You saved me, sir knight, I am yours!"

Not a syllable of this short but interesting colloquy had been heard by the shouting assembly, whose acclamations redoubled as the knight bent low over the little hand so trustingly confided to his keeping, and fervently pressed it to his lips.

Before night, however, the rumor of the young duchess' betrothal to the gallant Swan Knight had been noised abroad, and preparations for the marriage ceremony were begun without any further delay. Elsa, who had trembled with fear at the mere thought of an union with Frederick of Telramund, showed no reluctance whatever to pledge her troth to her valiant champion, nor did she even waver for a moment in her allegiance to him, when he informed her that she must never seek to know either his name or origin, which must remain a secret from her and from all the people, unless they would part forever.

The marriage was celebrated with much pomp, the young couple lived in blessed and peaceful union, and the love so suddenly kindled increased in depth and fervor, as one by one three beautiful children came to add to their happiness and gladden their home.

But Elsa, although utterly content with her husband's unalterable love and devotion, could not help but notice that many of her subjects secretly mistrusted him, and constantly tried, by every means in their power, to discover his name and station.

Little by little, she too began to ponder upon the subject, and the more she thought of it, the more she longed to know her husband's secret. Finally, curiosity prevailed over prudence, and while seated beside him one day, she turned toward him and abruptly asked the forbidden question.

"Elsa! Elsa! Is your faith dead?" cried the Swan Knight, in passionate, broken accents. "Can you no longer trust me? I love you so, and now I must leave you. Our happiness is at an end! But, before I go, your question shall be answered. Come with me!"

His pale face and despairing, reproachful glance brought

LOHENGRIN'S FAREWELL. *Pixis.*

Elsa to her senses. With a loving cry she flung herself on his breast, entreating him to forgive and forget her unfortunate curiosity, but he mournfully shook his head and replied:

"It is too late, Elsa, too late! You have doubted me, so I must leave you, but before I go you shall know all."

The knights assembled in the great banqueting hall near the Rhine, started up in surprise when their master suddenly appeared in their midst, leading the pale and weeping Elsa gently by the hand.

"Listen, oh, knights," he suddenly began, breaking the expectant silence. "The time has come when I must leave you; but, before I go, it is right that you should know that I, Lohengrin, son of Parsifal, the world-renowned king, was sent hither by the Holy Grail, to save your duchess from the oppressor's hand. Now the Holy Vessel summons me, and I must go, but ere I depart, I enjoin upon you to watch faithfully over my little ones and to wipe away their mother's tears. Farewell!"

Then, in the midst of the awe-struck silence which followed these words, while he held Elsa in a last fond embrace, the low strains of mystic music again came floating down the Rhine, and a moment later the swan appeared.

Slowly and reluctantly Lohengrin tore himself away from Elsa's clinging, passionate embrace, sprang down the steps and into the waiting swan-boat, which glided away to the sound of plaintive music, and bore him out of sight forever.

In vain Elsa wept, prayed, and beat her breast with her rosary, the sound of the tinkling silver bell never again broke the peaceful silence which brooded over the temple on Montsalvat, where Lohengrin had resumed his watch over the Holy Grail.*

* See Note 4 in Appendix.

The Prince's Vow.

OTTO, the youngest son of the noble family of Hesse, destined from his cradle to enter a monastery and there spend his life in a calling from which his ardent young spirit recoiled in horror, could not resign himself to meet his fate.

Alone, therefore, and in the dead of night, he effected his escape from home disguised as an archer, and bravely set out to seek his fortune. Several days' journey brought him at last to Cleves, where his distinguished appearance, and the great skill he manifested in handling the cross-bow, soon won the duke's favor.

Knights and ladies of high degree crowded around him, and enthusiastically applauded his unerring aim, but no praise seemed to gratify him half as much as the radiant smile with which the duke's lovely daughter hailed each successful shot. For, invisible to all the noble assembly, another archer, of proverbial dexterity, had slyly drawn his bow, and sent two darts to rankle in the impressionable hearts of Otto and the fair young duchess.

Hour after hour, and day after day, Otto most diligently practiced shooting beneath a certain window, where the duke's only daughter appeared from time to time to encourage him by a smile or by a fleeting gesture. One day, when our enamored young archer was thus agreeably occupied, the arrival of a knight and his suite caused him for a moment to stay his hand.

Instead of pausing to answer the duke's stately welcome, this stranger suddenly rushed forward and fell at Otto's feet with the joyful cry: "My lord and master, I have found you at last!" A second later, however, the knight knelt there alone, for Otto, with a passionate gesture of farewell to the maiden at the window, had darted through the open gate with the speed of one of his own arrows, and had vanished in the neighboring forest.

Slowly the knight rose to his feet, gazed at the fleet-footed youth until he was lost to sight, and then turned to answer the duke, who had been a silent but astonished witress of the whole scene. The usual courtesies were excnanged, the banquet spread, the topics of the day duly discussed, and when all the assistants had withdrawn and the knight found himself alone with his noble host, he began to explain who he was, and the cause of his strange behavior.

A few words soon revealed to the Duke of Cleves that his archer, Otto, was now the sole hope and heir of his noble race, his elder brothers having both died without issue. Various details were added by the knight, who asserted that an intense aversion for monastic life was the only thing which could have occasioned the young heir's precipitate flight.

"The lad is a remarkably good archer," exclaimed the duke, laughing heartily; "but methinks I can yet force him to acknowledge I am a better marksman than he."

And then, while slowly sipping his Rhine wine, the duke proposed a plan for the recovery of the fugitive prince. It was joyfully welcomed by the Count of Homberg, who bade him lose no time in putting it into execution. At the duke's call, archers, knights, and men-at-arms crowded into the hall, where they received orders to sally forth and not return until they had captured the missing youth.

"But, I solemnly charge you, not to injure a hair of his handsome young head," continued the duke impressively, as he gave them the signal to depart.

With a loud cheer, the host rushed out of the castle gates, and began to surround and beat the forest, while the duke turned to the knight and slyly exclaimed:

"Now, sir knight, I'll bait the trap."

With a nod and smile of approval, Count Homberg

watched the duke enter his daughter's apartment, and when he returned at the end of half an hour, gleefully rubbing his hands, he anxiously inquired :

"Well, most noble duke, is it all settled ? Did you experience any difficulty in winning your daughter's consent and connivance ?"

"None whatever," answered the duke, laughing so heartily that the armor hanging around the great hall fairly rang. "The altar is dressed, the candles lighted, the priests ready, and, unless I am very much mistaken, my men are even now bringing in the victim."

The words were scarcely out of his mouth when archers and horsemen burst into the hall, dragging Otto, whose torn garments, disheveled locks, and exhausted appearance fully corroborated their statement that he had led them a lively chase.

"Take him into the church immediately," commanded the duke, in his sternest tones. "I will not countenance disobedience ; drag him to the altar, where he will have to take his vows."

"Never !" exclaimed Otto passionately. "Never! You may drag me into the church and to the altar steps, but not one word will ever pass my lips. I'd rather die than take a single vow !"

"We will see, fair sir; we will see," said the duke, who paid no further heed to his vehement protests, and led the way to the church, bidding his men follow with the prisoner still vainly struggling to escape.

But when they had entered the sacred edifice, and Otto beheld a familiar, graceful figure, all clad in white, and enveloped from head to foot in a snowy veil, kneeling at the altar, he suddenly ceased to offer any resistance. Like a man in a dream, he was led up the aisle, and, obeying the duke's imperative sign, knelt beside the vision. Instead of the dreaded consecration service, the priests now began the marriage ceremony. Otto suddenly forgot his rash declaration, and with a firm and eager voice gladly took the vows which were to bind him forever, not to the church, but to a beloved and blushing bride.

The service concluded, the Duke of Cleves and Count Homberg stepped forward to offer their congratulations, explaining to Otto the change which had taken place in his fortunes.

"And now, Landgrave of Hesse, my noble son-in-law, unless you sorely repent taking your vows at the altar a few moments ago, in spite of your loudly declared determination to die rather than do so, it behooves you publicly to confess that I am a better archer than you, for *I* have hit the mark!" exclaimed the duke merrily.

"You may be the better marksman, sir duke!" exclaimed Otto, as he rapturously clasped his bride to his heart, "but you cannot deny that *I* have secured the prize!"

LÜTTICH

Saint Peter and Saint George.

SAINT PETER, weary of opening and shutting the Gates of Heaven, and longing to visit the fair spot on earth which bears the name of Lüttich, once summoned Saint George and entreated him to take his place for a little while.

Good Saint George, ever ready to oblige, cheerfully acquiesced, studied the fastenings, and opened and shut the gates until he felt sure he thoroughly understood their mechanism. Then he solemnly promised his colleague to refuse admittance to none who knocked, and patiently answer their every question.

Saint Peter was about to depart when Saint George suddenly detained him by exclaiming:

"Hold, Peter! I don't know one word of French! Suppose a Frenchman should knock at the gate!"

"No danger!" replied Saint Peter reassuringly. "No danger, my good fellow. Many a century has come and gone since I first took charge of the Heavenly Gates, but although persons of almost every nation have presented themselves, no Frenchman has ever yet appeared to seek admittance."

Then Saint Peter departed, and for a while Saint George undertook the office of porter: but although he was called upon to answer countless questions, and admit many souls, the Germans aver he had no occasion to do violence to his tongue, for no Frenchman knocked at the Gates of Heaven.

XANTEN.

Story of Siegfried.

At Xanten, in the Netherlands, where the Rhine lazily rolls its sluggish waters, there once dwelt a mighty king by the name of Sigmund, with his virtuous wife Sigelind and his promising young son Siegfried.

The prince's education, carefully carried on under his parents' supervision, was almost finished, when Sigmund suddenly decided to place him in apprenticeship with Mimer, a renowned smith, that he might learn all the intricacies of the manufacture of arms of every kind.

Like a dutiful son, Siegfried bent all his energies to the mastery of the new trade, and with such success that he could soon rival his teacher in skill. Pleased with his pupil's diligence and aptitude, Mimer frequently sought his society, entertained him with tales of olden times, and at last confided to him that Amilias, a gigantic Burgundian knight, encased in a ponderous armor which no sword had yet dinted, had sent a herald to challenge the smiths of the Netherlands to forge a weapon which could pierce his coat of mail.

Mimer confessed that he longed to try his skill, but mournfully added that his aged arm no longer possessed strength enough to wield the heavy hammer. Siegfried, who had listened attentively to the whole story, sprang to his feet as soon as Mimer had finished and impetuously cried:

"Be comforted, oh, master, for I will forge a sword which shall not only dint, but cleave the famed Burgundian armor."

At dawn the next day, therefore, Siegfried began his self-appointed task, and during seven days and nights the anvil constantly rang under the heavy blows of his hammer. At the end of this time he modestly presented himself before his master, bearing in his right hand a glittering sword of the finest steel.

Mimer examined it critically, and then, to test its edge, held it in a running stream, where he cast a fine thread which the water carried toward the blade. The thread no sooner touched the sword than it was severed. Delighted with the satisfactory result of his experiment, Mimer pronounced the weapon faultless, but Siegfried, dissatisfied with his labor, broke it into several pieces and declared he knew he could do better still.

Seven more days and nights were spent by the indefatigable young smith at his forge, and when he again appeared before his master he proudly brandished a highly polished sword which flashed in the sunlight like a streak of lightning.

Once more, Mimer examined and tested it: this time by casting twelve whole fleeces in the running stream, but when he saw them all neatly divided by the sharp blade he uttered a loud shout of triumph, and declared Siegfried's Balmung—such was the name the prince had given his sword—the finest weapon ever forged.

Therefore, when Amilias, the Burgundian, appeared in the Netherlands, Mimer fearlessly accepted his challenge, and approaching the mocking giant, dealt him a great blow.

Amilias did not even wince, but the smile on his broad countenance grew rather faint as Mimer twittingly inquired: "Well, how dost thou feel now, sir knight?"

"As if something cold had touched me," replied Amilias faintly.

"Shake thyself!" commanded Mimer.

The giant obeyed, and at his first motion his huge body fell asunder. The first blow from Balmung had cut through armor and knight. The head and shoulders now rolled heavily down the mountain side and fell into the Rhine, where they can still be seen when the waters are clear. As for the trunk, it remained on the mountain top, where it looks like a huge gray rock, for it is now petrified, and is frequently pointed out to admiring tourists.

The other apprentices, jealous of the praises Mimer lavishly bestowed upon Siegfried, now tried to devise some means of injuring him. One day, when the master of the forge was absent, and when the provision of charcoal necessary to maintain the great fire in the forge was almost exhausted, Veliant, the oldest apprentice, hoping to humiliate Siegfried by imposing upon him such a menial task, bade him take the mule, go to the mountain, and obtain a new supply of fuel from Regin the charcoal burner. But Siegfried, glad of the change, set out merrily, and after losing his way sundry times, and slaying a whole brood of young dragons, reached Regin's hut just as the sun was going down.

That evening, as they sat before the fire, Regin taunted the young prince with serving his inferiors in birth and station, until he worked him up into a passion, and wrung from him an avowal that he longed for freedom and a chance to distinguish himself in the world.

Regin then revealed to Siegfried that he was none other than Mimer in disguise, gave him back his freedom, made him exchange his toilworn garments for others, better suited to his rank, bound the sword Balmung to his side, and bade him seek a man, by the name of Gripir, who would provide him with a good war horse.

Gladly Siegfried obeyed this command, and strode rapidly up the mountain in search of Gripir, to whom he frankly made known his errand. The stud-keeper immediately signified his readiness to serve him, and conducted him to the mountain top, from whence he pointed out a herd of horses feeding in a pasture, bidding him take his choice among them.

Guided by the advice of an old, one-eyed man—Odin in disguise—whom he met on the way, Siegfried selected Greyfell, a descendant of Odin's favorite steed, the only one of the horses which successfully battled against the high waves in the river, and came bounding up to him. Proudly riding this matchless steed, Siegfried then returned to Regin to receive his further commands. That evening, seated by the camp-fire, and accompanying himself by the melodious tones of a harp which he touched with wondrous skill, Regin chanted the oft-repeated tale of the Curse of Gold, which is as follows:

Three of the Æsir, Odin, Hoenir, and Loki, once came down upon earth, disguised as mortals. As they traveled along, they freely distributed gifts to all they met. Odin gave knowledge and strength; Hoenir, gladness and good-cheer; but Loki, ever inclined to mischief, lingered behind them to scatter abroad the seeds of deceit and crime. In his wanton love of evil, he also slew a magnificent otter, which he carelessly flung over his shoulder, as he followed his companions to the hut of the giant Hreidmar, where they hoped to obtain refreshment.

But, no sooner had the giant's glance rested upon Loki's strange burden, than he uttered a terrible cry of rage, for the slain animal was his oldest son Otter, who frequently assumed this form. His cry immediately brought his two other sons, Regin and Fafnir to his side. With their assistance he quickly bound the three gods, who, being in human guise, could offer but slight resistance, for they possessed only human strength.

In spite of their promises and entreaties, Hreidmar refused to set them free, and declared they should remain in durance vile until they gave him gold enough to cover every inch of the slain Otter's skin. The only concession that the gods could obtain, was that Loki should be allowed to go in search of the ransom, while Odin and Hoenir remained as hostages in Hreidmar's hut.

Loosed from his bonds, Loki quickly wended his way to the source of the Rhine, where Andvari, a dwarf, was said to keep watch over an immense treasure. But when he reached the spot, he could find no trace of either treasure or dwarf. The only living creature in sight was a beautiful salmon, playfully disporting itself in the limpid waters.

Loki, the arch-deceiver, immediately suspected a fraud, and without further ado, sped down the Rhine to the North Sea, where he entreated Ran, the cruel sea queen, to lend him the net which she so often spread to catch the rich galleys floating so proudly over the surface of her husband's domain.

Won by his promises of future assistance, Ran soon consented to lend him her net. Armed with this infallible instrument, Loki quickly retraced his steps to the source of the Rhine. There he soon caught the salmon, which proved to be, as he had so shrewdly suspected, the dwarf Andvari in disguise.

Loki then demanded the jealously guarded treasure, which was surrendered as the price of freedom. He was about to depart when his covetous eye was caught by the glitter of a golden snake-ring which Andvari wore. To wrench this ring from the dwarf's finger and make his escape was the work of a moment, yet his flight was not so rapid but that he distinctly heard every word of the awful curse which Andvari pronounced upon the possessor of both treasure and ring.

Arrived at the hut where Odin and Hoenir anxiously awaited him, Loki poured out the gold on the otter skin, which spread out farther and farther, on all sides, until it covered a wide tract of ground. The treasure, however, was almost as unlimited as the skin, and when the last piece of gold had been laid down upon it, it was all covered with the exception of a single hair.

Hreidmar, whose eyes had greedily rested upon the countless treasures, now vowed the gods should not go until they had covered the last hair with gold, and thus fulfilled his conditions; so Loki, remembering the ring, produced it, placed it upon the uncovered spot, and thus obtained his own and his companions' liberty.*

Fearful lest anyone should deprive him of his treasure, Hreidmar never for a moment left it out of his sight. Day and night he lingered beside it, drawing it into his embrace, and gazing for hours at a time upon the runes engraved on his snake-ring. So frequently did he indulge in this latter pastime that his whole nature was soon changed, and one day, when Fafnir returned alone from the chase, he found, instead of Hreidmar, a great snake coiled all around the treasure.

A moment sufficed to draw his sword and kill the serpent, and it was only when the deed was done that he discovered it was his father whom he had thus slain. Simultaneously with this knowledge came the insidious thought that the treasure was his, and that if he could only remove it to a place of safety before his brother Regin appeared to claim a share, it need never be divided. Hastily gathering up the golden hoard, therefore, Fafnir transported it to Hunaland, where he spread it all out on a plain, since called the Glittering Heath, where he gloated over it night and day, until he, too, became a loathsome serpent.

The tale ended, Mimer, or Regin as we must now call him, revealed to Siegfried that he was Hreidmar's third and youngest son, who had been forced to seek refuge in the

* See "Stories of the Wagner Operas," by the author.

Volsung country, and there patiently bide his time, until a dauntless warrior consented to aid him in recovering the golden treasure.

In vain Siegfried reminded him of the awful curse which its possession entailed. Regin insisted that he was ready to bear the curse if he could only obtain the gold, and after much entreaty finally induced Siegfried to mount Greyfell and accompany him to the Glittering Heath.

From a mountain top on the opposite side of the river, the young hero first beheld the golden plain, where lay the goal of all Regin's hopes. Alone and on foot, he then descended the mountain and sprang into a skiff which was waiting to bear him across the river. The aged boatman (Odin in disguise), hearing his purpose, cunningly advised him to dig a trench in the dragon's track,—for the serpent had worn a great path on the hillside, in his daily journey down to the river to quench his devouring thirst,—to hide himself in this trench, and plunge his sword deep into the monster's side as he passed over him.

Siegfried, ever ready to receive good advice, put the old boatman's suggestion into practice, and soon lay in a deep trench, sword in hand, anxiously awaiting the serpent's descent to the river. He had not waited long, before a sound of rolling stones and a prolonged hiss fell upon his listening ear. A moment later, he felt the serpent's fiery breath touch his cheek, and then the loathsome folds of his huge body rolled over the trench, shutting out the air and daylight.

Undaunted by his proximity to the monster, Siegfried now boldly thrust Balmung up to the hilt into the body above his head. The blood gushed out of the wound in torrents, rapidly filling the trench, and had not the monster, in his last convulsive struggle, rolled over on one side, and thus allowed Siegfried to escape, he would have fallen victim to his own hardihood, and have been drowned in the slimy blood. This gore, covering him from head to foot, rendered him invulnerable, with the exception of a tiny spot, where a fallen lime leaf stuck fast to his shoulder.

When Regin, from his lookout on the mountain top, saw that Fafnir was dead, he hastened to cross the river and joined Siegfried. No trace of emotion passed over his face when he beheld the lifeless form of what had once been a well-beloved brother, and his eyes were soon greedily turned toward the heath where the glittering treasure lay.

A moment later, fearing lest Siegfried should claim a portion of this wealth, he stealthily drew Balmung out of Fafnir's bleeding side. But just as he was about to deal a deadly blow to the unsuspecting young hero, his foot slipped in the serpent's slimy blood, and he fell upon the trenchant blade, which put an end to his envy and existence at the same time.

Horror-struck, Siegfried gazed for a moment upon this sad sight, then vaulting upon Greyfell, he bounded away, leaving the Glittering Heath and its accursed treasure far behind him. He considered himself safe only when he had reached the distant seashore, and embarked with his steed upon a vessel steered by the gentle Bragi.

So sweet was the pilot's voice, and so entrancing his songs, that the waves ceased their play to listen, and the winds only breathed a soft accompaniment to his harp. Thus peacefully sailing over summer seas, they came at last to Isenland, where Bragi told Siegfried that Brunhild, the disobedient Valkyr, had been exiled to earth.

He then went on to explain, in his dreamy, poetical way, that this maiden, the queen of all Isenland, had been stung, together with all her household, by "the irresistible thorn of sleep," and doomed by Odin, the All-father, to slumber on until some hero should fight his way through the barrier of flames with which he had surrounded the palace, and break the charm by kissing her fair young brow.

Just as the story came to an end, the keel of the vessel grated upon the pebbly beach, and Siegfried, mounting his faithful Greyfell, leaped ashore, declaring his intention of riding through the flames to break the spell which rested upon the fair sleeper.

A moment later his swift steed had carried him away from the seashore, into the midst of the raging flames, through which he bravely forced his way to the very gates of the palace of Isenstein, where he found all, as Bragi had told him, wrapped in a deep and dreamless sleep. No sound of life broke the profound silence which had brooded over the place for years, and Siegfried penetrated unmolested into an apartment where the fair Brunhild lay wrapped in slumber.

No change had passed over her in all this time; her countenance was more beautiful, if anything, than on the day when the fatal thorn had stung her, and after a moment spent in breathless contemplation, Siegfried bent above her sleeping form, and pressed a gentle kiss upon her smooth brow. The blue eyes opened wide, the princess awoke, and knights, maids, and waiting men, simultaneously aroused from their prolonged repose, resumed the conversations and occupations broken off so long ago.

The deliverer was welcomed with songs and festivals, and every day some new game or banquet was devised in his honor. Six months passed by like a dream, and seemed all too short to Brunhild, who had fallen in love with the handsome young warrior as soon as her first conscious glance had rested upon him. But there were other great deeds for Siegfried to accomplish, and Odin, impatient at his inactivity, finally sent his two wise birds, Thought and Memory, to warn him that life was short, time fleeting, and that it behooved him to be up and doing.

No sooner had this warning fallen upon Siegfried's ear, than he mounted Greyfell, and without pausing to take leave of Brunhild, rode out of the castle of Isenstein, and away to the sea. There he embarked in a waiting vessel which immediately set sail, and bore him off to the Nibelungenland, the land of perpetual darkness and mist.

Landing here, Siegfried was immediately called upon to settle a quarrel between two young princes, Niblung and Shiblung, whose father had died leaving an immense treasure. This he had found in the course of his journeys, on a lonely plain called the Glittering Heath. These two princes, who had grown thin and pale watching the treasure, which was also guarded by Alberich (Andvari), king of the dwarfs, earnestly implored Siegfried to divide the hoard between them. The hero consented upon condition that the sword, which lay on top of the gold, and which he immediately recognized as his own Balmung, should be given him in exchange for his services.

The brothers made no objection, and he began the division of the treasure, which was carried on quite satisfactorily to both parties until nothing but the accursed ring remained. The princes, quarreling for its possession, fought until both fell mortally wounded upon their vast piles of gold, and died clasping their glittering treasures in a last fond embrace.

While Siegfried was mournfully contemplating this sad sight, Alberich the dwarf, fearing lest the newcomer should attempt to carry away the great hoard, donned his Tarnkappe,—a magic mantle which had the power of making the wearer invisible to mortal eyes,—and stealing behind the hero, dealt him a great and treacherous blow.

Siegfried soon recovered, and seeing no foe, concluded that the attack must have been made by the dwarf. Patiently biding his time until he felt a sharp current of air touch his cheek, he promptly stretched out his strong right hand, caught his invisible little opponent, divested him of the Tarnkappe, which he appropriated, and made him solemnly swear to serve him only, and to guard the immense treasure faithfully for his use.

Shortly after this encounter Siegfried came into contact with the Nibelungen warriors, whom he defeated, thanks to his Tarnkappe and invincible Balmung. This victory gave him the sovereignty over the land of mist and darkness, where he rested for a while, ere he returned home, accompanied by a kingly retinue of a thousand stalwart Nibelungen knights. The journey was accomplished in safety, and when the numerous galleys reached Xanten, on the Rhine, there were great rejoicings, and the long absent Siegfried and his mighty followers were entertained with sumptuous feasts. Siegfried lingered here by his parents' side, recounting his adventures by land and sea, and taking an active part in jousts and games, until, weary of this aimless existence, he determined to go in search of new adventures.

The main part of the Nibelungen warriors were sent back to the land of mist and darkness, to await his summons, only ten of their number being privileged to accompany him to the famed Burgundian land. Over hill and down dale they traveled, following the sinuous course of the Rhine, until they reached the city of Worms, the Burgundian capital, where they were hospitably received by King Gunther, and by every member of the royal family.

One person only, Hagen, the confidant and adviser of the king, viewed the strangers with displeasure, and strove, by every means in his power, to disparage them before his master. But, in spite of all his evil insinuations, Gunther received Siegfried with all the courtesy due his rank, and ordered sundry festivities and games in his honor, in the course of which all had cause to admire the strength and agility displayed by the Nibelungen king. Kriemhild, sister of Gunther, than whom no more beautiful maiden ever dwelt upon the banks of the Rhine, daily watched and applauded his prowess, culled choice roses from her famous garden, and twined them into garlands for the handsome young victor, who showed himself humble and gentle before her alone, and whose burning love glances kindled an answering flame in her impressionable heart. Even in her dreams, he was ever before her, and sharing the superstition so general in her day, she anxiously sought a favorable interpretation for them all. What was not her chagrin therefore, when, after an agitated night, her dream was interpreted tragically. She had dreamed that a beautiful falcon, flying toward her from the north, nestled contentedly in her bosom, whence it was cruelly torn away by two dark eagles, which suddenly swooped down upon it and left it lying at her feet, a bleeding and mangled corpse. Ute, the queen mother, skilled in interpreting dreams, declared she would marry a northern king, who would love her, and rest happy in her love, until treacherously slain by two cruel foes. The first part of the prophecy caused Kriemhild's heart to flutter with joy; for was not Siegfried a king from the north, and did she not love him and long for his love in return? But her tender spirit quailed when she heard the tragic end, so she strove, by all the means in her power, to banish the recollection of this ominous dream.

She was greatly assisted in this process by several exciting events, for, according to some versions of the story, a terrible dragon suddenly appeared and bore her off to a cave in the Drachenfels, whence she was heroically rescued by Siegfried. Other traditions aver that two kings declared war against Burgundy, and were defeated, thanks to the courage of Siegfried, who returned to Worms in triumph.

Shortly after these events the Burgundian court was further excited by the arrival of a herald sent by Brunhild, queen of Isenland, to promise her hand and kingdom to any knight who could outdo her in casting a spear, hurling a stone, and in leaping.

In answer to the manifold questions asked him, the herald warmly lauded the charms of his fair queen, related how she had been stung by "the thorn of sleep," surrounded by a barricade of raging flames, and finally released by the kiss of a beautiful stranger, who had braved every danger to approach her, had lingered contentedly by her side, but had at last suddenly and mysteriously disappeared.

This story greatly interested Gunther, the Burgundian

king, who bade the herald return with all speed to Isenland, to inform Brunhild that he accepted her challenge, and would soon present himself, ready to win her hand or die.

After vainly trying to deter him from this rash enterprise, by revealing to him that Brunhild, being a Valkyr, was endowed with more than human strength, Siegfried determined to accompany him to Isenland, in the guise of a vassal, and lend him all the assistance in his power for Kriemhild's sake.*

Brunhild, who had dispatched her herald in hopes that her challenge would reach the ear of Siegfried and bring him back to her feet, scornfully viewed the Burgundian king, and haughtily bade him prepare for the appointed contest. Siegfried, who had remained by the vessel, hastily donned his Tarnkappe, which he had brought with that purpose in view, and stealing unseen to Gunther's side, bade him go through the motions and fear naught, for he would aid and sustain him.

Brunhild's first blow overthrew Gunther and his invisible supporter, but before she had time to cry out "Victory," Siegfried placed Gunther upon his feet once more, and hurled the spear at her, butt-end foremost, with such force, that Brunhild staggered and fell, and was obliged to confess herself beaten.

But, although her first attempt had proved unsuccessful, and the king she scorned had shown himself no despicable foe, Brunhild still hoped to defeat him. Catching up a huge stone, therefore, she threw it with incredible force, and bounding after it, alighted beside it as it fell.

A murmur of admiration arose, and all the spectators eagerly watched to see whether Gunther could rival her in strength and agility a second time. Invisible to all, Siegfried bent, caught up the stone, threw it much further than Brunhild had done, and grasping Gunther by his broad belt, landed him beside the stone with one mighty bound. The Burgundian king had won, and, in the midst of deafening

*See "Myths of Northern Lands," by the author.

SEIGFRIED AND KRIEMHILD.
Royal Palace, Münich.

acclamations, the proud Brunhild was forced to confess herself outdone.

Furious at being thus caught in her own trap, and determined to exterminate the strangers rather than become the wife of their king, Brunhild secretly began to assemble her troops, beguiling her guests into a false sense of security by the sumptuous festivals which she gave in their honor.

Siegfried, however, perceiving these criminal intentions, stole secretly away to the Nibelungen land, whence he soon returned with an imposing force of knights, in time to save Gunther, and to compel Brunhild to keep her promise.

The bridal party now proceeded to Worms, whither Siegfried preceded them to announce their coming. The timid but warm welcome he received from Kriemhild encouraged him to sue openly for her hand. When Gunther arrived their marriage was celebrated and Brunhild learned for the first time that Siegfried was not, as her husband had told her, one of his vassals, but a mighty king, and the hero who had slain a dragon and become invulnerable by bathing in its blood.

When all the wedding festivities were ended, Siegfried bore his happy bride away to the Nibelungen land, where he gave her all the Nibelungen hoard, reserving for himself nothing but the fatal ring. The course of their peaceful and happy life was interrupted, after several years, by a pressing invitation to visit their Burgundian kindred, an invitation far too cordial to be refused.

So the Nibelungen king and queen set out with a royal retinue, and, after a delightful journey over the smooth sea and along the Rhine, they reached the city of Worms in the midst of great rejoicings. The harmony which reigned at first among the various members of the royal family was soon disturbed, however, by the treacherous Hagen, who, having once overheard by what stratagem Brunhild had been won, now revealed the secret to her, thus cunningly enlisting her aid to compass Siegfried's death.

Next, he artfully insinuated himself into Kriemhild's good graces, and under pretext of better guarding her husband's precious life, won from her the admission that although Fafnir's blood had rendered her husband invulnerable, there was one little spot on his shoulder—where the lime leaf had stuck—where a blow might prove fatal. At his urgent request, Kriemhild embroidered a tiny leaf on Siegfried's garment, on the exact spot where the real leaf had rested, while he vehemently swore he would keep her secret and constantly watch over her husband's safety.

But one day, when the royal party were hunting in the Odenwald, and when Siegfried was bending over a little fountain to slake his burning thirst, the treacherous Hagen stole behind him, thrust his spear through the embroidered leaf into the stooping form, and thus basely slew him.

Siegfried's lifeless body was carried home on a shield and laid before Kriemhild's door, and when she found it there she almost died of grief. To discover the murderer,—for she suspected foul play,—she bade each warrior lay his hand upon the beloved remains, and when at Hagen's touch the blood again began to flow, she vehemently denounced him as a traitor and assassin.

According to some versions of this tale Siegfried's body was burned, and Brunhild, regretting what she had done, stabbed herself and was buried with him. According to others he was laid at rest in a sumptuous tomb, and Kriemhild, who would fain have returned to the Nibelungenland, was persuaded to remain with her kin in her native country. A few years later, guided by her family's wishes, she sent for the mighty Nibelungen hoard, which was conveyed to Burgundy in several large vessels, and placed in a great tower of which Kriemhild only held the key. But Hagen, the vile murderer, who was as avaricious as treacherous, soon stole the treasure, and fearing lest he should be forced to restore it, buried it deep in the Rhine, near Lochheim, where it remains to this day.

SIEGFRIED'S BODY BORNE BY THE HUNTSMEN. *Pixis.*

Some years later, under the influence of a magic draught, or urged by the thirst for revenge, Kriemhild married Attila, king of the Huns, and, under pretext of a friendly visit, beguiled the Burgundians into her realm. In trying to execute her orders and slay Hagen, the Huns fell foul of the Burgundian heroes, who died only after they had slain many of their foes, Gunther and Hagen perishing by the hand of Kriemhild, who however died by the sword as soon as Siegfried was avenged.

The Drachenfels, where Siegfried slew the dragon; the city of Worms, which owes its name to the corpse of the gigantic worm Fafnir, found on the Glittering Heath; the Rose Garden, where Kriemhild, the happy maiden, wove garlands for her lover; the Odenwald, where Siegfried fell; the church of St. Cecilia, where his tomb can still be seen; and Lochheim, where the Nibelungen hoard is buried in the Rhine, are the principal places along this mighty river which are connected with the great German epic, the Nibelungenlied, the story of the noble Siegfried, born in the Netherlands, at Xanten, on the Rhine.*

ELBERFELD.

The Angel Page.

A LAD of faultless proportions and peerless beauty once sought a brave and noble knight, humbly entreating permission to serve him as page. Charmed by his graceful manners and frank request, the knight engaged him, and never, for a moment, did he have cause to regret having secured his services.

The cheerful alacrity with which the little page performed every duty, the intense devotion which enabled him to discover and anticipate almost every wish, soon won his master's approval, and before long they became inseparable

* See Note 5 in Appendix.

companions. The years passed swiftly by; never before had the knight enjoyed such continuous prosperity, and never had success so persistently attended him, as since the day and hour when the youthful page had first entered his gate.

One day when master and follower were riding along the banks of the Rhine, they suddenly noticed the approach of a band of dastardly men, who had often, but vainly, sought to harm the virtuous knight. Their troop was so numerous and so cleverly disposed, that a single glance sufficed to show the knight the utter impossibility of hewing his way through their serried ranks, or of making his escape.

"Would to God you were safe within my castle walls, my faithful little page!" he sadly cried. "We are lost, my lad, but it behooves us to sell our lives as dearly as possible, and to die like heroes, instead of cravens. Get behind me, oh, page, and should a chance present itself, remember I bid you flee!"

"Master, master, follow me! I will show you a way to escape, follow me!" cried the little page, galloping along the river bank, and suddenly spurring his reluctant steed into the rushing tide.

"Rash youth, return!" called the knight, bounding forward in the vain hope of overtaking the venturesome page. "Better die, fighting bravely, than to perish miserably in the waves. Return, my page, return!"

"Fear nothing, master, follow me!" still cried the little page, and his silvery tones rose so confidently above the noise of the wind and waves, that the knight unconsciously obeyed. A few moments later the horses had found a firm footing, and guided by his page, the knight safely forded the Rhine, and reached the opposite shore, as the baffled foe came down to the water's brink.

In vain the pursuers urged their steeds into the deep waters; no trace of ford could be found, so they were forced to abandon the pursuit. The knight's warm expressions of gratitude and admiration only deepened the affection of the little page, who seemed perfectly happy when in his presence, or when engaged in some of his numerous errands of mercy.

Not long after this miraculous escape from death, the knight's heart was torn with anguish, for his wife, his beloved young wife, lay dangerously ill. The learned physicians, summoned in haste to her bedside, gravely shook their heads, and declared she must die, for the only remedy which could give her relief—the milk of a lioness—could not be procured in that country.

The rumor of the strange and unobtainable prescription rapidly spread throughout the castle, and came to the ears of the faithful little page, who immediately sprang to his feet and rushed out of the hall. An hour later—before any decided change for the worse had taken place—he suddenly appeared at the lady's bedside, flushed and panting, but bearing a full cup of lioness' milk, which the learned doctors administered to the patient without delay. In a very few moments the color stole back into the lady's pallid cheeks, the light to her eyes, and she soon sank into a sweet sleep, from which she awoke fully cured, and restored to life, health, and love.

Then the knight eagerly sought his little page, and gratefully poured out the thanks with which his heart overflowed. "But tell me, my noble, faithful page, how could you so speedily procure a remedy which all my wealth and the doctors' influence could not command?" he inquired, after the first expression of his undying gratitude.

"Noble master, I knew that a lioness was suckling her cubs in an Arabian den, and so——"

"Arabia!" exclaimed the knight, interrupting him, "Arabia! Did you find your way thither, and effect your return within one short hour's time?"

"Even so, oh, gracious master," modestly replied the

little page, with his beautiful, candid eyes fixed on his master's pale, astonished face.

"Lad, who are you, then?" suddenly demanded the knight, a nameless terror invading his heart. "Who are you? Speak; and conceal nothing!"

"Master, beloved master! ask not who I am, nor whence I came," cried the little page, sinking down at his feet, and stretching out imploring hands. "Question me not! Let me remain at your side, oh, master! and remember that no harm has befallen you since I have been in your service."

"Lad, cease this pleading and answer me. Who are you?" insisted the knight, carefully avoiding his passionate glance of entreaty.

"A spirit, oh, master! A spirit of light, who for you, and your service, left a home in the realms above. But now, oh, master! I must go. Farewell, farewell!"*

"Lad, lad, leave me not! Remain!" now cried the knight in his turn. "Ask what reward you please, but do not forsake me. Remain, my faithful little page, for I cannot live without you!"

"You have questioned my origin and have mentioned a reward. The charm is broken, oh, master! and now I must go. In exchange for the services I have performed so cheerfully and so lovingly, I ask you to place a silver bell in the dense forest, that its tinkling sound may guide the weary wanderers, and enable them to find their way home. Dedicate the bell to the Almighty and to his angelic host, oh, master! and receive my last farewell."

The lad vanished, but none saw him leave the hall or pass through the castle gates, and no trace of him was ever found. The angel page had faded from mortal sight, and returned to the heavenly home, inhabited by countless spirits as good, faithful, and pure as he.

His last request was piously fulfilled by the noble knight, who seemed absorbed in mournful recollections of the past,

* See Note 6 in Appendix.

for his eye constantly roamed in search of the beautiful page who had left him, and when, at evensong, the silvery tones of the little bell pealed forth in the quiet air, they fell upon his ear like angel's words and filled his heart with restless longing.

Little by little the knight's strength failed. His step grew slow and feeble, and one day, when the shades of night were falling and the first tinkle of the little bell fell upon his ear, he softly murmured: "My page, my faithful little page!" and his soul was released and allowed to join the angel spirit he had learned to love so well. After that, and for many a year, the bell continued to peal forth its silvery chimes, some echoes of which are still said to linger in the Elberfeld forest, and many a weary wanderer has had cause to bless the virtuous knight and his angel page.

DÜSSELDORF.

The Critics Silenced.

A GREAT crowd once assembled on the market place at Düsseldorf, to view the unveiling of the equestrian statue of the beloved Elector, John William.

Gabriel Grupello, the artist, stood at his post, and at the prince's signal dropped the veil. The statue, a masterpiece, excited much admiration, and the artist's heart swelled with pride when the Elector, in token of approval, publicly seized and shook his hand.

But the courtiers, jealous of this unwonted mark of distinction, eagerly sought something to depreciate, and as they dared not criticise the effigy, which the Elector had pronounced perfect, they took their revenge by disparaging the steed. One found fault with the hoofs, another with the withers, a third with the neck, a fourth with the ears;

in short no part of the unfortunate quadruped could meet with the courtiers' entire approval.

Silently Grupello listened to all their comments, and when they had quite finished he turned to the Elector, gravely entreating permission to erect a scaffolding around the statue once more, and to be allowed three days' work, screened from all inquisitive eyes and secured from every interruption. The Elector graciously complied with this request, and during three days the heavy clang of the hammer resounded incessantly on the market place.

The courtiers, passing to and fro, heard the sound and complacently congratulated themselves upon the valuable hints they had bestowed upon the artist. The last day came, the hammering ceased, the scaffolding fell, and once more, the Elector and his suite gathered around the statue.

"Well, my noble lords and gentlemen," cried the Elector, turning to his followers, "are you satisfied now?"

"Yes, the hoofs are quite right now!" exclaimed the hoof-critic approvingly.

"And the arch of the neck is no longer strained, but flexible and proud," said another suavely.

"See!" cried a third, "the ears now seem quite natural!"

Each courtier warmly praised the particular part he had once condemned, and all, thinking the success owing entirely to themselves and to their timely suggestions, openly professed their complete satisfaction.

With downcast eyes Grupello listened to their praise, but, when they had quite finished, he raised his head and boldly cried:

"Behold, your Royal Highness! neck, hoofs, ears, and withers are quite unchanged, for a statue of bronze, once cast, cannot be altered."

"You have not changed it, Master Grupello!" exclaimed the Elector, astonished. "Pray tell me what you were hammering so vigorously, then?"

"Oh!" replied the artist, carelessly shrugging his shoulders, "I was merely demolishing the reputation of the critics, who were jealous of the praise your Royal Highness so generously bestowed."

COLOGNE.

The Cathedral Legend.

ENGELBERT THE HOLY, bishop of Cologne, longed to signalize his rule and immortalize his name by some great work. He determined, therefore, to erect a cathedral which would tower far above and outshine all others, and with this laudable purpose in view, sent for a renowned architect.

Elated by the honor thus conferred upon him, this man readily undertook to produce a suitable plan within a certain space of time, and withdrew from the bishop's presence full of eagerness to begin his work. But, when he had returned to his own humble little dwelling, spread a huge sheet of spotless parchment upon the table before him, and prepared his rules, compasses, and other drawing implements, the inspiration he so confidently expected entirely failed him.

Hour after hour the architect pondered, but the great sheet still remained a perfect blank. To stimulate his ideas he finally concluded to take a little walk, and thoughtfully wandered along the crooked, narrow streets, and out of the Frankenpforte to the banks of the Rhine. A stretch of fine, smooth sand and the prevailing solitude checked the architect's uncertain steps, and invited him to linger for a while. Idly, at first, he began tracing the outline of a cathedral in the sand ; then suddenly he grasped his cane more firmly and drew more rapidly, until, in his excitement, his breath came in quick, short gasps. Dome, turrets, and spire were added one by one, and when all was finished, he raised his head and proudly exclaimed :

"There is the cathedral plan ! Surely none can ever equal it."

"No ; none but the cathedral of Mayence, of which that is a very fair copy," said a mocking voice close beside him.

The architect, who until then had believed himself quite alone, now turned with a start and beheld a wizened little old man, who bent over his plan with a sarcastic expression on his sharp face. His first impulse was, of course, to give utterance to his anger, but a second glance at the completed plan brought the instant conviction that the criticism was true.

Hastily the architect effaced the outline, smoothed the sand, and patiently began to trace a second plan. Under his practiced hand, choir, nave, altar, and chapel rapidly assumed beautiful and harmonious proportions. Like one inspired, he added ornament and tracery, carefully elaborating his design, and when the last touch had been given, he stood off a few paces and triumphantly cried :

"There ! No such an edifice as that has ever yet pierced the blue vault of heaven."

"No; none except the cathedral of Strasburg," snickered the same derisive voice which already, once before, had dashed his hopes to the ground.

"Strasburg !" exclaimed the architect. "Strasburg, ay—yes ! True, too true !" and his head sank down upon his breast, and the light of pleasure died out of his eyes. But he was a sanguine man, and a moment later he had recovered his wonted energy and begun a third plan, muttering that he would surely have time to complete it before the sun set and darkness overtook him. His hand fairly trembled with eagerness, and his eyes almost started from their sockets, as he tried to represent the visions of beauty which now thronged his brain. The cane moved faster and faster, the lines covered the sand like network, the red disk of the sun sank beneath the distant horizon, and its rosy glow was reflected in the sparkling river as the last line was rapidly traced.

"There !" he cried. "This is no treacherous effect of

COLOGNE.
Bridge of Boats,

memory, but a creation of my own brain which will make my name immortal."

"Ha! ha! ha!" chuckled the little old man, whose presence the architect had again entirely forgotten in his abstraction. "You are mistaken again, sir architect; for what you so proudly call a creation of your own brain looks singularly like the cathedral of Amiens."

Beside himself with anger, and completely baffled, for he could not but acknowledge the similarity, now that it was pointed out to him, the architect threw his staff at the stranger's feet and impetuously cried:

"Perhaps you, who laugh at me, could draw a better plan!"

The clawlike fingers immediately closed over the staff, and in the rapidly gathering twilight the stranger traced the plan, cut, and elevation of a stupendous cathedral. With dilated eyes the architect breathlessly followed his every movement; and although the lines were so quickly and faintly traced that they were lost to sight almost as soon as made, he still saw enough to be convinced that the plan far surpassed anything that he had yet seen.

"Well, what do you think of my plan?" suddenly asked the old man, when he had quite finished.

"It is simply stupendous!" exclaimed the architect. "But who are you, who can thus, in a few moments, create such an exquisite plan? You are surely the greatest architect on the face of the earth, or——"

"His Satanic Majesty, the greatest architect in the Lower World, at your service, sir architect. Moreover, if my plan pleases you, it is yours. You shall reap all the honors and profits which it cannot fail to bring you, if you will only consent to pledge me your soul in exchange."

"Avaunt! Satan, avaunt!" cried the terrified architect, vehemently crossing himself again and again. With a snarling cry of rage the fiend then vanished, and the architect found himself alone once more, by the rushing river. No trace of his companion remained except a faint odor of brimstone, which seemed to linger on the quiet evening air. With hasty, trembling steps, the architect returned home, and all night long he tossed about on his sleepless couch, vainly striving to recollect the plan of the cathedral, which hovered vaguely and tantalizingly before him. But, in spite of all his efforts, he could not reproduce even the most simple detail.

Day after day passed, the appointed time was almost gone, and still the architect was no nearer his goal than at first. Once more he wandered out through the Frankenpforte to the banks of the swift-flowing Rhine, and there, in the gathering twilight, as he had hoped, in spite of a momentary spasm of fear, the fiend once more appeared before him.

"The plan is still at your disposal, sir architect," he murmured in soft, insinuating tones. "Subscribe to my conditions, and you shall have it."

As in a dream, the architect beheld the finished cathedral, and heard the cries of an enthusiastic multitude praising his name. Overcome by the temptation, he quickly gasped:

"I consent—the plan! Give it—quick!"

"Meet me here, at midnight, to-morrow," answered the Tempter, "and as soon as you have signed your name to a certain little pledge, which I shall have the honor of laying before you, the plan will be yours." The thought of submitting such a marvelously beautiful plan to Engelbert the Holy, and of the glory which would ever rest like a halo upon his name, at first occupied all the architect's ideas; but when night closed in, and he found himself all alone in his room, the recollection that his soul would be lost forever came upon him with all its force.

With loud groans, and many tears, he sank upon his knees, to entreat aid from Heaven; but when he would have prayed, he could find no suitable words and could only repeat, over and over again, the short conversation which had taken place between him and the fiend. His housekeeper, awakened by his groans, grew pale with horror as she crouched by the key-hole and heard every word.

Tremblingly she put on her hooded cloak, stole out of the house door, locked it behind her, and thrusting the key into her pocket, hobbled off to church, where she poured out the whole story into the astonished ears of her father-confessor, and wound up by imploring him to save her master's soul.

The priest, who had listened very attentively, pondered the matter for a while, and then began to explain to the tearful, anxious woman that a plan sufficiently beautiful to induce her master to pledge his soul for its possession must be obtained almost at any price. However, he admitted that a human soul should be rescued, if possible; and producing a piece of the true cross, set in gold and precious stones, bade her give it to her master, with minute directions for its use. The holy relic concealed beneath the dark folds of his mantle, the architect stole out alone, late at night, to keep his appointment with his Satanic Majesty. Not a star twinkled in the firmament above, and the wind whistled and moaned as it blew over the river, and touched his pale face with its clammy breath. Not a sound was heard in the city, save the dismal howls of a few dogs, until the bells slowly tolled the midnight hour.

As the twelfth stroke died away, the Evil One suddenly appeared with a huge roll of parchment tucked under his arm.

"The plan! the plan!" gasped the architect, shivering with something besides the cold.

"It is here. You shall have it, in a moment," answered Satan. "Just prick your finger with your penknife, use your blood to sign your name to this pledge, and the plan is yours."

The architect ransacked his pockets, but could not find his knife. Satan, who had anxiously watched his fruitless search, uttered an impatient ejaculation, and hastily cried:

"Here, hold this plan for a moment, while I look for a sharp stone."

For a moment he groped around in the darkness, but when he had found what he wanted, and raised his head, he recoiled in horror. The architect stood before him, clasping the plan close to his breast and brandishing the relic above his head as he vehemently cried: "Get thee behind me, Satan! Back, I say! In the name of the One who died upon this cross, I bid thee depart." Cowering in fear, his ugly features distorted by rage, Satan exclaimed:

"Villain! You have outwitted me, but I shall yet have my revenge. The plan is yours, it is true, but the cathedral shall never be finished without my aid and consent. The story of your fraud will be noised abroad, but your name, instead of enduring forever, will soon be buried in oblivion."

With a threatening gesture Satan then vanished, while the architect hastened home with the precious plan which he had secured at such a terrible risk. Engelbert the Holy approved of it warmly, and the work was begun without delay. Countless workmen were employed, enormous sums were expended, and the architect, fondly hoping to outwit the Evil One a second time, had his name engraved in deep characters on one of the large stones of the tower. In his eagerness to see the effect, he sprang upon this block before it was properly secured, and as he leaned over, it tipped and fell to the ground, carrying him with it and crushing him to death beneath its weight.

Owing to this accident the work was stopped, but, although often renewed, hundreds of years passed by ere the cathedral of Cologne was entirely finished. It is, moreover, commonly reported that it would still be incomplete, had not Satan consented to its termination, and even contributed funds for the construction, by establishing a famous lottery in its behalf. But, although the cathedral begun in 1225 was finished in 1880, the name of its real architect is still unknown.

COLOGNE CATHEDRAL.

The Devil's Wager.

AMONG the numerous legends recounted to explain the long unfinished state of the Cologne Cathedral, is another amusing specimen.

The devil had not forgiven the wily architect who had once so cleverly defeated his calculations; and was fully resolved to make a second attempt to secure his soul. Disguised, therefore, as on a former occasion, he went to call upon the architect, who, recognizing him, could not restrain a certain feeling of elation at the thought of having escaped him; a feeling which was greatly increased by the first words spoken by his Satanic Majesty.

"Well, sir architect, your work progresses finely, in spite of the few condemnatory expressions I made use of on the memorable occasion when you got the better of me. You must really excuse the temper I then showed; but, you see, it was the very first time that I had been outwitted, and until then, I scarcely realized that you were more than a match for me."

"You flatter me," stammered the architect; overcome by his polite bow, yet rather doubtful whether the speech was intended as a compliment or as an insult.

"No, no!" replied the devil. "Not at all, my dear sir, you are fully as smart as I; and if you have no objection, I would like to make a bet with you where you could not so easily outwit me a second time."

Bewildered by these compliments, and forgetting in his conceit that he owed his safety to divine intervention only, the architect agreed to the bet. So the devil engaged himself to bring water from Trèves to Cologne, by a new aqueduct, before the cathedral was finished, the architect's soul being the prize of the winner.

This bet duly settled, Satan vanished, and the architect, doubling his force of workmen, labored early and late at the cathedral, and even had a great stone, upon which his name had duly been engraved, hoisted up on the nearly finished tower. One evening, just after this stone had been set into place, and before it was properly secured, the architect climbed up to the top of the tower, and glancing toward the heights, saw a silvery stream of water come rushing toward the city with the force and rapidity of a torrent.

"The devil has won!" he exclaimed, springing upon the great stone in his dismay. A moment's oscillation, and stone and architect fell to the ground, where the latter was crushed to pieces.

Tradition further relates that the devil, in the shape of a huge black hound, darted forward to seize the architect's soul ere he was dead, but came just too late to secure his prey. A very ancient bas-relief commemorates this tradition, and the traveler can there see the hound vainly trying to secure the architect's soul, which, however, escapes forever from his power.

The Devil's Stone.

THE devil, who plays so important a part in all the legends of the cathedral, was so angry when he saw the work advancing that he flew to the Seven Mountains, caught a great block of stone in his nervous grasp, and hurled it with all his might against the nearly completed building. His animus was such that the ponderous block would surely have struck and wrecked the building, had not a benevolent Providence interfered by suddenly sending so strong a wind that the stone deflected from its course and fell harmlessly short.

This stone, which can still be seen, and is known as the Devil's Stone, bears the imprint of Satan's hot hands, and the people of Cologne aver that ever after that, Satan was duly careful to allow for the wind whenever he aimed for a certain goal.

The Fire Bell.

In one of the great towers of the Cologne cathedral hung the great bell which rang morning, noon, and night to call the faithful to prayers, and solemnly tolled the flight of time. Constant use gradually dulled its sound, however, and finally the city council declared that Wolf, the great founder, should fashion a new bell, for which they appropriated twenty-five thousand pounds of pure metal.

Wolf made the mold, melted the metal, and invited all the people to witness the casting of the new cathedral bell. As he directed the stream of liquid metal into the mold, he proudly looked around him, and hoping to make a good impression upon the unsophisticated people, hypocritically exclaimed: "God speed the casting!"

As he was an utter atheist, however, this prayer was not granted, and when the mold was broken, the bell was found useless, as it was cracked from top to bottom. A second mold was prepared, a second casting made, and as the same mockery was again gone through with, the second bell also proved an utter failure.

Angry at this double mischance, Wolf prepared to make a third casting, and in his excitement he exclaimed as usual: "Devil take the work!" which impious words made the people shudder with horror.

In spite of the founder's impiety, however, the bell this time proved quite flawless, was hung in the tower, and Wolf was invited to be present that his hand might ring the first melodious peal. Pleased with the honor, the founder gave a mighty pull to the rope, but instead of the harmonious sound he expected, the mighty bell gave forth such a harsh, discordant tone that the people anxiously crossed themselves, and looked up at the tower with a shudder of horror.

Wolf himself, horrified at the sound, started back in dismay and fell from the tower, but the great bell remained there, not to summon the faithful to the house of God, but to warn the citizens of Cologne that some great danger was threatening them. Its harsh, discordant tones are never heard, therefore, except in case of fire or war; and when they rend the quiet air, the women and children cross themselves and pray, while the men rush forth to give the required aid.

> "Since then there hangs that fated bell, a warning to the bad ;
> A lesson to the wicked 'tis, its tale so deep and sad ;
> The offspring of the skill of hell, the child of curses dire,
> 'Tis now but toll'd in time of storm, of dread, or doole, or fire."
>
> —*J. G. Seidl.*

The Legend of the Cross.

IN the cathedral of Cologne are a number of holy relics, which are exhibited for the edification of the faithful on all solemn occasions. Here, in a costly shrine, are the skulls of the Magi, which, transferred from Constantinople to Milan, found a permanent resting place in Cologne already in the twelfth century.

The cathedral also boasts of the possession of a fragment of the true cross, of which the following curious legend is told :

Although driven out of the garden of Eden, and prevented from ever returning to its grateful shade by the angel with the flaming sword, Adam and Eve often longed to see its glories again. Feeling the dreaded approach of death, and hoping to prolong his life, Adam once bade Seth hasten thither, to secure some balsam from the tree of life, directing him to follow the footprints burned into the soil by his flying feet. Seth, ever obedient, soon came to the gate, where the angel with his flashing sword bade him pause and state his errand.

Sadly shaking his head, the heavenly messenger then replied that four thousand years must elapse ere pardon would become manifest, and that the wood of the cross, upon which the Lamb of Atonement would be slain, would grow from the grave where Adam would sleep. As Seth was about to turn aside discouraged, the angel bade him cast a glance into Paradise, and see what Adam had forfeited. Seth perceived the matchless garden, and caught a glimpse of the tree of life, whose root went down into the depths of hell, where Cain was suffering the punishment of his crime, and whose summit, almost lost in the skies, supported the graceful form of a woman, clasping a beautiful child to her breast. This babe cast upon him a glance of ineffable compassion.

The guardian angel, stretching out his hand, then plucked three seeds from this lofty tree, and gave them to Seth, bidding him return home, and plant them upon his father's grave. Shortly after, Adam died and was buried, the seeds were planted, and three trees, a pine, cedar, and cypress, springing out of the grave, twined round each other, until they formed but one immense trunk.

Moses used a twig of this tree to perform his miracles, David sat beneath it bewailing his sins, and Solomon had it cut down to furnish one of the lofty pillars for the Temple. Owing to some error, however, the pillar was first too long. then too short, and was finally discarded and cast by Solomon's order into the Cedron, whose waters carried it away to the South. The Queen of Sheba, on her way to Jerusalem, saw the mighty log, secured it, and offered it to the king, who not being able to use it in spite of all his efforts, had it sunk in the pool of Bethesda, whose waters then received their miraculous power. The trunk, however, rose again to the surface just before the Crucifixion, and was used to fashion the cross upon which the Lord died.

Buried upon Calvary, the cross remained untouched until Helena, mother of Constantine, came to seek it, three hundred and twenty-eight years later, and distinguished it from the crosses of the malefactors, lying beside it, by the miraculous effect it had upon a dying woman, whom it restored to life. The cross, thus recovered, remained in Jerusalem until borne away by Chosroes, King of Persia, from which country it was recovered by Heraclius, in the year 615. It was then that the true cross was divided into innumerable fragments, which have gradually been scattered in various churches throughout the world, where they are always regarded as relics of great value.

The Eleven Thousand Virgins.

ONE of the most noted churches of Cologne is dedicated to St. Ursula, and is richly and fantastically decorated with paintings representing various scenes of her life, and with the bones of her eleven thousand martyred companions.

Ursula was the only child of Vionetus, or Thionetus, King of Brittany, and of his beautiful wife Daria. The maiden showed great instincts of piety, and as soon as she was old enough, learned to read all the theological books and treatises, and became as well versed in theology as the most learned priest. She was also very beautiful, but early in life she registered a solemn vow to serve the Lord only, and to forego marriage and all worldly pomps for his sake. When she was but fifteen years of age Ursula lost her mother, and shortly after that her father, whom the Venetians call the Moor, received an embassy from Agrippinus, King of England, who wished to secure Ursula's hand for Conon, his only son. Vionetus, knowing that a refusal might be considered so insulting as to entail a bloody war, did not dare to say no; yet he could not bear to force his child into a detested alliance. While he was pondering what answer he could give, Ursula, discovering the cause of his perplexity, volunteered to give her own reply. After having duly prayed she summoned the ambassadors, and told them she would consent to the proposed alliance,

LANDING OF ST. URSULA AT COLOGNE. *Memling.*

provided the heathen prince would embrace Christianity, would give her ten handmaidens of spotless purity and noble birth, each accompanied by a thousand virgins, would supply an equal number of virgin attendants for her own train, would grant her three years of freedom that she might make a pious pilgrimage to Rome, visiting all the holy shrines by the way, and would claim her as wife only when the journey was ended.

The ambassadors, having received this answer, hastened home, where they described the Princess Ursula's beauty and attainments in such glowing terms, that the heathen prince immediately received baptism, and collecting the eleven thousand virgins from all parts of his kingdom, sent them over to Brittany to attend their future queen.

Ursula received the maidens gladly, and bidding them assemble in a flowery meadow, she expounded the Gospel so convincingly that she soon converted them all. The English prince, hastening to Brittany at her summons, was told to remain for a while and comfort her father, while she and her maidens embarked in a number of vessels, in which they intended to sail for Rome. Dismissing pilot and sailors, Ursula declared they needed no other guidance and assistance than God's, and singing pious hymns in chorus, the maiden band sailed away. Now, either because Ursula was deficient in geography, or because she was indeed guided by an unseen hand, she steered her vessel northward, instead of southward, and with the other vessels in her wake entered the Rhine, where, aided by favorable winds, she sailed against the current, disembarking only once at Cologne.

Here she was favored by the vision of an angel, who appeared at the foot of her bed, holding the martyr's palm, to warn her that on her return she and her eleven thousand virgin companions would suffer martyrdom at the hands of the Huns. Calmly resuming her journey on the morrow, Ursula sailed up the Rhine to Basel, where, according to some accounts, she was met by the captain of a Christian legion, who escorted her across the mountains. Other versions relate that the procession of spotless maidens was preceded by six angels, who smoothed the road under their feet, spread tents for their protection at night, and provided food and refreshment on the way.

Still singing hymns in chorus, the maidens arrived in Rome, where Pope Cyriacus joyfully received and blessed them, and where they were joined by the prince and his attendants, who had also undertaken the pilgrimage, and had hastened to Rome by another way. The eleven thousand virgins, having finished visiting all the shrines, now prepared to return northward, accompanied by Prince Conon and his attendants, and by Pope Cyriacus and sundry cardinals and priests.

Two Roman generals, heathens, seeing the maidens depart, and fearing lest their example and preaching should convert all the northern barbarians, sent a secret message to the King of the Huns, who was then besieging Cologne, to bid him slay Ursula and her train as soon as they came to that point on their way down the Rhine.

The maiden procession, attended by the prince and Pope, passed over the Alps, crossed Switzerland, re-embarked at Basel, and sailed down the Rhine where the wild Huns, after slaying all the men, attacked the pious maidens. Exhorted by Ursula, they all died like martyrs and went to heaven to receive the promised palm and crown. Ursula, last of all, was pierced by three arrows from the Huns' bows, and only one of her maidens managed to escape from their murderous fury. This maiden, Cordula by name, was hiding in the hold of one of the vessels, when she was favored with a vision, saw the skies open, and beheld all her companions enter Paradise, waving their palms and singing hymns of praise. At this sight she repented of her cowardice, and after a fervent prayer left her hiding place and went in search of the martyrdom which she soon found.

"The maiden spoke and sought the shore ;
In one short hour she lived no more.
Upon thy lovely banks, O Rhine,
Poured her pure blood like new-pressed wine.
Can it be doubted that she got
The high reward she so well sought?
Or that, amidst the maiden choir,
She now, in glory, strikes the lyre?"
—*Rheincronik—Hagan.*

The bones of the eleven thousand holy virgins were hastily interred, but none knew the exact spot where they had been buried, until Kunibert, bishop of Cologne, having fervently prayed that he might discover the holy relics, saw a dove come down from the sky, and after fluttering overhead for a moment, flit off to a corner of the church, where it began to scratch diligently. Guided by this sign, the bishop began a search, which soon proved successful. The bones of the eleven thousand virgins now serve as decoration for the church, and St. Ursula's remains, having been found interred separately, were placed in a sarcophagus, on which the miraculous dove is represented.*

A Prompt Retort.

THE Church of the Minorites in Cologne, which, according to the legend, was erected by the cathedral workmen during their hours of rest, is supposed to have been begun in 1220 and finished forty years later.

In this church was buried the celebrated theologian and philosopher, Duns Scotus, whose epitaph gives a short *résumé* of his career, for beside the date of his death, 1309, it bears the Latin inscription, "Scotia me genuit, Anglia me suscepit, Gallia me docuit, Colonia me tenet."

According to tradition, this sage was buried in a trance, and many years later, when the vault was opened to receive a new inmate, it was discovered that Duns Scotus had left

* See Note 7 in Appendix.

his coffin and dragged himself to the foot of the stairs, where he had evidently perished of cold, hunger, and thirst. Thus sadly and tragically ended the life of one of the wisest men of his time, who was also noted for great quickness at repartee. He was a favorite of Charles the Bold, who often invited him to his table, where he tried to call forth some of the noted sallies of the philosopher's keen wit. On one occasion, the Duke of Burgundy, in a facetious mood, asked the sage sitting opposite him what was the difference between Scot and sot, wording his question like Bacon, "What is there between Scot and Sot?"

"The table only," replied the philosopher promptly, to the great discomfiture of his princely interlocutor, who however did not dare to resent the answer which he had provoked.

The Magician and the Courtiers.

In the Church of St. Andrew in Cologne can be seen the tomb and relics of the famous magician and astrologer Albertus Magnus, who lived and died in the neighboring convent of the Dominicans, where he once displayed his marvelous power for the entertainment of William of Holland.

Invited in midwinter to a garden feast in the convent, William of Holland wonderingly accepted the invitation, and accompanied by his courtiers, all clad in their warmest garments on account of the inclemency of the season, he resorted thither at the appointed time. The guests were immediately led into the gardens,—a cheerless picture of wintry gloom,—where at a motion from the magician's wand the scene was suddenly changed to all the glory of midsummer.

Throwing aside the warm garments, which the tropical heat rendered unendurable, the courtiers flung them carelessly down on the grass, and gayly partook of the rich viands and cooling drinks brought by the monks for their delectation. Jest, song, and feasting beguiled the time so successfully that the guests started with surprise when the convent bell suddenly began to ring the "Ave Maria." At the first stroke of the bell, Albertus Magnus' magic had been entirely dispelled, and the courtiers, standing knee-deep in snow, tugged at their garments, which were half incased with ice, longing to throw them over their shoulders to preserve themselves from the icy blasts which again swept down from the north.

Their sudden dismay and frantic efforts greatly amused William of Holland, who, in token of thanks for the monks' garden party in midwinter, gave them the tract of land between Cologne and Rodenkirchen. The courtiers who were sent to carry this deed to the convent on the morrow, were politely invited into the refectory, where the prior poured out some of his choicest wine for their refreshment. Charmed with the flavor of this vintage, the messengers drank toast after toast, until the prior, fearing they would not leave until they had drained the cask, implored Albertus Magnus to devise some means to make them depart. The magician, therefore, stepped forward and again filled their cups, but when the guests would fain have tasted this wine they saw lurid flames rise out of each vessel, and in their terror each turned and clutched at his companion, not noticing at first that each had caught the other by the nose.

The flames subsiding suddenly, they were covered with confusion at their absurd position, and were so furious at having thus been turned into ridicule that they left immediately, and never returned to tax the convent hospitality again.

The Sacrilegious Painter.

THE Church of St. Mary of the Capitol, founded by Plectrude, mother of Charles Martel, upon the site once occupied by the Roman Capitol, possesses as altar-piece a crucifix to which great miracles are attributed. Some young painters, idly talking together one day, dared one of their number to enter the church and renew the sacred emblem's freshness by giving it a new coat of paint.

The artist, a heedless young fellow, immediately accepted the challenge, and knowing the priests would not permit him to touch their holy image were he to present himself in the daytime, he entered the church alone at midnight. Just as the city clocks were tolling the hour, he dipped his brush in the paint, but no sooner had the bristles touched the crucifix, than his arm fell paralyzed to his side.

Gazing upward in terror at the figure on the cross, he fancied he saw such a reproachful glance fall upon him that he fell down before the altar in convulsions. A priest found him there early in the morning, but, in spite of every care, he expired unconscious, when the clocks were again tolling the midnight hour, and since then no painter has dared to touch the sacred image on the altar.

The Christ Child and the Boy.

A POOR widow of Cologne daily brought her only child, a little boy named Hermann Joseph, to pray before the image of the Virgin and Child, in the Church of St. Mary of the Capitol. The little fellow, deeply impressed by his mother's stories, and by the beauty of the image, was very anxious indeed to make some offering, such as he saw laid upon the shrine, but, as they were very poor indeed, he had nothing to give.

It happened one day, however, that Hermann Joseph, for the first time in his life, received a great rosy-cheeked apple. This seemed such a priceless treasure to him that he rushed off alone to the church, and kneeling before the image, begged Mary, with all a child's innocent faith, to let her beautiful babe stoop down, and take in his little hand the gift he had brought.

This simple prayer was granted, and the Virgin bending down, the Christ Child took the apple with such a radiant smile that little Hermann Joseph returned home beside himself with delight. In hopes of pleasing the Child, he daily brought a tiny offering to lay at its feet, scouring the hedgerows for the daintiest wild flowers, searching for wild strawberries, and gathering the brightest pebbles he could find.

When Hermann Joseph was ten years old, however, his mother informed him that she was too poor to continue sending him to school, and that he must now learn a trade, so he could make his own way in the world ere long. The poor child, who loved his books, and had hoped to become a priest, ran tearfully into the church, and, falling down upon his knees, confided his sorrow to the Virgin and Child.

When he had ended his prayer, a gentle voice fell upon his ear, and looking upward he saw, as well as heard, that the Virgin was speaking to him. She bade him lift a stone behind the altar, beneath which he would find a sum of money sufficient to enable him to go to school and become a priest as he wished.

Overjoyed at this promise, little Hermann Joseph sought and found the money, which enabled him to continue his studies and enter a monastery. There, absorbed in his learned researches, he forgot the Virgin and Child, and spent all his time in abstruse study. One day, however, his memory suddenly deserted him, and finding he could remember nothing he read, he closed his books in despair.

Then the recollection of his happy childhood came back to him, and realizing how forgetful and ungrateful he had proved, he returned to Cologne, where, flinging himself on his knees before the image, he humbly implored forgiveness for his sins. He lingered there all day long on his knees, and fell into a doze toward evening; he dreamed the Virgin spoke to him as of old, promising him a happy life in Paradise, where the Lord would repay him for all his childish offerings by giving him heavenly flowers and fruit in lavish profusion.

This dream comforted Hermann Joseph greatly, and when he awoke and found his memory entirely restored, he returned fervent thanks. He returned to his convent, and resumed his studies, which, however, never again made him forget to worship the Holy Mother and Child.

In commemoration of this legend, a statue has been placed in the church of St. Mary of the Capitol, representing the Infant Jesus bending down to accept Hermann Joseph's first childish gift.

According to another version of this legend, the child Hermann Joseph died while he was very young indeed, and the mourning mother was comforted by a dream, in which the Infant Jesus spoke to her, promising her child should be his playmate in heaven, and reap a rich reward for his childish gifts. Knebel has versified this form of the legend, and his poem concludes with the lines:

"And thus he spoke in dying:
'O mother, dear, I see
The beautiful Child Jesus
A-coming down to me!

"'And in his hand he beareth
Bright flowers as white as snow,
And red and juicy strawberries.
Dear mother, let me go!'

"He died. And that fond mother
Her tears could not restrain;
But she knew he was with Jesus
And she did not weep again."

The Resurrection of St. Maternus.

THE Church of St. Gereon, in Cologne, is also known as the Church of the Martyrs, in honor of the three hundred and eighteen soldiers of the Thebaid legion. They suffered persecution there with their captain Gereon, under the Emperor Diocletian, and their bones still serve to decorate the building.

The first church on this site is said to have been erected by order of the Empress Helena, over the bones of St. Maternus. The legends relate that when this good and holy man died the people, unable to live without his wise counsels, implored St. Peter, who was then bishop of Rome, to restore him to life.

When St. Peter heard this appeal, he looked fixedly in the direction of Cologne and cried in loud tones: "The time of rest has not yet come, Maternus. Arise, and fight for the Cross." Then, turning to the messenger, he gave him his staff, and bade him hasten homeward, and lay it on the grave, promising that the saint would come to life again, although he would already have lain forty days in the tomb.

St. Peter's prediction was duly fulfilled, the good old saint rose from the dead, lived as many years after his resurrection as he had spent days in the tomb, and when he died, at last, it was with the full consciousness that he had obeyed St. Peter's injunctions, fought the good fight to the end, and deserved the rest which was awaiting him in the many mansions.

The Church of the Apostles.

JOST VON BUHL, the wealthy merchant of Cologne, was very unhappy indeed, as he remorsefully thought of his many sins, and wondered how he could make the scales of justice incline in his favor when the great and terrible Day of Judgment came. All night long he pondered this question, and when morning dawned, he hastened down to the river side, purchased a whole boat-load of fine blocks of stone, and had them carted up to the place where the Church of the Apostles, which had fallen into ruins, was slowly being rebuilt. He, himself, went with the carters, and when they halted before the place, stepped up to the monks who were gazing in open-mouthed astonishment at the long procession of carts and said: "Good Fathers, is it quite true that one good deed will outweigh many bad ones, when the Holy Apostles weigh our sins and virtues in their scales on the Judgment Day?"

"Yes; it is true," answered the monks wonderingly.

"Well, then," exclaimed Jost von Buhl, "I'll give you these stones to rebuild your church, trusting they will prove ponderous enough to make the scales tip in my favor, and outbalance my sins on the last day."

The church which the wealthy merchant thus helped to rebuild in the thirteenth century was daily visited, about one hundred years later, by the beautiful young wife of Mengis von Aducht, who came there to implore the Virgin to grant her dearest wish and give her a child.

One day when this fair lady, Richmodis, had been praying more fervently than usual, the Virgin suddenly leaned down from the altar and gave her a skull. She accepted it and gazed upon it in sad resignation, thinking it surely portended an early death instead of maternity. But while she was thus silently gazing down upon it, she saw three delicate white roses spring out of the skull, change to white-winged angels, and softly fly away.

Pondering deeply on this mystery, Richmodis returned home, was taken ill, died, and was buried, by order of her inconsolable husband, in the church she loved so well. The night after her interment, while Mengis sat mourning alone in his empty house, the sexton, an avaricious man, stole into the church, lantern in hand, opened the tomb, and prepared to rob Richmodis of her costly jewels.

But just as he bent over the corpse to draw the wedding ring from her finger, he saw her slowly rise. As he fled in terror, she crept out of the tomb, crossed the market place, and knocked loudly at the door of her house. The mourning knight von Aducht was roused from his abstraction by the sudden appearance of his frightened servants, who breathlessly declared that their beloved mistress stood in the street waiting for admittance.

Mengis von Aducht heaved a deep sigh, gazed at them in wonder, and mournfully said: " Alas! the beloved dead never return, and I would sooner believe that my horses were gazing out of the attic window, than credit the idle tales you tell."

Hardly had the words left his lips, however, when a heavy tramping was heard along the stairs and overhead, and a moment later his faithful steeds thrust their heads out of the attic window, whinnying plaintively as they felt the cool night air.

Convinced by this miracle of the truth of the servants' statements, the knight now rushed to the door, caught his recovered wife in his arms, carried her into bed, and a few days later she was entirely restored to life and health. She even lived to bear three beautiful children, who were so good and lovely that all deemed them angels, and she often told them the story of her reception of the skull, which portended her death, and of the three white roses which sprang out of it and represented them, imploring them to do all in their power to become angels at last, that the whole vision might come true.

As for Mengis von Aducht, he ordered horses' heads to be carved in stone, and placed under the gable of his roof, as a constant reminder of the night when his steeds climbed up to the attic and gazed out of the window into the street, where his newly risen wife was patiently waiting for readmittance into his house and heart. These stone heads can still be seen, and are one of the curiosities always pointed out to strangers in the quaint city of Cologne.

The Stain of Sin.

ANNO, bishop of Cologne, lay all alone in his bed chamber in the Episcopal palace, one night, but while all his attendants were plunged in slumber, he alone could not sleep. The thought of his sins kept him awake, and in the wee small hours of the night he winced at the thought of the tyranny he had shown in robbing the people of all their former privileges.

While he was musing thus, the Angel of Death suddenly entered his room, pronounced the mystical words which separate soul and body, and a moment later the bishop saw his own corpse lying stiff and cold, and was hurried away by the angel through unlimited space. In a few seconds he was brought into a vast hall, illumined by tall tapers, and filled with the intoxicating perfume of the most precious incense.

Anno gazed about him in surprise, and saw that he was in a goodly assembly of all the noble bishops who had passed away before him. He recognized among others, the bishops of Cologne, St. Maternus, Severinus, Kunibert, Hildebold, Bruno, St. Herbert, and his own predecessor Hermann, beside whom was a vacant seat. Conjecturing that this place was reserved for him, Anno was about to sit down, when Arnold, bishop of Worms, detained him, and, pointing to a hideous stain on his breast, declared in solemn tones:

"None but the stainless can sit here. Return to earth, oh, brother! remove the stain, and then we will welcome you."

Reluctantly, for he was very sorry to leave this peaceful spot, Anno returned to earth, resumed his abode in his lifeless clay, and when morning came hastened to atone for the sins of the past by restoring all their former privileges to the inhabitants of Cologne, and doing penance for his sins.

The next night, when all was still, the Angel of Death again came to visit him, and led him away to the heavenly mansion, where, seeing the disfiguring stain had vanished, the bishops gladly received him in their midst to dwell with them in bliss forever.

The Heinzelmännchen.

In the good old days, when fairies, elves, and dwarfs constantly visited the earth, when wishes were immediately granted, the virtuous always rewarded and the wicked invariably punished, the inhabitants of Cologne were particularly favored, as they were under the protection of the Heinzelmännchen, a tiny race of benevolent beings, who stole noiselessly into their houses at night, and deftly finished all the work which, though begun, had been set aside before it was ended.*

Relying upon their aid, the bakers set their dough to raise, slept soundly, and when they awoke found piles of newly baked loaves; the miller's grain was ground, and the flour tied up in sacks; the housewives' rooms were swept and dusted, the spinner's flax all spun, and a tailor in town always found the garments he had begun to cut out, duly made and pressed, lying neatly folded upon his table.

Now, the tailor's wife was a very inquisitive woman, and very anxious to see the benevolent Heinzelmännchen, who labored so kindly for them. As she was a heavy sleeper and could not easily wake up, she strewed dry pease all over the floor ere she went to bed one evening. The tiny Heinzelmännchen, racing to and fro in their busy haste, stepped on the pease, tripped and fell, making such a clatter with the irons, tongs, scissors, etc., that the tailor's wife, waking up, hastened to take a peep at them.

The Heinzelmännchen, seeing her, and guessing that it was she who had strewn pease on the floor, were so indignant that they left the house and town forever. Since

* See Note 8 in Appendix.

then the people of Cologne have been obliged to do their tasks unaided, and all the work which is not finished at nightfall is sure to be found in the same unsatisfactory state in the morning, for the Heinzelmännchen have vowed never to visit the town again.

The Novice.

A KNIGHT and his beautiful little eight-year-old daughter Beatrix once paused at the gate of a convent in Cologne where dismounting, the knight intrusted his child to the holy nuns, bidding them take good care of her, and admit her into their order, if, at the end of ten years, he had not returned from Palestine to claim her.

Ten years passed by, and the beautiful child had become a lovely maiden, whom all the nuns loved dearly, and to whose deft fingers they owed the floral decorations which daily decked the Virgin's altar in the convent chapel. The nuns, wishing to give Beatrix every facility to steal in and out of the chapel to carry her flowers, had even intrusted the key to her keeping, and when the ten years were ended, they readily prevailed upon her to become a novice.

A few days after, when Beatrix was in the convent garden, gathering flowers, the portress bade her step into her cell, and gaze out of her window—the only opening beside the door in the long wall—and see the bright pageant filing past. Beatrix, eager to catch a glimpse of the gay world which she only dimly remembered, leaned out of the casement, and soon attracted the attention of a handsome young knight, who threw her a kiss. A few days later the little novice stole into the chapel at midnight, laid the keys at the Virgin's feet, told her she was about to steal forth into the world to join one who loved her dearly, and implored her forgiveness, and a kindly welcome should she ever return. Then, stealing out into the street, the little novice vanished, and it was only fifteen years later that a veiled lady rang at the convent gate, inquiring of the portress whether the convent had not sheltered a novice by the name of Beatrix some fifteen years before.

The portress, a garrulous old crone, immediately informed her that Beatrix was there still, honored by all for her many virtues, and, that although she had refused to take the veil for many a year, she was to take her conventual vows on the morrow. Then, at the stranger's request, the portress pointed out the entrance to the chapel, which opened out into the street, and watched her glide into the empty place of worship.

The returned Beatrix, for it was she, fell upon her knees, and implored the Virgin's pardon. To her utter astonishment she then heard the image on the altar relate that for fifteen long years, the Virgin, in her guise, had faithfully fulfilled the duties which she now bade her resume, instructing her to take the vows on the morrow.

The nuns, coming into the chapel at dawn, found the novice Beatrix, who had spent the night in prayer at the foot of the altar, and tenderly led her away to array her for the ceremony, little thinking that she had been absent fifteen years, and that it was the Virgin who had served the novitiate in her stead.

The new nun now lived such a holy, exemplary life that she became the pattern of all the sisterhood, and finally died in such great odor of sanctity that she was canonized.

The Priests' Gate.

THE city of Cologne was once strongly fortified. Now the mighty walls have all been razed, the moats filled, and the space they occupied is used as a public park or promenade. Several of the old city gates have been allowed to stand, however; the most noted among these monuments being the Hahnenthor and the Pfaffenthor, of which latter the following story is told:

At one time the burghers of the city were very anxious indeed to maintain their freedom, which the various archbishops had tried to restrict in many ways. Engelbert the Holy, coming to the Episcopal see, determined to get the better of this rebellious element, and with this purpose in view took measures to secure its noted leader, Hermann Gryn.

As he dared not make away with him openly, he had recourse to a stratagem, and sent a message to the worthy burgher, inviting him to a convent near the city gates, where he wished to hold a secret interview with him and discuss the best plan for settling their continual feuds. Hermann Gryn promised faithfully to be present at the appointed hour and place, but, instead of keeping the matter secret, as the prelate had requested, he imparted it to the city council, telling them he was not without fear of foul play, and begging them to come to his rescue, should his absence be too prolonged.

Courageously then, Gryn wended his way alone to the convent, knocked, and was admitted. They led him along dark passages, until he came before a heavy iron door, which the monks told him opened into the archbishop's private rooms. Here they bade him enter alone, as their presence was not desired at the interview.

Hermann immediately complied with what seemed a very natural request, but when he found himself in total darkness, and heard the iron door quickly shut and locked behind him, he was seized with dismay. He then remembered that the monks kept a lion as a curiosity, and concluded that he had treacherously been exposed to its fury.

A moment later a loud roar broke the silence, proving that his conjectures were true; so he quickly drew the sword which he wore hidden under his cloak, resolved to defend

COLOGNE.

City Hall.

his life. A terrible struggle took place in the darkness, but the man finally slew the lion, and stepping over its carcass began to explore his prison, which was lighted at the farther end by a small grated window. When evening came, and the worthy burghers saw no signs of their beloved leader's return, they went in haste to the convent, where the brothers told them that Hermann Gryn had imprudently ventured into the lion's den and been slain. Deceived by the monks' pretended sorrow, the burghers began to bewail their loss as they slowly moved away, but, suddenly, their mourning ceased, for through a grated window they saw a hand frantically beckoning to them, and heard Gryn's voice calling them to the rescue.

To storm the convent, break in the doors, rescue Gryn, and learn from his lips the whole story of the monks' perfidy, did not take the enraged citizens very long, and in their indignation they seized and hung the lying brothers under the great arched doorway, which has since been known as the Pfaffenthor or priests' door.

To commemorate Hermann Gryn's brave face to face encounter with the lion, a bas-relief representing the scene was placed directly above the main entrance of the City Hall of Cologne, where it can still be seen.

BRAUWEILER.

The Game of Chess.

As Otto III. was but a child when his father died, leaving him heir to the Western Empire, the cares of the government were intrusted to his mother, and to a handsome and capable young nobleman named Ezzo, who acquitted himself nobly of this charge.

The young emperor was brought up at court under his mother's eye, but his lovely sister, Mathilda, was sent to the convent at Brauweiler, where she spent many years under the care of the nuns, leaving this quiet retreat only to witness the coronation of her brother, which took place as soon as he was of age to reign alone.

Count Ezzo, who, as already stated, was young and handsome, no sooner saw the lovely princess than he fell deeply in love with her, and his heart beat high with pleasure when he noticed that she seemed to prefer his society and conversation to that of all the other courtly knights. His happiness was of short duration, however, for Mathilda soon returned to her convent home, and he became so melancholy and absent-minded that the emperor began to marvel at the sudden change in his usually genial companion. Thinking to divert him from the sad thoughts, whose cause he did not in the least suspect, Otto one day challenged Ezzo to a game of chess, laughingly exclaiming that the victor of three successive games might ask the vanquished for any boon he chose, which the latter would be forced to grant.

Pale and trembling with eagerness, for he now saw a way to urge his suit, which, until then, had seemed hopeless, Ezzo began the game, and played so skillfully that he beat his sovereign thrice. Then, falling at the monarch's feet, he asked for the hand of Mathilda, which Otto, mindful of his promise, agreed to bestow upon him, providing he could win the young lady's consent.

Seeing the ill-suppressed anxiety and impatience of the suitor, Otto then laughingly bade him prepare to bear an important missive to the Brauweiler convent, telling him to be sure and wait until he received an answer to it in person. Ezzo, needless to state, was soon ready, and rode in hot haste to the convent, where, as bearer of an imperial message, he was allowed to see the Princess Mathilda alone.

The answer to the letter must have been all he could wish, for he soon informed the prioress that he had come to escort the princess to court, where she was to be married. The prioress, hearing this news, shook her head in dismay, and vainly tried to prevail upon Mathilda to select a heavenly rather than an earthly spouse. As the young couple were about to ride away she again renewed her entreaties, and seeing no signs of relenting in the princess' beautiful, blushing face, she angrily exclaimed :

"I'd sooner believe this withered staff could again bud and bear leaves, than that any good will accrue to you out of this alliance."

Ezzo, seeing a cloud pass over his beloved's countenance at these ominous words, hurled after her instead of the customary blessing, suddenly caught the staff out of the holy mother's hand, thrust it deep in the earth near the convent door, and exclaimed, "Let it remain there, holy mother, and we will see whether or not God approves of the union of loving hearts, and sanctions earthly marriages," ere he rode gayly away at Mathilda's side. The marriage preparations were soon ended, the nuptial ceremony took place, and as the solemn benediction was pronounced over the newly married couple, the mulberry staff put forth its first tiny little leaf. Little by little it grew and developed, until it became a mighty tree, and flourished as proudly as Ezzo and Mathilda, who lived happily together, and whose many children grew up to be as good and happy as they.

The mulberry tree is still standing near the Brauweiler convent, at a short distance from Cologne, and whenever it shows any signs of decay, if true lovers kiss beneath its shade, it is sure to send forth a fresh shoot, which in due time replaces the withered and dried up tree.*

* See Note 9 in Appendix.

ARNOLDSWEILER.

The Minstrel's Ride.

ARNOLD, the minstrel, was once invited to accompany Charlemagne on a hunting expedition to the great Bürgelwald forest, where plentiful game was to be found, so that he might amuse the emperor and his guests, while they sat at meat and rested from their strenuous exertions.

At noon, one day, the emperor bade Arnold sing to him, and was so charmed with the minstrel's great talent, that he promised to grant him as much land as he could ride around ere the meal was ended. Arnold immediately sprang on the emperor's own steed, which was offered him, and rode rapidly away, scoring the tree-boles with his sword as he dashed by.

As the minstrel urged the horse to its utmost speed, the animal had not gone very far ere it began to show signs of fatigue, but Arnold, who had foreseen this, and cleverly stationed relays of horses along the road he intended to pursue, urged him ruthlessly on, nor paused except to change steeds, when he came to the first station he had marked out. Riding thus at full speed, and changing horses ere their energy quite flagged, he rode around all the Bürgelwald, and when he returned to the camp the emperor laughingly remarked that he had returned too soon, was evidently too modest, and concluded by asking how much land he now claimed.

"The whole forest!" exclaimed the minstrel, falling at the emperor's feet, and then he boldly confessed the stratagem which he had used.* The emperor freely forgave him when Arnold informed him that he had acted thus merely to secure the revenues of the Bürgelwald for the benefit of the poor and sick. Charlemagne, touched by his humanity, gave him also the neighboring castle, which became the home of Arnold's descendants, who all cared for the poor

* See Note 10 in Appendix.

as diligently as the minstrel, in whose honor the neighboring village of Arnoldsweiler is named.

ZÜNDORF.

The Crystal Palace.

In the bed of the Rhine, between Zündorf and the little island of the same name, is the crystal palace of Father Rhine, if the report of a village midwife is to be believed. One night, when she was about to retire, this woman was suddenly called away from home by a taciturn man, enveloped in a great cloak, and carrying a lantern of curious pattern.

Following him closely in the pouring rain, she stumbled along in the darkness until she felt cold water eddy around her ankles. She was about to jump back in terror, when the man caught her in his arms and plunged with her right into the river. When she opened her eyes again, she found herself in a beautiful crystal palace, all set with precious stones, where she was shortly bidden to take good care of a beautiful golden-haired nymph or Undine.

The nurse was so efficient, that before many hours had passed her patient was comfortably settled, and able to talk a little. In soft whispers the golden-haired lady now confided to the old nurse that her husband was the mighty water spirit whom mortals call Father Rhine,* while she was the only daughter of the Lord of Rheidt.

One day, clad in foamy green, and disguised as a mortal, Father Rhine had appeared at the village dance, invited her to tread a measure with him, and whirling her around in ever widening circles had reached the river edge and suddenly plunged with her into the stream, where he had conveyed her to his crystal palace and made her his happy wife.

The fair young lady then cautioned the old woman to

* See "Myths of Northern Lands," by the author.

accept no more than the usual reward for her services, no matter how eagerly her husband might press her to accept rich gifts, and closed her eyes in feigned sleep as Father Rhine appeared. Seeing his beloved wife entirely out of danger, the river god beckoned to the nurse to follow him, led her into his treasure chamber, where lay great heaps of gold, silver, and precious stones, and bade her help herself.

The old woman, mindful of the advice just received, passed by jewels and gold, selected the small silver coin which was her usual guerdon, and resisting all her mysterious conductor's entreaties to take more, signified her readiness to depart.

Taking her by the hand, Father Rhine then passed along a dark corridor, rose with her through the limpid flood, deposited her, dripping but safe, on the shore near her native town, and vanished, after flinging a whole handful of gold into her lap. Ever since then, the simple people delight in telling of the marvels of the crystal palace beneath the flood, for the old woman often described it minutely for the benefit of her admiring listeners, always producing a handful of gold in proof of the truth of her tale.

GODORF.

The Will-o'-the-Wisp.

THE marshy peninsula which extends between Godorf and Rodenkirchen is said to be the favorite resort of the sprite known all along the Rhine as the Herwisch, and in England as the Will-o'-the-Wisp. This mischievous little creature is said to delight in leading unsuspecting travelers astray, and in playing all manner of pranks, but, like most practical jokers, he is quick to resent any attempt to make fun of him.

One day a maiden, passing across this stretch of ground

at nightfall, began to sing all the songs she knew, to beguile the loneliness of the way and inspire her with courage. Having soon come to the end of her scanty répertoire, she carelessly sang a mocking ditty about the Herwisch, who, enraged at her impudence, came rushing toward her threateningly brandishing his tiny lantern.

With a cry of terror, the girl began to run, closely pursued by the sprite, who, in punishment for her derisive song, flapped his wings in her face and frightened her so badly that she became an idiot.

Since then, the young people of Germany have never dared to sing the mocking refrain, and carefully avoid mentioning the Herwisch's name after nightfall, lest they should in some way arouse his anger.

AIX-LA-CHAPELLE.

The Magic Ring.

CHARLEMAGNE, king of France, and emperor of the West, had married a beautiful Eastern princess by the name of Frastrada, for whom he had conceived an intense passion. Thrice before had Charlemagne been married, and he little suspected that his affections, which he had long deemed extinct, could revive with such fervor. All wondered at his devotion, but none suspected that the gold ring inscribed with cabalistic signs, which Frastrada continually wore, was the magic talisman which had worked such a charm.

The new queen, however, did not long enjoy her power. A dangerous illness overtook her, and when on the point of death, fearful lest the ring should pass into the hands of another, while she was buried out of sight and forgotten, she slipped the magic treasure from her finger into her mouth and breathed her last.

Solemn preparations were made to inter her with great pomp in the cathedral of Mayence, but when they would fain have carried her thither, the emperor, who had seemed quite stupefied with grief, flung himself on his knees beside the corpse, clasped it in his arms, and passionately declared that he could not bear to consign it to the dark and lonely tomb, where it would be lost to his sight forever. In vain the councilors and courtiers argued and entreated; in vain Turpin, the prime minister, represented that the people had need of him ; the emperor refused to leave the apartment where the dead queen lay, or to partake of any food. Exhausted at last by his lengthy fast and extravagant grief, Charlemagne fell asleep at his post, and Turpin, who had been watching for this opportunity, and who, by this time, felt convinced that the queen possessed a charmed gem, noiselessly stole to her bedside.

But, although he carefully examined hands, neck, and ears, no such jewel was to be seen. He was about to give up the search, when, bending over the corpse, he suddenly perceived a glimmer of gold through the parted lips of the dead queen. Trembling lest the emperor should awaken before he had accomplished his purpose, Turpin hastily extracted the ring and concealed it on his own person.

A few minutes later Charlemagne awoke. His first glance fell upon the corpse, from which he turned with a slight shudder ; his second upon the faithful Turpin, who was anxiously watching him.

"Turpin, my faithful friend !" he suddenly cried, leaving his seat and casting himself into the prime minister's arms. "Your presence is like balm to my wounded heart! You shall remain by my side forever !"

This first outburst over, the emperor quietly allowed himself to be led from the mortuary chamber, pausing at the door for a moment to give orders for the long delayed burial. Then, accompanied by Turpin, who was forced to ride constantly by his side, Charlemagne saw Frastrada's remains consigned to the tomb prepared to receive them, over which was placed the Latin inscription which is still legible in spite of the many years which have since come and gone.

The courtiers, ever watchful and inclined to jealousy, soon noticed Turpin's wonderful influence over the emperor, and knowing naught of the magic ring, were at a loss to account for it. As for Turpin, wearied beyond all expression by Charlemagne's constant demands upon his attention, and fearful lest the ring should eventually pass into less scrupulous hands, he could find no rest either night or day, and vainly sought to devise some safe plan to rid himself of the troublesome gem.

One night, when the emperor had left his palace at Ingelheim, and was camping out in the forest on his way to the north, Turpin left the tent where his master lay sound asleep, and wandered out into the moonlight alone. It was the first time, since the ring had come into his possession, that he had been able to elude Charlemagne's watchfulness and enjoy a moment's solitude, and his heart swelled with a feeling of relief as he plunged into the pathless forest. While he cogitated how he could best dispose of the magic ring, Turpin wandered on and on, until, at last, he found himself at the opening of a beautiful glade. The moonlight flooded this retired spot and shone like silver over the deep and quiet pool, which lay thus embosomed in the dark woods. Lost in admiration at the tranquil beauty of the scene, Turpin sat down on a stone and feasted his eyes in silence.

But soon the ever present idea of the magic ring came to disturb his contemplative mood. With a sigh he drew it from its hiding place in his breast, and for the first time he noticed, by the pale light of the moon, that beside some cabalistic signs the ring bore the image of a tiny swan. Suddenly the thought struck him that the opportunity so long and vainly sought was now at hand, and that the deep and placid waters before him would soon close over and conceal the ring forever. A moment later, the jewel flashed beneath the rays of the moon, a slight splash was heard in the night air, ever widening ripples broke the mirror-like surface of the pool, and a snowy swan appeared, sailing with stately calm over the ruffled waters.

Immensely pleased to be rid of this care Turpin now retraced his steps to the emperor's tent. There he soon had the satisfaction of perceiving that the spell was broken, and that Charlemagne had returned to the old undemonstrative friendship which had united them for many a year, and no longer paid him the unwelcome attentions of a passionate and jealous lover.

The emperor, however, betrayed some signs of restlessness, and when the sun had risen bright and clear, he suddenly proposed that they should tarry in that spot another day, and enjoy the pleasures of the hunt in the mighty forest. His proposition was hailed with enthusiasm, and soon after the forest echoes were all rudely awakened by the joyous clangor of the hunting horns, as a royal stag started from the covert, closely followed by huntsmen and hounds. In vain the frightened animal exerted its utmost speed, the hounds still pursued, until, panting and exhausted, he was brought to bay in the very glade which Turpin had visited the night before. Charlemagne, who had been foremost in the chase all morning, and who alone had been in at the death of the stag, now checked his steed, and remained motionless in his saddle, gazing in spellbound admiration at the sunny stretch of water which reflected the blue sky, and at the stately swans gliding over its smooth surface. "Ah! how beautiful!" he exclaimed. "I would fain linger here forever."

Then he dismounted, cast himself down upon the smooth grass by the edge of the pool, plunged his hands into the cool tide, and quenched his ardent thirst. There he remained in dreamy content all day long, summoning his courtiers thither by winding his horn. When the shadows began to lengthen, and the lurid glow of the setting sun was reflected in the miniature lake, he made a solemn vow to build a palace near this spot, that he might revel in its beauty and never be forced to leave it again.

The vow was kept, and the palace became the nucleus of Charlemagne's capital and favorite city Aix-la-Chapelle. When many years had passed, and the great emperor felt the approach of death, he commanded that his body should be laid to rest in the cathedral vault, not far from the spot he loved so well, and pronounced an awful curse upon the sacrilegious hand which should attempt to open his tomb or to remove his remains.

Strangers visiting Aix-la-Chapelle are cautioned against visiting the magic pool by moonlight, for, at the mystic hour when Turpin dropped the ring into its placid waters, the spell recovers all its former power, and the traveler who has once been subjected to its sway may wander where he will; his longing heart will always lead his reluctant feet back to the charmed spot.

The Cathedral Legend.

THE cathedral of Aix-la-Chapelle, with its delicate yet lofty spire, had been duly begun, and the work was well under way, when it was brought to a sudden standstill from lack of funds to complete it. In vain all the councilors of the city put their wise heads together, they could not find any way of raising money, and were about to give up the attempt in despair, when a little old man suddenly appeared in their midst, proposing to give them a barrel of gold in exchange for the soul of the first living creature which entered the cathedral after it was all finished.

At first the magistrates recoiled horrified, and demurred, but when Satan, for it was he, demonstrated that if they did not accept his offer, he would immediately make use of the money to purchase up many venal souls, they decided to take the gold and reveal to no one the way in which it had been procured. Satan, having thus obtained their solemn promise to deliver up to his tender mercies the soul of the first living creature which entered the cathedral, promptly supplied all the necessary funds. The work progressed rapidly, and soon the people of Aix-la-Chapelle began to talk of the dedication of their cathedral.

All at once, however, the general joy was turned to sorrow, and all the inhabitants of the city, who had been strangely anxious to penetrate within the closed doors, now loudly declared they would never set foot inside the sacred building. Seeking the reason for this sudden revulsion, it was soon ascertained that one of the councilors had confided the secret of Satan's interference to his wife. She in her turn had intrusted it to the keeping of a friend, whence it had, of course, spread over the town like wild fire, filling all hearts with nameless dread.

The Pope and bishops, finding no one willing to enter the cathedral, and not wishing to risk their own precious souls, were at a loss how to proceed, when a monk suddenly came into their presence and proposed a plan which was hailed with enthusiasm by every member of the clergy. By their order the preparations for the dedication were speedily ended, and when all was ready, and the people of Aix-la-Chapelle duly assembled in front of the cathedral, a huge box was brought and placed close beside the doors, which were set ajar.

Then the box-lid was cautiously slipped aside and a captive wolf, springing out of his narrow quarters, rushed into the empty edifice. The assembled multitude saw the monks shut the door, heard a howl of rage, and saw the building shake violently from foundation to spire. While they were gazing open-mouthed at this miracle, the doors burst open and the devil escaped, snarling with anger at being outwitted,

AIX-LA-CHAPELLE CATHEDRAL.

and banging the door so noisily behind him that it was cracked from top to bottom.

Satan having fled, and his power being ended, the priests fearlessly entered the cathedral, thrust out the dead body of the wolf, and solemnly proceeded to dedicate the beautiful building to the service of God. Since then, however, one of the cathedral doors has been disfigured by an unseemly crack, while another, of more recent date, bears the effigy of a wolf, apparently playing with a pine-cone, which the mediæval artist intended as a symbol of his soul.

The devil, however, did not forget that he had been outwitted, and patiently bided his time, hoping he would find some means of revenge. After several years' cogitation, he resolved to pick up a great mound of earth which then stood near Leyden, carry it to Aix-la-Chapelle, and drop it on the city at nightfall, thus crushing cathedral and inhabitants at once. The journey was long, the mound heavy and cumbersome, and, owing to the dusk and the size of his burden, Satan could not very well descry the position of the town. He therefore asked an old woman, whom he met by the way, to point out its exact location.

She recognized her interlocutor by the peculiar smell of brimstone hovering around him, told him he had gone far out of his way, and pointing to the right, where she declared the city lights were twinkling, she bade him walk on another mile.

Misled by these directions, the devil strode on, dropped his burden upon what he supposed was the city, and chuckling with glee, returned home. Imagine his chagrin, therefore, when passing near there one day, to discover that he had flung the mound down in the center of a plain near the city, where it now forms the much frequented summer resort known as the Lousberg.

Charlemagne, it is said, was so pleased with the cathedral erected in his favorite city, that he donated three thousand pounds of sterling silver for the manufacture of a suitable bell. The work was intrusted to a dishonest founder, who appropriated the precious metal for his own use and substituted pewter.

The emperor, wishing to be the first to ring the new bell, pulled the rope as soon as it was hung, but, dismayed at the dull clang it produced, he called the founder and bade him ring it. Hoping to deceive the monarch, the dishonest artisan tugged so lustily at the rope that the huge clapper fell down upon him, and killed him in punishment for his dishonesty.

Ever since then the bell, whose silvery tones had been intended to summon the faithful to church, has been rung for fires only, and whenever its discordant clang is heard the people start up in dismay, for they know some great misfortune has occurred.

Charlemagne, at his own request, was buried beneath the cupola of this church, where his body rested undisturbed until the Emperor Otto III. ordered the opening of his predecessor's tomb. Charlemagne's body was found perfectly preserved, sitting upright on an ivory throne, with all his regal emblems around him, his sword Joyeuse at his side, and an open Bible on his knee. The chair upon which he sat is now exhibited in the cathedral, for the emperor's body was placed in a sarcophagus, where it has remained ever since. As for the sword and regalia, they were transported to Vienna, where they figure among the imperial crown jewels.

Eginbard and Emma.

AMONG all the scholars trained in Alcuin's school at Aix-la-Chapelle, none was more apt and diligent than Eginhard, who won not only his master's praise but also the approval of Charlemagne. As soon, therefore, as his education was completed, the emperor offered him a position at court, where he became his private secretary and knew all the secrets of state.

Young Eginhard, honored by all for his learning and integrity, soon won the affections of Emma, Charlemagne's daughter; but, fearful of the emperor's displeasure, the lovers met only in public, and then had but little occasion to exchange tender words and glances. One winter night, however, overcome with longing to see his beloved, Eginhard stole softly across the courtyard, and visited her in her tower. Forgetful of time in the pleasures of unchecked conversation, he lingered beside her until dawn, and when he would fain have left her, shrank back appalled, for the ground was all covered with newly fallen snow.

Not daring to cross the yard, lest his footprints should betray his carefully guarded secret, and compromise his lady-love, Eginhard stood hesitating at the door, until Emma, with ready woman's wit, declared she would carry him over, for the double track made by her feet would occasion no ill-natured comments. This plan was immediately carried out, and Charlemagne, after a sleepless night, gazing idly out of his window, saw his daughter carrying Eginhard across the yard.

In open council, that selfsame day, the emperor recounted what he had seen, and asked how he should deal with the culprits; but when his advisers recommended banishment or death for the presumptuous young secretary, he declared that in his eyes all mortals were equal and that he deemed it wiser to bestow upon him his daughter's hand. The young people were then summoned, and amid the general silence the imperial decision was made known.

Longfellow has given us an admirable poetic version of this charming legend, which he concludes thus:

> "And the good emperor rose up from his throne,
> And taking her white hand within his own
> Placed it in Eginhard's, and said: 'My son,
> This is the gift thy constant zeal hath won;
> Thus I repay the royal debt I owe,
> And cover up the footprints in the snow.'"
>
> —*Tales of a Wayside Inn.*

The Emperor's Sin.

CHARLEMAGNE, the great and glorious emperor of the West, had sinned so deeply that he dared not even confess his wrong-doing in order to obtain absolution and recover his long lost peace of mind. In spite of all his efforts to reveal it, his lips refused to speak, and that transgression, buried in his heart and branded in his memory, made him feel like an outcast from the Church.

Tortured by remorse, he finally sought the presence of St. Egidius, a holy man of Aix-la-Chapelle, and penitently kneeling before him, began to confess all his sins. The minor transgressions were quickly disposed of, and soon nothing remained to be told except that one awful sin whose shadow darkened all his life. Instead of words, however, the emperor could only utter heart-rending groans, while scalding tears coursed down his pale face.

Touched by his evident remorse, and longing to help him free his soul from its burden of sin, Egidius finally gave him his tablets, bidding him write the confession he had not strength to utter. But the emperor sadly shook his head, pushed the tablets aside, and, as soon as he could speak, confessed that, much as he would like to do so, he could not obey, as he had never learned to write.

Egidius, not at all surprised,—for in those days only a few learned men knew how to read or write,—then offered to teach Charlemagne the art, so that he might at last confess his sin and obtain forgiveness. The emperor received this proposal with joy, and patiently learned to trace his letters, although his mighty fist, accustomed to swing the battle-ax and brandish the mighty sword Joyeuse, was but little fitted for such work.

The mastery of the art of writing cost him far more exertion than would have been required to win a victory over a horde of fierce barbarians, and great beads of perspiration often appeared on the imperial brow, ere he succeeded in learning to trace the words which would reveal his great sin.

While Charlemagne, weeping and groaning, was painfully tracing the record which his lips refused to utter, Egidius knelt in a corner of the cell in silent prayer. The emperor having finished his confession, and added a fervent plea for forgiveness, dropped his stylus, rose from his seat and humbly laid the tablets before St. Egidius, who stared upon them with a face of blank astonishment. He had seen Charlemagne tracing heavy, unformed characters, yet the surface of the tablets was perfectly smooth and no trace of writing was to be seen.

While he was thus gazing fixedly upon it, a few words in golden letters suddenly appeared, and eagerly looking at them he saw: "God forgives all who truly repent." A low exclamation of surprise attracted the attention of Charlemagne, whose head was bowed in deep contrition, and looking up, he too read the comforting assurance that his sin had been forgiven.

The Emperor's Ride.

TEN long years had passed since the emperor had ridden out of his favorite city, at the head of his army, to go and fight the heathen, and now, instead of the welcome tidings of his return, dark rumors of defeat and death spread throughout the whole country. Convinced of the truth of these reports, the lords of the empire assembled to discuss what had better be done, and, after much deliberation, sent an embassy to the Empress Hildegarde. They bade her, for her subjects' sake, choose another husband to rule the nation wisely, instead of Charlemagne, who would never be seen again.

Hildegarde, at first, indignantly refused to consider this proposal, but finally, seeing the justice of their wishes, she consented, for the good of the country, to marry any man they recommended; stipulating, however, that she should be allowed to spend three more days in strict solitude, mourning for the beloved husband whom she would never behold again.

Well pleased with this answer, the lords withdrew, and began making preparations for the coming marriage, while Hildegarde wept for Charlemagne, who, by the way, was not at all dead, but very busy fighting the heathen, whom he had almost entirely subdued.

During the night, while poor Hildegarde wept, an angel of the Lord suddenly appeared to Charlemagne, and bade him return in hot haste to Aix-la-Chapelle, if he would not lose both wife and scepter at once. Thus warned, the emperor sprang on the steed which the heavenly messenger had brought, and sped over mountain and valley with marvelous rapidity, arriving at Aix-la-Chapelle just as the third and last night of Hildegarde's respite was drawing to a close.

Instead of entering his palace, however, the emperor dismounted and passed into the silent cathedral, where he seated himself in his great golden chair, with his sword across his knees, as was his wont when dispensing justice. There he waited until the sacristan came to prepare the church for the wedding, which was to take place soon after sunrise.

This man, startled by the sight of the imposing figure seated upon the imperial throne, and thinking it an apparition, staggered, and would have fallen, had he not steadied himself by the rope of the great bell, which, thus suddenly set in motion, sent peal after peal through the awakening city.

The people of Aix-la-Chapelle, startled by the untimely and frantic ringing, rushed out of their houses to see what had occurred, and as they entered the church they uttered loud cries of joy, for there sat Charlemagne in all his wonted state.

These cries soon reached the ears of the unhappy Hildegarde, who, still dissolved in tears, and deeming they were intended to welcome her unknown bridegroom, shrank back in fear; but her sorrow was changed to boundless joy when she saw her beloved husband once more, and heard how Providence had miraculously interfered to save her from a hated second marriage.*

Roland's First Adventure.

CHARLEMAGNE once summoned all his knights before him at Aix-la-Chapelle, and told them he was very anxious to secure a priceless jewel set in the shield of a robber knight who ranged the Ardennes. He bade them go forth separately and try to secure it, promising that the successful knight should have any reward he cared to claim.

As it was then a time of peace, and there was no fighting on hand, the knights were only too glad to sally forth in quest of the robber knight, each secretly hoping to secure the jewel and return in triumph to Aix-la-Chapelle on the appointed day.

Milon, Charlemagne's brother-in-law, was specially anxious to win the prize, and, accompanied by his young son Roland, who acted as his page, he scoured the Ardennes forest for many a day. All his search proved in vain, however, and weary and discouraged, Milon dismounted from his steed, removed his armor, and lay down under a tree to sleep, bidding Roland keep watch beside him.

The lad obeyed, but soon, seeing his father asleep, and longing for some exciting adventure, he donned the armor, sprang on the war horse, and rode into the forest. There he encountered the robber knight, whom he recognized by the jewel glittering brightly in the center of his shield.

Too brave to retreat, although somewhat dismayed at the prospect of an encounter with an antagonist so much taller and stronger than he, Roland laid his lance at rest, charged

* See Note 11 in Appendix.

gallantly, and, when unhorsed, continued the struggle afoot. An inadvertent movement on the part of the robber knight finally permitted the young hero to deal him a mortal blow; and after cutting off his hands and head, wrenching the jewel from the shield and hiding it in his bosom, Roland returned to the place where his father was still sleeping soundly.

Carefully removing all traces of blood, and putting the armor back as he had found it, Roland awaited his father's awakening. Without saying a word, he then accompanied him on a further quest, and viewed his dismay when he found the lifeless body of the antagonist he had so long and vainly sought.

On the appointed day all the knights appeared before Charlemagne in Aix-la-Chapelle, each accompanied by a page bearing the head, hands, or some part of the armor of the robber knight of the Ardennes. One and all declared they had found him slain in the forest, where, according to the traces, a terrible encounter must have taken place.

Last of all came Milon with dejected mien. He was closely followed by Roland, however, who held a shield in which the resplendent jewel was set. At this sight all the people set up a loud shout of joy, and Charlemagne bade Milon step forward and claim his reward. Amazed at this reception, the knight turned to gaze in the direction where all their glances were fixed, and seeing the jewel, openly declared that, as he had not won it, he deserved neither reward nor praise. Roland, closely questioned by his imperial uncle, now revealed how he had obtained the prize; and when asked to name his reward, said he would fain be admitted among the number of knights privileged to accompany Charlemagne wherever he went, and to fight always by his side.

A Generous Deed.

RUDOLPH, count of Hapsburg, was riding alone one day, and came to a rushing torrent near Aix-la-Chapelle. He plunged his spurs into the sides of his mettlesome steed, and was about to stem the raging current, when he suddenly became aware of the presence of a feeble old priest, who was tucking up his gown to ford the stream.

The count paused to warn him of the danger, but the old priest calmly continued his preparations, declaring that as a dying man had sent for him to administer extreme unction, it was his duty to risk his life, even, in order to save a soul.

Touched by the priest's simple faith, and the strong sense of duty which urged him to confront any peril, the count sprang from his steed, bade the old man mount, and watched him until he had safely crossed the stream and was out of sight. Then Rudolph returned home on foot, wondering whether he would have the courage to do his duty as faithfully as that feeble old man.

Early on the morrow, the priest appeared before his door, leading the steed, which he brought back to the count with many thanks. He said that owing to its fleetness he had reached the bedside of the dying man in time to induce him to ask forgiveness for his sins, and trust in the mercy of the Lord. Rudolph of Hapsburg listened attentively to the old priest's tale, and then made him a present of the horse, vowing that it should ever after be used to carry the priest and his brothers on their constant errands of mercy.

Many years later, when this count of Hapsburg had become emperor of Germany, and was surrounded by the pomps of his imperial court, a wandering minstrel sang the tale of this kindly deed, and the people cheered enthusiastically when they heard that it was their beloved emperor, who had given his favorite steed to further the good work of the priests of Aix-la-Chapelle.

The Golden Eggs.

FREDERICK, emperor of Germany, having abdicated in favor of his son Maximilian, the people crowded around the new ruler, seeking to win his favor by the gifts which they hastened to offer him. One deputation after another laid their offerings at his feet, and last of all came a messenger from the Jews, the usurers of the town, bearing a basket all filled with eggs of the purest gold.

The people gazed in awe at the gift, which was of fabulous value, and were greatly surprised when, instead of the gracious thanks they fully expected, the emperor sternly bade his guard seize the messenger, lock him up in the dungeon, and capture all the usurers in town.

The Jew money-lenders, falling at his feet, implored his mercy, wringing their hands, inquiring how they could have incurred the royal displeasure, and offering great sums for their release. But Maximilian paid no heed to their prayers and ironically said, as he bade the guards lead them away:

"The hens which lay such desirable eggs should be kept in a place of safety."

LÜLSDORF.

The Cruel Sister.

CLOSE by the village of Lülsdorf, near the right bank of the Rhine, is the ruined tower of an old castle, built in the fifth or sixth century, which was once inhabited by a knight and his two daughters. These maidens were of very different characters and dispositions, for one was gentle and lovely, while the other was hard and vindictive.

The gentle maiden was engaged to be married, and on the eve of her wedding strolled by the riverside, where she was joined by her elder sister, who, unknown to anyone, had fallen deeply in love with the prospective bridegroom.

While pretending a friendliness she was far from feeling, the jealous sister lured the morrow's bride out of sight of the castle, and bade her stretch out her hand and pluck a beautiful water lily growing almost out of reach. Then, as the gentle girl leaned far over the water, she suddenly and treacherously pushed her in. The struggling maiden tried to scramble ashore again, and piteously implored her jealous sister to help her, promising all she could think of as a bribe to induce her to lend a rescuing hand, but all in vain. When she had sunk for the third and last time beneath the deep waters, the wicked sister crept home in the gathering darkness, entered the bride's room, locked herself in, and issued forth on the morrow only, decked in bridal array and closely veiled.

As the sisters were of the same height and figure, and as their voices were exactly alike, no one suspected the fraud. The marriage ceremony took place, and when it was ended, the newly married couple returned to the castle, where they were entertained during the nuptial feast by the songs of many minstrels who had hastened thither at the report of a wedding.

One of these minstrels, the last to arrive, pausing by the river to mend a broken harp-string, had found in the sedges the corpse of the beautiful bride, which had been washed up by the tide. By virtue of his art, for tradition reports he was a magician as well as a musician, he fashioned a harp out of the maiden's body, using the strands of her golden hair for strings.

> "The body which lay outstretched on the sands,
> Became a beautiful harp in his hands,
> For he took the maiden's snow-white breast
> And he made it a place for the chords to rest.
> And on her small fingers so fair to see
> He fixed the strings as well might be;
> Which out of the locks of her golden hair,
> He twined with a skill so wondrous rare."
>
> —*Snowe's translation of German poem.*

With this marvelous instrument he now appeared before the wedding guests, and letting his fingers wander over its strings, produced a melody so plaintive and soul-stirring that the veiled bride suddenly burst into tears. The bridegroom, pushing the veil aside to wipe them away and comfort her, suddenly discovered the fraud, and wildly inquired what it meant.

But the harper continued his strain, unmoved by all the commotion around him, until the pleading tones became so urgent that the murderess, goaded to madness by their importunity, confessed her crime ere she sank to the floor in violent convulsions from which she died.

ZÜLPICH.

Clovis' Vow.

ZÜLPICH, as the ancient Tolbiac is now called, is the site of Clovis' famous battle against the invading Teutons. It was here he uttered the solemn vow that if the God of his Christian wife Clothilde would only grant him the victory, he would be baptized, and would serve him only all the rest of his life.

The victory remained with the Francs, and Clovis, mindful of his vow, was duly baptized in the cathedral at Rheims, where the archbishop, St. Remi, solemnly bade him bend the knee before the Lord of heaven, and henceforth burn what he had worshiped, and worship what he had been wont to destroy.

LÜFTELBERG.

The Charitable Girl.

A LEGEND relates that this eminence received its name from Lüfthilde, a charming and charitable girl who did much good to the poor. She employed all her spare moments in spinning fine thread which she sold at a high price, and

VOW OF CLOVIS. *Blanc.*

devoted all the money which she thus earned to buy remedies for the sick, who considered her far more skillful than any leech.

Charlemagne, out hunting one day, had the misfortune to wound himself sorely, and would have bled to death, had not this deft-handed maiden been summoned. By her timely assistance she saved his life. Full of gratitude for her services, the emperor bade her mount his horse, promising to give her as much land as she could ride around ere sundown. Lüfthilde, nothing daunted, urged the emperor's steed to its utmost speed, and rode all around the forest now known as the Lüftelberg.

To prove that she had really been all around it, she dropped her spindle, and kept twisting her thread, which was found to describe the exact boundary of the land which the emperor gave her in fee. This she appropriated for the use of the poor, founding an order of nuns, who employed all their time in caring for the sick.

VILLICH.

The Box on the Ear.

In the tenth century Adelheid was abbess of the nunnery at Villich, and by her energy kept all her nuns in very good order and hard at work. A broken-hearted young lady once asked permission to enter her convent, saying that her betrothed had perished in battle in a distant land, and that, as she was now entirely alone, she would fain retire from the world.

She was therefore admitted, took her vows, and as she was the possessor of a beautiful voice, was soon appointed leader of the convent choir. One day, while she was singing in her stall, her glance fell down upon the congregation, and there, among the people, she suddenly beheld her lover, who had not been slain, but only sorely wounded. Her surprise was so great that she paused abruptly in her pious strain, and a loud, discordant cry broke from her trembling lips.

The abbess, who was a quick-witted woman, and equal to any emergency, immediately perceived the cause of the nun's confusion. To bring her promptly back to a realizing sense of time and place, she raised her hand and dealt her a sound box on the ear.

Startled into propriety by this stinging blow, the nun went on with the service, singing as truly as before, and tradition recounts that never again did she dare to raise her eyes during the service, or sing a note out of tune, for fear of feeling the abbess' heavy hand.

> " And lo ! a miracle ! the maid
> Casts down her shameful eyes :
> Then raised her song in sweet accord,
> To all the nuns' surprise.
> —*Adelheid von Slotterfoth.*

BONN.

The Vehmgericht.

In the crypt of the cathedral of Bonn, which is said to have been founded by Constantine, were once held those famous midnight meetings of the German secret society called Vehmgericht, which, in the Middle Ages, took the law into its own hands, and executed summary justice, acting as powerfully and independently as the Inquisition in Spain.

The Lord of Freyerwahl, a lawless robber knight, had long committed every sort of crime with impunity, and everyone had learned to fear and detest him.. One day, while riding through a village, he caught a glimpse of a lovely young girl, the niece of the priest, whom he kidnaped that selfsame night, after setting fire to the parsonage to prevent immediate pursuit. The poor village priest lost all he had in the flames, but his deepest sorrow was caused by the total disappearance of his orphaned niece, of whom he could obtain no tidings. One year after this calamity, which he had never ceased to mourn, the priest was summoned by an emissary of the Vehm, and led into the crypt of the Bonn cathedral at midnight. While waiting for further developments, he took note of the silent masked figures, the sable-hung walls, open grave, ax, block, rope, and roll of parchment, which he knew were the emblems of the secret society.

All at once, the silence was broken by the entrance of a prisoner, who was accused of kidnaping a young lady and condemned to marry her. The knight of Freyerwahl, for it was he, angrily refused to do so, but, in spite of all his struggles, the girl was brought in, and, at an imperious sign from the judge, the priest performed the marriage ceremony.

As soon as the service was ended, and while the priest was rejoicing to see his niece once more, the judge went on to declare that the slight reparation just made to the poor girl's honor in no way balanced the crimes committed by the accused, who was then and there sentenced to death and executed. The guilty lord of Freyerwahl's remains were duly interred in the cathedral, but the only inscription placed above them was his name, with the words: "Died by order of the Vehm, 1250."

The Three Sleepers.

BONN, the birthplace of Beethoven, is noted for the extreme laziness of its inhabitants, who love to indulge in their propensity for prolonged sleep. Three young men of this town were said to be specially affected with somnolence. They considered it an unendurable hardship to be forced to wake up and rise some time during the day, and resolved to withdraw to a cave outside the city, where they settled themselves comfortably for a long nap.

Day after day passed by and they slept peacefully on; but at the end of seven years one of them slowly opened his eyes, and sleepily muttered, "Do you hear that ox bellow?" Then he sank back again in sound sleep.

Seven years later, the second youth half opened his eyes and hesitatingly answered, "It is not an ox, but a cow!" ere he too relapsed into oblivion. The silence of the cave was again unbroken, save by the sleepers' long-drawn breath, until another seven years had passed, when the third youth dreamily inquired, "What ox? What cow? Can't you let a fellow sleep in peace?" and turned over to resume his slumbers.

The three Bonn sleepers are still said to occupy the same cave, one of them waking for a moment every seven years. In turn they volunteer a few words, forming a conversation as thrillingly interesting as the one recorded above, which proves how very witty lazy young men are apt to become.

The Devil and the Wind.

His Satanic Majesty, on his usual rounds one wintry morning, entered the cave of the Wind. Many were the pranks which these two mischief-makers had enjoyed together. On this occasion the Evil One seemed unusually talkative and restless. After a few moments' stay, he suddenly rose from his chair and addressed the Wind, who, according to his customary tactics, had incessantly bustled about the cave, upsetting everything in his eager haste to welcome his distinguished visitor from the Lower Regions.

"My dear Wind," Satan exclaimed, "it is a beautiful frosty day. Leave this dark cave and come out for a little walk with me."

The Wind, at this proposal, gave an ecstatic twirl on the

tips of his toes, flew across the cave, and stormily embraced his guest, crying:

"A splendid idea, my dear friend, and quite worthy of your superior genius. I have been pining for exercise, and was just wishing for an excuse to leave this narrow cell."

"Very well," replied the Devil, laughing at his friend's impetuous embrace. "Come along, then."

Arm in arm, the two cronies left the cave and sallied out into the quiet and peaceful world. A heavy frost lay like a white mist over the frozen ground, and the trees, shrubs, and grasses along the roadside were all covered with myriads of icy pendants, which glittered in the early beams of the sun and reflected all the brilliant hues of the rainbow.

"Ha! ha!" chuckled the Wind in Satan's ear. "My dear Devil, do look at those silly trees, shrubs, and grasses, all decked out in their finest jewels! Just see how proudly they display their glittering apparel before an admiring world. Foolish things! They little suspected I would be out to-day. What say you, my friend, shall I trouble their joy a little and upset their silly complacency?"

The Devil, that notorious killer of all innocent pleasure, gladly hailed the proposal.

"Now, just watch me!" exclaimed the Wind, and he drew in such a great, long breath that it seemed as if he must burst.

The trees, shrubs, and grasses suddenly forgot their harmless pride, and the Sun, who had seen the Devil and the Wind putting their heads together, and foresaw that some evil would result from this ominous consultation, drew down the corners of his great smiling mouth, and quickly placed a thick misty veil before his eyes, to shut out the sight which he knew, only too well, would next greet him.

"Ah, Wind, cruel Wind," he sighed; "why not let the earth rejoice in her jewels? Why seek to destroy what is already so perishable?"

The diamond-incrusted vegetation, missing the glad sunlight, and dreading the enemy's power, now began to shiver softly with nameless apprehension. A moment later the Wind, tearing his arm out of his friend's, rushed forward with fury, shook plants and trees until they writhed and twisted in his relentless grasp, and all their bright pendants lay shattered in a thousand minute fragments on the ground.

"Ha! ha! ha!" then laughed the Devil and Wind in chorus.

"Well done! Friend Wind," added Satan, as his companion, having dashed all the bright jewels to the earth, and ruthlessly broken and twisted many tender limbs, now joined him again. "I congratulate you upon your swift executive powers. Really, my dear fellow, I nearly died laughing when I saw those trees writhe in your grasp. And the groans they uttered when you wrenched the diamond crowns from their heads and dashed them to pieces on the frozen ground! It was too funny for words. Ha! ha! ha!"

Arm in arm, once more, and still laughing heartily in chorus, Satan and the Wind continued their walk. The Sun, peeping out timidly from behind the misty folds of his veil, gladly saw them depart, and as soon as they were quite out of sight, he brushed it entirely aside and smiled down encouragingly upon the shivering trees gazing so mournfully upon their ruined finery.

"Courage! courage!" he smiled. "The fiends are gone. Courage my friends, courage. You have my warmest sympathy."

And he shone down upon them so brightly and steadily that the trees, softened by his kind words and looks, slowly dropped great reluctant tears, which sparkled quite as brilliantly as their glorious jewels. These warm tears fell down upon the frozen ground and broken pendants, which soon melted at their contact, and finally disappeared, leaving no trace whatever of their once beautiful presence.

In the meanwhile, Satan and his companion had journeyed on, losing no opportunity, however slight, of doing some damage or of playing some scurvy trick. Nothing and no one seemed safe from their pranks. The Wind impudently kissed the maidens' cheeks until they fairly glowed with indignation, and slyly pinched the little children's fingers and toes until they began to cry. A moment later, he stole treacherously behind a poor old woman, turned her tattered shawl up over her head, and twisted her garments so tightly about her that she could scarcely move a step. Then, laughing and whistling, he snatched the hat right off a venerable alderman's head, and tossed it far away. But, when the old gentleman, puffing and blowing with his unwonted exertions, would fain have laid his pudgy fingers upon his truant headgear, the Wind snatched it away again, forcing the poor old alderman to continue his aggravating pursuit. Weary at last of this sport, the Wind joined his companion, who had watched the alderman's frantic efforts with intense amusement, and had fairly held his sides with laughter, and they both resumed their journey, which finally brought them into the city of Bonn. The Devil, shrewdly glancing right and left, took note of all he saw along the way, and a well-pleased, sardonic grin passed over his expressive features whenever he saw quarreling or strife.

The two companions came at last to a place where the street grew broad and wide, the present Market Place, on one side of which stood a great building used in those days as a Jesuit monastery.

"My dear Wind," suddenly exclaimed Satan, stopping short before the heavy oaken door, "would you mind waiting for me here a few minutes while I run in and see how my dear friends, the Jesuits, are getting on?"

"Not at all!" exclaimed the Wind, who was not sorry to rest a little after all his exertions.

At Satan's touch the oaken door flew open wide, and a moment later the Wind found himself alone and began to walk slowly up and down the street, whistling softly to himself. Satan, in the meanwhile, had begun his round of inspection within. He listened at key-holes, peeped over the brothers' shoulders, glanced through their books and papers, softly whispered a word in this ear and a sentence in that, while the smile on his ugly face deepened and broadened, for he was only too well pleased with all he heard and saw.

"Ha! ha!" he chuckled softly to himself. "These fine fellows are after my own heart, and are so busy dispatching my business that really I cannot tear myself away from them. I must stay here and watch them carry out these little plans of theirs. But to avoid awakening any suspicions, I'll assume the Jesuit robe and cowl, and will even adopt their motto, 'The end justifies the means.' Ha! ha! ha!"

The Wind, awaiting his friend's return, grew impatient. His step grew quicker, his whistle shriller, and as it was very cold he began to blow on his own fingers to keep them warm. Several hours passed, and still no sign of the Devil's return.

"He must have forgotten that I am waiting out here in the cold," exclaimed the Wind, and stepping to the heavy oaken door, he applied his lips to the key-hole, and uttered a long shrill whistle, which roused all the echoes in the old building, caused the Jesuits to draw their cowls closer around their ears and thrust their hands farther up their wide sleeves, while the Devil laughed maliciously to himself as he pictured his friend's impatience.

"There, that will surely fetch him!" cried the Wind complacently, drawing himself up and resuming his interrupted walk, but minute after minute passed and still the door remained closed. To while away the time, the Wind spasmodically tried a few of his former pranks upon the passers-by, but as no one was there, to laugh at his sallies, they no longer afforded him so much pleasure. Repeatedly he whistled at the oaken door, shook it until the boards creaked and groaned, and the Jesuits within crossed themselves in sudden terror. The Wind, in his impatience, then changed his whistle into a prolonged howl, which grew louder and louder, until the good people of Bonn fairly shuddered. But finally, exhausted by these frantic efforts, he ceased howling, and breathed forth long, plaintive sighs, which rose and fell as he trudged backward and forward awaiting the Devil's return.

Years ago the Jesuits forsook the ancient convent, but the Wind, waiting at the door, failed to recognize his old friend in his new garb, and remained at his post. There he still paces, back and forth, sometimes angry, sometimes reproachful, sometimes playful. But go when you will, night or day, summer or winter, you will be sure to find him waiting for his old ally, in front of the old Jesuit convent, on the Market Place in Bonn.

KREUZBURG.

A Strange Bird.

LONG before the Kreuzberg had become a holy spot, and was studded with the crosses to which it now owes its name, the site of the convent was occupied by a cunning fowler. He snared birds of all kinds, which he knew by name and whose habits he could accurately describe.

This fowler was so passionately fond of ornithology that he was never so happy as when he could discover a new specimen, and so proud of his learning that he openly declared he could name any winged creature on earth, and challenged the devil to do as much.

Satan, who had long been watching to secure the fowler's soul, seeing an opportunity to reach his ends, now promised to supply him with all the birds he wanted, in exchange for the possession of his soul at death. He bargained, however, that he would relinquish all claim to it, if the fowler ever brought him a bird he could not name.

At first the fowler, finding his snares always full of game, was delighted with his bargain, but little by little the haunting fear that the devil would claim his soul troubled him so sorely that he wondered, night and day, how he might outwit the fiend. After many days of deep thought, he finally decided to take one of his own little grandchildren, smear him with tar, roll him in loose feathers of every kind and hue, and then present him to the devil, bidding him class the bird and tell its name.

This plan, cleverly carried out, greatly puzzled the devil, who, after vainly scratching his head with his clawlike fingers, and impatiently curling and uncurling his long tail, was finally compelled to declare he was unable to class the strange specimen before him, and must therefore relinquish all claims upon the fowler's soul.

Thus delivered from an awful fate, the fowler revealed the deception he had used, and when the devil took leave of him in a very indignant mood, the happy man solemnly swore that he would never again attempt to deal with the Evil Spirit.

The High Cross.

On the highway leading from Bonn to the castle of Godesberg is a tall cross, erected by one of the knights of Drachenfels. This nobleman had left his wife to take part in the Crusades, and after more than twenty years' absence returned home to find that she had married one of his rivals shortly after his departure.

Burning to avenge this insult, the knight would fain have challenged his supplanter, but he was dead; his wife was in a nunnery, and their sole heir was a youth of seventeen, who little suspected the crime his parents had committed.

Riding along the highway one day, the Lord of Drachenfels met a youth, whom, by his likeness to his faithless wife, he immediately recognized as her son. Carried away by passion, he immediately attacked and slew him; but when the youth lay dead before him, he suddenly realized what he had done, and fled in remorse.

A passing peasant found the corpse and went to the convent, where the unhappy mother, learning her loss, sank back unconscious and died twenty-four hours later.

> "There was a nun in Villich fair,
> Who had lived a life of sorrow;
> They brought her a lock of that stripling's hair,
> And she died upon the morrow."
>
> —*Planché.*

As for the murderer, continually haunted by his young victim's face, he wandered restlessly from place to place. Then, after erecting a memorial cross, known as the Hoch Kreuz, on the very spot where the youth fell, he withdrew into a monastery, where he spent the remainder of his life in doing penance for his sin.

> "This cross was built on this fatal spot;
> More of the tale man knoweth not."
>
> —*Planché.*

GODESBERG.

The Deserted Wife.

On the hill near Bonn, where the ruins of the castle of Godesberg are now to be seen, the Romans once erected a temple to Jupiter, which, however, was changed into a Christian church as soon as the people were converted. This sacred edifice having fallen into ruins, the emperor Julian built a fortress on its site; which, in due time, made way for the present building, of which nothing but picturesque ruins now remain.

Godesberg castle came by inheritance to Gebhard, archbishop of Cologne, who, notwithstanding his clerical vows, fell deeply in love with a fair maiden. As the Reformers were very busy in those days, and in contradiction to the Catholics, permitted their priests to marry, Gebhard, who was no bigoted Catholic, gladly allowed himself to be converted to the new faith.

The Catholic party, resenting his defection and denouncing his first action, which was to marry his lady-love, deprived him of his clerical power and emoluments, which he had forfeited by his marriage. It also declared open war against him, hoping to wrest from his grasp the extensive property which he had inherited, and to which it had no just claim. Forced to defend himself, Gebhard now fought bravely, but, in spite of all his efforts, he soon found himself deprived of all his property, except the castle of Godesberg, where he retreated with his dearly won bride. Even there, however, he was not long allowed to enjoy her company in peace, and seeing himself obliged to go forth again, and do battle against his opponents, he confided her to the care of the last scion of the Neuenahr family. Gebhard was defeated and forced to flee, his castle surrounded, and after a long siege it was captured by the Catholics, who, enraged at the obstinate resistance made by the inmates, then reduced it to its present ruined condition.

The deserted bride, separated forever from her husband, withdrew into a sisterhood of which she was made canoness, to spend the remainder of her life in utter seclusion.

GODESBERG CASTLE.

RAMERSDORF.

The Dancers Cursed.

THE inhabitants of the little hamlet of Ramersdorf had been wont to assemble every Sunday afternoon on the village green, where the young people danced merrily. But when the year one thousand came, all hearts were oppressed by a nameless fear that the end of the world was near at hand. These gay doings all ceased, and the abbot of Löwenberg gladly saw his church crowded from morning till night with humble suppliants for divine mercy.

The much dreaded year came and passed. The sun continued to rise and set, and seeing no signs of coming dissolution, a reaction set in, and the young people gayly prepared to resume their former Sunday afternoon pastime. Scarcely had the music begun, however, when the abbot appeared among them, and peremptorily bade them cease. But when lads and lasses laughingly disregarded his orders, he turned upon them and solemnly cursed them, saying he hoped Heaven would compel them to dance without ceasing for a whole year and a day.

Frightened by this curse, the young people would now fain have paused in their merry round, but to their dismay they found they had no more control over their feet. So they whirled around faster and faster, hour after hour, day and night, until the fatal year was ended, and the extra day came to a close. The dancers then fell in a senseless heap in the middle of the hollow worn by their untiring feet; but, although they were eventually restored to consciousness, they remained helpless idiots as long as they lived.

Needless to say, since this awful punishment, the young people of Ramersdorf have ceased dancing on Sunday on the village green, and there is no place in Germany where the Sabbath quiet is more strictly observed.

HEISTERBACH.

The Bird of Paradise.

In the monastery at Heisterbach, where many holy men spent their lives in meditation and prayer, there once lived a monk by the name of Alfus. He had taken refuge in the cloister early in life, and had diligently studied and prayed, until a great light had dawned upon his soul, and he had amassed a store of knowledge which made him famous for many a mile around.

But, in spite of all his learning, his mind remained so pure and simple that he thought he knew nothing at all, and his faith was like that of a little child Such was his usual condition of innocent trust; yet, being human, he too had seasons of temptation, when torturing doubt would assail and rankle within his soul.

In the course of a long life he had frequently noticed that familiarity lessens enjoyment, that the eye wearies at last of the most beautiful sight, the ear of the sweetest sound, that the most intoxicating perfumes finally pall upon the senses, and that the mind grows weary of even the most elevated train of thoughts.

"Will it be thus in heaven?" he anxiously questioned, in one of these dark seasons of doubt. "Will not the beauty of the heavenly mansions cease to please our eyes, and the grand tones of the celestial harmony lose all charm for our ears? Will not the joys of heaven itself grow dim in the course of eternity?"

Although Alfus faithfully struggled against these insidious doubts, and strove to regain his simple faith, he was continually haunted by fear and unable to taste a moment's peace. Hoping to divert his thoughts by a long walk, he left the monastery very early one morning. The sun had risen bright and clear, the pure white clouds floated dreamily across the azure sky, casting faint fitful shadows over mountain and river, the dew glistened on the nodding blades of grass and radiant flowers, and the birds rapturously trilled their morning carol as he pensively walked down the hill and entered the dense forest.

The whole earth seemed to breathe forth peace and joy, but Alfus' heart was not at rest, and these serene sights and sounds only added poignancy to his grief.

"Ah!" he sighed, "with what rapture I first gazed upon this scene! What emotions and holy thoughts were awakened by the first glimpse of this matchless river! What lofty purposes were kindled in my heart at the sight of these grand hills! But now, alas! all is changed. The rapture I once experienced I no longer feel. The grandeur which almost oppressed me has lost its power, and I frequently pass along without vouchsafing even a glance to this magnificent view."

While musing thus, Alfus wandered through the forest, paying no attention to the road he was following. A slight feeling of fatigue made him pause at last, and glance about him; but although he was quite familiar with every inch of ground about the monastery for many a mile around, he could not remember ever having seen this spot before. All around him tall trees of an unknown species gently rustled their leafy branches. At his feet delicate ferns and wild flowers dipped under the weight of some gorgeous butterfly or busy bee, and while he stood there, forgetful of fatigue in his breathless admiration, a bird, perched on a neighboring tree, suddenly began to sing. This unearthly song was so sweet, so thrilling, so low, so distinct, so utterly unlike any music he had heard before that Brother Alfus sank down on a mossy stone and listened to it with intense rapture. The song lasted but a second, then abruptly ceased, leaving the monk sick with longing to hear it once more. But the bird had vanished, no sound now broke the forest silence, so he reluctantly rose to wend his way back through the woods to the old monastery.

It was very strange, however. His step, elastic and full of vigor as he strode down the hill that very morn, was now hesitating and slow, his beard was strangely gray, and all his body seemed feeble and stiff. The scene, too, seemed changed, and where he had scrambled through underbrush, he now saw tall trees of at least a century's growth.

Slowly and painfully, Alfus trudged on, and as soon as he reached the edge of the forest, he eagerly looked up to the monastery. But behold! that too was changed. The buildings seemed larger, the entrance gate wider, and the walls looked old and weather-beaten.

What could have happened? How could such changes have taken place during an absence, which, at the utmost, had only lasted a few hours? Alfus passed his hand over his eyes as if to clear his sight, and anxiously resumed his walk. Some women were washing at the village fountain, and he, who knew every man, woman, and child, for miles around, wonderingly gazed into faces which he had never seen.

"Look!" cried one of them, nudging her companion. "That old monk wears the dress of the order, yet I do not remember ever having seen him before. Who can he be?"

Alfus paid no heed to this remark, nor paused to question the women, but hastened on as fast as his trembling limbs would allow him, and timidly rang the monastery bell. In spite of his trouble, he noticed it no longer gave forth the silvery peal he knew so well, and when a young monk, a stranger, opened the door, he gazed upon him aghast, and exclaimed in tremulous tones:

"Why! where is Brother Anthony? Why does he not open the door as usual?"

"Brother Anthony!" exclaimed the monk. "We have no Anthony here. I am the porter, and for the past five years no one else has opened the door."

For a moment poor Alfus stood on the threshold as if petrified, but at the sight of two cowled figures, slowly pacing along the cloister wall, he rushed forward, calling them by the familiar names of his fellow-monks, whom he fancied he recognized. But no one answered his cry, and when he peered eagerly beneath their cowls he realized his mistake and despairingly cried:

"Brethren, I entreat you, speak, and tell what has happened! I left the monastery, as usual, this morning only, for a little stroll in the woods, and come back to find all changed. Where is the abbot? Where are my companions? Is there no one here who remembers Alfus?"

"Alfus—Alfus," thoughtfully repeated an aged monk, who sat in the warm sunshine. "Alfus, yes; there was once a brother of that name in this monastery, but that was long ago. I remember, when but a lad, hearing the old monks tell how he wandered out one summer morning, and vanished in the forest, whence he never returned. Although they sought carefully for him for many a day, no trace of him was ever found, and the abbot said that God must have borne him up to heaven in a chariot of fire, like Elijah, for he was very holy indeed. But all this happened a hundred years ago."

At these last words a sudden light seemed to illumine the face of poor Alfus, who slowly sank down upon his knees, clasped his tremulous hands, and exclaimed:

"Now I understand it all, oh, gracious Lord! Truly a thousand years are but as a day in thy sight. A whole century passed while I held my breath to listen to the song of the bird which sings at the gate of Paradise. Forgive my unbelief, O Lord; grant that I may enter into thy rest, and do not refuse to receive my penitent soul."

Brother Alfus then stretched out his trembling hands, a radiant smile illuminated his pale face, and when the wondering monks, crowding around him, would fain have helped him rise, they found his soul had flown away to join his companions in the heavenly mansions, and there enjoy an eternity of unchanging bliss.*

* See Note 12 in Appendix.

The Church Pillar.

"If you will only give me that stone, good friar," exclaimed a knight, as he struck his gauntleted hand against a stone in one of the pillars of the church at Heisterbach on the Rhine; "if you will only give me that stone, you shall have a purseful of gold in exchange."

"Give you that stone, sir knight! What value can it possibly have in your eyes?" exclaimed the poor old friar, gazing at the knight in open-mouthed astonishment.

"Alas, good friar! a demon of sleeplessness and unrest haunts my pillow wherever I go. Here only I find repose, here only it dares not persecute me. When the opening service is ended, and I lean my head back against this stone, as a preparatory move toward directing all my attention to your sermon, my eyelids droop gently over my eyes, and my weary limbs relax in profound sleep. Some magic power must be concealed in this hard stone, good friar. I beseech you, therefore, grant my prayer."

The simple-minded friar, who fancied the knight was in earnest, gravely pondered the matter a while. Then he excused himself and went to consult the abbot, his superior, who listened to the whole story with a humorous twinkle in his eye and finally said:

"Brother, go and tell the noble knight that our church pillars cannot be molested, but that, since he has derived so much comfort from it, he had better take advantage of the stone's narcotic powers as often as possible, for the service which precedes the sermon may, in time, do good to his soul and prepare him to enjoy everlasting rest."

The Last Abbot.

THE once magnificent abbey of Heisterbach is now nothing but a picturesque ruin, said to be haunted by the unquiet spirit of the last abbot. Long years ago, his companions folded their weary hands over their silent hearts and sank to rest. The summer winds have long whispered through the waving grasses which grow over their graves, and the winter snows have silently spread their white pall over all, but still the aged abbot can find no peace.

Night after night, when the cool evening breezes blow over the Seven Mountains and ripple the waters of the Rhine, when the silvery moon-beams gently steal along the ruined walls, the abbot appears, and slowly wanders in and out among the tombs. His hair is white, the light has long died out of his sightless eyes, and as he noiselessly moves along, he counts with his staff the grassy mounds beneath which his departed brethren have lain for many a year.

This task finished, he heaves a mournful sigh, and sadly whispers that the number is not yet complete. One grave is lacking still, but the aged abbot is doomed to haunt the place until the last crumbling wall has fallen into dust, and the great stones have all dropped asunder. When no trace of the ancient abbey remains, when tradition alone will remind the traveler of its former existence, the abbot's watch will be over, and he too will sink into his grave and be at rest.

A poetical version of this legend is as follows.

" Sadly through yon graveyard creeps
The abbot old and hoar,
His long beard in the night wind sweeps ;
His heart knows joy no more.

" No more he hears—no more he sees ;
A long staff guides his way.

What seeks he there? why braves the breeze?
'He counts the graves,' they say.

"And ever as he counts, it seems,
As still were wanting one.
He shakes his hoary head, and deems
Next day his race is run.

"Not yet is made that couch, his own
Warm tears his wan cheeks lave;
When yon firm fabric's overthrown
He'll only find his grave."

—*C. Rheinhold.*

NONNEN-STRÖMBERG.

The Hermit Sisters.

BACK of the little town of Königswinter on the Rhine rise the seven hills known as the Siebengebirge, from whence beautiful views can be had of the Rhine and the surrounding country. The charm of the mountains is further enhanced by a halo of legend and romance which makes them particularly attractive to lovers of tales of olden times. One of these tales is as follows:

The lord of Argenfels had two beautiful daughters, Bertha and Mina, with whom he spent all his time, for he was already well advanced in years, and could no longer take any part in the military plans then afoot. All the country was in a great state of excitement at this time, for St. Bernard, the eloquent preacher, had been urging a Crusade at Spires, and his enthusiasm had decided many knights to join the emperor, Frederick Barbarossa, in the attempt to deliver the Holy Sepulcher from the hands of the Saracens.

The knight of Argenfels, debarred by age from taking an active part in the expedition, nevertheless gave his money lavishly to further the cause, and warmly welcomed the knights continually passing his gates on their way to the general tryst at Frankfort-on-the-Main. One evening, he gave shelter to a handsome and brave young lord who dwelt on the Wolkenberg, one of the Seven Mountains. He no sooner saw the lovely Bertha than he entirely lost his heart to her. As he had but little time to spare, and must leave on the morrow, the knight made such good use of his time, that when he rode away, it was as the betrothed of the fair maiden, who was to marry him as soon as he returned from the Holy Land.

The Crusade begun so hopefully proved very disastrous indeed. Many brave knights died in distant lands, and the Lord of Wolkenburg, among others, fell into the hands of the Saracens and was detained in prison for seven long years. You can imagine how the ardent lover pined, and how solemnly he finally registered a vow to dedicate a chapel to St. Peter, if he would but deliver him from captivity and allow him to join his betrothed once more.

At last his prayers were answered, and as soon as he was released he hastened back to his native land. From afar he eagerly looked for the first glimpse of the lordly towers of Argenfels, and perceived with a sharp pang that they were a mass of blackened ruins. Springing out of the boat at the landing he hurried up the hill, and learned from an old shepherd that the castle had been besieged and taken by a robber knight, that the old lord of Argenfels had fallen in the fray, and that his lovely daughters must have perished also, as they had never since been seen.

The broken-hearted Lord of Wolkenburg then sadly withdrew to his lonely castle in the Seven Mountains, but, finding his sorrow unbearable, he resolved to consecrate the remainder of his life to God, and retire to some remote spot where he might erect a hermitage. He penetrated far into the woods in search of a suitable place, and came at last to a little hut, where, to his intense surprise and delight, he found his beloved Bertha and her sister.

After the first exchange of loving greetings had taken place, and the first rapture of meeting was over, the maiden told him how she and her sister had escaped from the besieged castle of Argenfels by an underground passage. They had taken refuge here, in the dense forest, to escape from the pursuit of their enemy, who had made war against them to get Bertha into his power.

Needless to say, the knight of Wolkenburg did not turn hermit, but married his lady-love, and built the chapel dedicated to St. Peter which crowns the Nonnen-Strömberg, one of the Seven Mountains, where Mina founded the convent in which she permanently took up her abode.

The Cruel Parents.

ON the Nonnen-Strömberg lived a cruel and unprincipled knight, who, having lost all his sons, dragged his only daughter out of the convent of Villich, where she had already taken a nun's vows, and told her she would be forced to marry so that his race should not become entirely extinct.

In vain the poor young nun wept and protested; her father declared she would be forced to obey, and to prevent her escape he kept her a close prisoner, while he looked around him for a suitable husband.

A knight of the neighborhood, fully as wicked as he, finally suggested that his son should be the bridegroom, and in spite of the young man's resistance, commanded him to be ready on a certain day, taking measures to secure obedience by force, should such a course become necessary. The youth, who had lost a beloved betrothed, and had secretly taken vows in the monastery of Heisterbach, was dragged to the altar in robe and cowl, where he was joined by a tearful nun. Both stood motionless and irresponsive, while a priest, bribed for the purpose, read the marriage service and gave them the nuptial benediction. He had scarcely uttered the last words, when the young couple, falling on their knees, fervently exclaimed: "In God alone we put our trust!" With a terrible crash the ground opened under them, and received their bodies, while their pure souls were seen by all the witnesses soaring gladly up into the open heavens, where hosts of angels met them with psalms of joy.

The dishonest priest, terrified at this vision, rushed out of the chapel and down the mountain, which ever since then has been known as the Nonnen-Strömberg, and his lifeless body was found in a ravine on the morrow. As for the cruel fathers they lived unhappily, died miserably, and their souls, we are told, were claimed by Satan, whose faithful followers they had long been.

OEHLBERG.

The Thunderbolt.

Balther von Bassenich, having quarreled with the bishop of Cologne and put him to death, the emperor, indignant at the outrage, besieged and took his castle, which was immediately set afire. As the emperor's entrance had been effected at night, and in silence, Balther little suspected anything wrong, and was greatly surprised when his only daughter Liba roused him from sleep, imploring him to fly.

In the dense smoke which already filled the castle, father and daughter made their way to a secret passage, along which they traveled all night, ere they came to its mouth, which opened into a cave. Here father and daughter remained in concealment, subsisting upon mountain roots and berries, and when they deemed it safe enough, they withdrew further into the heart of the forest, where they built a little hermitage, in which they took up their abode.

As the knight of Bassenich was now old and feeble, Liba was obliged to provide for all his wants, ranging the forest in search of berries, and thinking constantly of her lover, Schott von Grünstein, who must be mourning for her as one long dead. One evening, while father and daughter were sitting on a broad stone, talking over the past, the knight expressed a great desire to die, declaring he knew his sins would be forgiven, for he had sorely repented of all the evil he had done.

While he was talking thus, a storm gathered overhead, and suddenly a thunderbolt crashed down upon them, slaying both father and daughter. Schott von Grünstein, who was wandering idly in the forest, came to see where the bolt had struck, and to his surprise and amazement found a charred and blackened corpse and close beside it a kneeling female.

Drawing near, and frightened by her immobility, he touched her and recognized his beloved Liba, who was quite dead! After piously laying her to rest beside her father, near the rock which is known as the Treuenfels, the disconsolate lover took up his abode in their little hermitage, and spent the remainder of his life in seclusion, longing for the time when he might join his beloved in heaven.

LÖWENBERG.

The Wild Hunt.

THE Löwenberg, another of the Seven Mountains, was once the daily hunting ground of a neighboring knight, who was so fond of the chase that he even hunted on Sundays, and once pursued his quarry to the foot of the altar where a priest was celebrating mass.

Outraged by the insolence of the knight, who then and there slew his game, the priest solemnly cursed him. At the same moment the ground opened beneath the hunter's feet, and a pack of hounds from the Infernal Regions fell upon and tore him to pieces.

Ever since then, on stormy nights, this Sabbath-breaker's restless ghost hunts wildly through the air, followed by a spectral train of huntsmen and hell hounds, for he can find no rest, though dead, and is condemned to lead the Wild Hunt forever.

This legend, which originated in the myth of Odin, leader of the Raging Host, is told with slight variations of many places along the Rhine, where sudden wind storms, rising during the night, are still considered by the credulous peasantry as the passing of a mysterious heavenly host.*

DRACHENFELS.

The Story of Roland.

THE great crag known as the Drachenfels or Dragon Rock, where from the river a mighty cave can be seen, owes its name to the legends connected with it, which are very numerous indeed. Some authorities aver that it was here that Siegfried slew the Dragon; according to others, this cave was the den of a famous monster, who, in heathen times, feasted daily upon the tender damsels left bound near his lair, duly decked with flowers, for they were the victims offered up in sacrifice to him.

It happened one day, however, that the maiden chosen by lot to appease the hunger of the dragon was a Christian. Instead of fainting away and thus becoming a helpless prey, as her predecessors had done, this maiden boldly faced the monster, holding up a cross before his gaping jaws. Terrified at the sight of this holy emblem, the dragon started back, lost his balance, fell into the river, and was drowned. The people, awed by this miracle, and pleased to be rid of their

* See "Myths of Northern Lands."

exacting foe, allowed the maiden to preach to them, and were eventually all converted to the Christian faith.

A third legend relates that the dragon lingered in the cave year after year, opening its jaws to swallow ships and crew whenever an unsuspecting mariner steered his vessel too near that dangerous shore. This little pastime was continued until far in the Middle Ages, when, one day, he swallowed a ship loaded with nothing but gunpowder. The effect we are told was instantaneous and disastrous, for no sooner had the inoffensive looking black stuff reached the pit of his stomach—where lay the inexhaustible supply of fire which dragons were then wont to belch forth at will—than it suddenly exploded, scattering the monster's remains far and wide.

This cliff is now surmounted by a beautiful new castle, the Drachenburg, and by the crumbling and picturesque ruins of what was once a mighty stronghold, occupied by the Lord of Drachenfels and his only daughter Hildegarde.

A passing knight entered this castle at nightfall, claiming the hospitality of the inmates. No sooner had he beheld the lovely young châtelaine than he fell desperately in love with her and resolved, if possible, to win her for his wife. In order to produce a favorable impression, the knight exerted himself to entertain both father and daughter by recounting exciting adventures by land and sea, and in doing so, unconsciously revealed his identity; for the deeds of young Roland, Charlemagne's beloved nephew, were the theme of every wandering bard.

As soon as the Lord of Drachenfels discovered the exalted rank of his visitor, he cordially pressed him to stay a few days; an invitation which Roland gladly accepted, as it gave him time to urge his suit with the fair Hildegarde.

Walking with him through the romantic "Nightingale Valley" at the foot of the castle, one warm summer eve, she listened blushingly to his passionate declaration of love and gladly promised to become his wife.

DRACHENBURG CASTLE.

But, before the lovers could be married, a messenger from Charlemagne came to summon Roland to war, for the Saracens threatened to invade France and overthrow Christianity in Europe. This summons was so urgent that no true knight could hesitate to obey, and Roland regretfully parted from Hildegarde, promising to return as soon as possible to claim her for his bride.

Time passed on. The rumor of Roland's high deeds first made Hildegarde's heart swell with pride, then came a long weary time of waiting with no tidings at all, and lastly a messenger tearfully reported that Roland had died, fighting bravely in the Valley of Roncevaux.

At these tidings poor Hildegarde's heart was almost broken. She felt that all earthly happiness was over, and that she could only find solace in prayer. Finally she prevailed upon her father to let her enter the convent of Nonnenwörth, which was situated on an island in the Rhine, within sight of her ancestral home.

The time of probation was shortened for her, by special dispensation, and soon, having taken conventual vows, she spent all her time in the chapel praying for the soul of her beloved. She always added a special entreaty that the end might come, and her longing heart be permitted to join her lover in the heavenly mansions.

Roland had not perished in the Valley of Roncevaux, as history relates, and although sorely wounded, he slowly made his way back to the castle of Drachenfels, where he presented himself one summer evening, his heart thrilling with joy. He was greatly astonished, therefore, to see all the servants shrink away from him in speechless terror; but, too impatient to pause and question them, he rushed impetuously into the great hall where the Lord of Drachenfels sat mournfully alone, and breathlessly asked for Hildegarde.

A few moments later the light died out of his eyes, and the smile faded from his lips, for he knew that Hildegarde had left him, and realized that, as she had already taken the irrevocable vows, he had lost her forever.

That selfsame night Roland rode sadly out of the castle of Drachenfels, and when he had reached an eminence overlooking the island of Nonnenwörth, on the opposite side of the Rhine, he slowly dismounted from his steed. Seated upon a stone, he spent the night gazing at the convent, and wondering whether the twinkling light he saw was burning in Hildegarde's cell.

Early in the morning he saw the long procession of nuns issue from the convent door and file into the chapel, and fancying he could distinguish Hildegarde's graceful form among the rest, he determined to build an hermitage on the very spot where he sat, and spend the remainder of his life there, in watching over his beloved. This resolution was soon put into effect, and Roland, the brave knight, having disposed of all his property, laid aside armor and sword, assumed the garb of an hermit, and spent all his time in penance and prayer, gazing continually upon the convent at his feet and at the river which flowed between him and his beloved.

One winter morning, he saw the nuns march slowly into the churchyard, bearing a coffin. His heart was oppressed with fear, for the graceful form which he had identified with Hildegarde was missing in their ranks. At sundown the convent priest, visiting him as usual, informed him that one of the nuns was dead, and in answer to his eager inquiries revealed that it was Hildegarde. In faltering tones Roland then confessed who he was, how dearly he had loved the dead, and informed the priest that when he died he wished to be buried with his face turned toward the spot where Hildegarde lay.

Troubled by this request, the priest hastened thither on the next day to offer further consolations to the mourner, but found them useless, for Roland lay cold in death, but with a radiant smile upon his pallid face. The priest buried him as he had requested, and ever since then the height where the hermitage once stood has been known as Rolandseck. This name was long borne by a castle erected near there, of which nothing but ruins now remain to remind the traveler of this touching tale of undying love.*

A later legend of Drachenfels relates that Adelheid, the only daughter of another castle owner, was wooed by a base and cowardly wretch, who, having been ignominiously dismissed from her father's presence, persuaded her to meet him alone in the woods near by. To deprive everyone else of the bride he could not secure, this man stabbed her mortally, intending to perish also, but, frightened by the awfulness of death, he had not the courage to slay himself, and fled instead.

He must have died shortly after, however, and it is supposed he felt some remorse for his crime, for his ghost nightly haunts these regions. It steal noiselessly down into the village below the castle, to lay a cold finger upon the forehead of those about to die, thus warning them that their end is near, and that it is time to make their peace with God and seek forgiveness of their sins.

RHEINBREITBACH.

The Three Miners.

In the mountains just back of Rheinbreitbach are the oldest copper mines in Germany, which, exhausted and filled with water, are no longer a scene of busy labor as they were a few centuries ago, when the miners daily came there from their homes in Rheinbreitbach to work all day in the dark passages underground.

Three of these miners, who were very good friends, always walked back and forth together, and worked side by side, never failing to breathe a short prayer ere they went down

* See Note 13 in Appendix.

into the shaft. But one morning, when there was a special pressure of work, they omitted the prayer, hurried down to their post, and were hard at work when they were startled by a long, ominous, rumbling sound, and by the shaking of the ground around them.

Simultaneously they rushed toward the shaft to escape, but they were too late, for a huge mass of fallen earth and stones blocked up the passage in which they found themselves caught as in a trap. After the first moments of utter despair, they encouraged each other to work their way out, for they had food enough to last them twelve hours, and their lamps had been freshly filled.

Before they began they said their usual prayer, to atone for the morning's omission, and set bravely to work, but in spite of all their efforts, food, strength, and light soon failed them, and clasping each other's hands they lay down in the darkness saying, "God's will be done."

They had lain thus a long, long while when a light suddenly appeared at one end of the gallery, and with dilating eyes they beheld the approach of the mine specter, Meister Hämmerling, of whom they had heard many a tale. Drawing near them, the ghost addressed them in sepulchral tones, gave them a basket in which they would find all the food they required, a lantern which would supply the necessary light, and bade them work their way out of the mine, promising that the first wish they uttered when they again beheld the light of day would be granted them.

Meister Hämmerling vanished after speaking thus, but basket and lantern remained, and the three miners, refreshed and encouraged, set to work again with renewed zest, although their families in Rheinbreitbach mourned them as dead. During seven years the lantern burned brightly, night and day, the provision basket was never empty, and the workmen digging their way out, and having no way of counting time, little suspected how long they had been buried alive.

Finally the day came when a blow from their pick-ax let

in the light of day. Then the lantern was extinguished, the basket found empty. The three men returned hearty thanks for their delivery, ere they sought their homes in Rheinbreitbach. Walking along briskly one exclaimed: "All I now wish is to press wife and children to my heart once more ere I die."

"And I," exclaimed the second, "shall be ready to leave the world forever, when I have once more seen my family at table with me as usual."

"All I now ask," exclaimed the third, "is to linger for a year and a day with my loved ones, and then to be at rest."

A few minutes later the three miners entered the village, where their appearance caused a great sensation, and where all crowded around them, scarcely able to believe the testimony of their own eyes.

As soon as the first miner had embraced his wife and children he fell down dead, the second passed peacefully away after his first meal, and the third, having often recounted his adventures in the mine, slept to wake no more on earth at the end of a year and a day.

ST. APOLLINARISBERG.

The Greedy Abbot.

On the top of a hill, near Remagen on the Rhine, in full view of the river, rises the pretty church dedicated to St. Apollinaris, which was formerly a great resort for pilgrims. This church is beautifully decorated with ancient and modern works of art, and among the latter are some of Ittenbach's and Müller's exquisite paintings.

The first artist who decorated this building is said to have been so entranced by the view obtainable from the church tower, that he painted his own portait there, that his eyes might ever rest upon hill and dale, and follow the sinuous course of the glistening river.

The particular sanctity of this church is attributed to the relics of St. Apollinaris which it contains, and which one of the bishops intended to convey to Cologne in the twelfth century. But the ship containing the holy remains came to a sudden stand-still in the middle of the river, directly opposite Remagen, and as no efforts could avail to make it continue its journey down the stream, the bishop declared the saint had evidently elected to remain there.

Not very far from the church, at the foot of the mountain, is the celebrated Apollinaris fountain, whose waters are bottled and sent to all parts of the world to aid digestion. A curious legend is told about these waters and a mediæval abbot, who ruled the people roundabout, but, instead of giving them a good example, practiced every vice, and was particularly addicted to over eating and drinking. This prelate once saw a beautiful young girl called Sabine, whom he began to compliment and talk to in a way utterly unbecoming an old man and a priest. The girl, who was virtuous and gentle, rejected his unwelcome attentions; plainly informing him that she was engaged to a young huntsman, whom she loved and was about to marry.

The abbot, furious at this check, immediately began to intrigue to force her to resign her lover, and either obey him or enter a convent; but Sabine, who had frankly told her betrothed of the prelate's visit and conversation, implored him to secure for her the protection of his influential master, the virtuous lord of Aarberg.

No sooner had this nobleman heard the young huntsman's appeal than he promised to aid him, and after transferring Sabine to a place of safety, he waited for a good opportunity to punish the wicked old abbot. This opportunity came very soon, for finding that he had been outwitted, the prelate tried to console himself by eating and drinking more than usual. He soon brought upon himself such a terrible attack of indigestion, that complaining of extreme dizziness and a strange loss of appetite, he prepared for a journey to some medicinal springs at a distance.

On his way thither he passed the castle of Aarberg, and the master, warned of his coming, seized him and put him into prison. There the abbot fumed and raged as much as he pleased, but none came at his cry. Lunch, dinner, and supper hour passed without bringing any of the dainty dishes to which he was so accustomed and devoted.

His cries finally became so imperious that a jailer appeared, and, in answer to his clamors for food and drink, bade him satisfy his hunger and thirst with the loaf of black bread and the jar of water which had been placed there for his use.

Vanquished at last by hunger,—for the violent exercise he had indulged in had made him ravenous,—the abbot tasted the bread and water, and lying down upon the hard stones slept far more peacefully than at home. Several days he spent thus; no one but the jailer appeared, and no other fare was vouchsafed him than the usual prisoner's allowance of bread and water.

At last, the lord of Aarberg came, blandly inquiring about his health, and asking whether his appetite had returned. The prelate threatened to complain to the emperor, but was silenced when the nobleman coolly answered that in that case he would feel himself called upon to attract the Pope's attention to sundry little matters which had come under his immediate observation, and which doubtless would not receive his complete approval. Then the lord of Aarberg, again inquiring concerning his guest's appetite, and hearing him declare he was famished, made a sign. Sabine now stepped into the cell, bearing a tray loaded with appetizing viands, which fairly made the abbot's mouth water. Just as he was about to partake of this food, however, his host stopped him to inquire how much a journey to the mineral springs, with the usual fees to the local physician, would cost.

"Six hundred ducats!" exclaimed the abbot gruffly, for he was in a great hurry to enjoy his dinner.

"Then, abbot," continued the lord of Aarberg, "since you have recovered your health without taking the journey, and the water from my fountain has entirely restored your appetite, you owe me those six hundred ducats, which I will trouble you to give me before you begin your meal."

The abbot vainly demurred, but finally, seeing his tray vanish at a sign, he paid the required sum and was allowed to eat in peace. The six hundred ducats were immediately handed over to Sabine as a marriage portion, and the lord of Aarberg courteously escorted the abbot home, dropping a very strong hint to the effect that, should he ever molest Sabine or her husband again, he would not fail to report the matter to the Pope, who would certainly not let him off with a mere fine.

This warning proved effectual in hindering the abbot from further misdeeds; and when he died shortly after from over eating and drinking, the people openly rejoiced at the thought that he had ceased to trouble them forever.

OCKENFELS.

Taken at his Word.

THE ivy-covered ruins of the castle of Ockenfels, not very far from Linz, once belonged to a stern, hard-hearted knight, Rheinhard von Renneberg, who departed for the war, leaving his only daughter Etelinda in charge of the castle chaplain. During his absence Rudolf of Linz fell in love with the maiden, and, encouraged by the chaplain, he declared his passion. The young people were anxiously awaiting Rheinhard's return to ask his consent to their union, but when they heard he was coming on the morrow, with a stranger, whom he had selected as his future son-in-law, they knew he would never listen to their plea.

The chaplain, certain that Rheinhard would ruthlessly part the lovers, now advised them to marry immediately, and after he had given them the marriage benediction, led them into a secret vault, known to him alone. There he left them with light, water, and food, promising to come and release them when the count's first outburst of anger was over, and it would be safe to encounter him. The young people were quite happy at first, for they little suspected that the cruel lord had thrown the chaplain into a foul dungeon as soon as he had heard the story of his daughter's marriage. He said he would keep him there until he revealed where the young people were concealed, and swore a solemn oath that he hoped he might die a sudden death, if ever he consented to forgive his daughter or her husband.

At the end of several days the young couple, having neither water nor provisions left, and being plunged in darkness, cautiously stole out of their hiding place by night, passed unseen through the castle, and took refuge in the forest, where they dwelt in a cave. Here Rudolf snared birds and gathered roots and berries for the subsistence of his lovely wife. During two years they remained there, but when a severe winter came and their scant garments no longer sufficed to protect Etelinda and her babe from the cold, Rudolf made up his mind to brave her father's anger, and to make an attempt to obtain some relief for her sake. He had not gone far before he met Rheinhard, hunting in the forest, and sternly bidding him follow, he led him to the cave. There Rheinhard found his daughter, almost frozen to death. Touched by her sufferings, he forgave her freely, and took her back to Ockenfels.

As soon as he arrived there, he hastened to the dungeon into which he had cast the poor chaplain, intending to set him free; but, losing his balance, he fell and broke his neck; thus meeting with sudden death as soon as he had forgiven his only daughter.

LANDSKRONE AND NEUENAHR

The Wonder Bridge.

WHERE the German river Ahr flows into the Rhine, stand the ruins of the once lordly castle of Landskrone, directly opposite the fortress of Neuenahr. In the beginning of the Middle Ages the knights inhabiting these two castles were very good friends indeed, and, in order to see each other daily, and as often as they pleased, they spanned the rushing stream with a high arched bridge, the marvel of the whole countryside, where it was known as the Wonder Bridge.

But these knights died, their successors quarreled, and soon no one crossed the bridge, within whose crevices the birds deposited seeds which sprouted and grew, covering the gray stones with an intricate tangle of flowering shrubs and creepers. Year after year passed by, and the bridge, with its burden of blossoms, arching over the rushing waters, was so picturesque that it deserved more than ever the title of the Wonder Bridge.

When several centuries had elapsed, one of the castles became the property of a young knight, who accidentally met the young lady of the other castle at a tournament, and fell desperately in love with her. Unfortunately, however, this damsel's father was very conservative indeed, and so rigidly kept up the family feud that the young people dared not openly proclaim their love. They parted sadly when the festivities were ended, and returned to their respective homes. Gazing out of his window, toward the abode of his beloved, the knight's glance suddenly fell upon the Wonder Bridge, so long unused, softly illumined by the light of the moon. He resolved to try whether it would not prove as serviceable to lovers as to faithful friends. So he ventured out of the long closed postern gate, and slowly and patiently worked his way through the flowery tangle, startling the sleepy birds, who had so long been undisturbed, and causing them to flutter away from their cozy nests.

The maiden, standing at her casement, saw her lover draw near in the silvery moonlight, which flooded the long unused path, and hastened noiselessly out to meet him. Night after night the lovers now enjoyed a clandestine meeting, and finding that there was no hope of winning the maiden's father to consent to their union, the knight finally persuaded her to accompany him back over the bridge.

Gently and lovingly he helped her across the stream, and led her into the chapel of Landskrone, where a waiting priest soon made them man and wife. The Wonder Bridge, having faithfully done its duty, and served lovers and friends, finding itself now utterly useless, gradually crumbled away into ruins, dropping its stones into the waters, one by one, until now no traces of it remain.

Many years after the marriage of these true lovers,—who lived happily together, and never repented having made use of the means of communication ready to hand,—long after the bridge had fallen into decay, the castle of Landskrone was besieged by a great army. The lord of Landskrone held out bravely, until at last his garrison was so reduced by famine and death, and his walls so rapidly caving in beneath the enemy's heavy battering rams, that he could not but perceive that he would soon fall into their hands.

Too proud to surrender, yet wishing to save his only daughter, he led her to a secret passage, where he promised to join her as soon as the enemy broke into the fortress, and escape with her to a foreign land. In her subterranean retreat the maiden tremblingly listened to the din of battle overhead, and when it suddenly ceased she anxiously watched for her father's coming. Hour after hour went by, and still he did not appear. A cool spring, trickling along one wall, furnished her water to drink, and a fissure in the rock overhead renewed her supply of fresh air and permitted her to distinguish the difference between night and day.

The pangs of hunger soon began to make themselves felt, however, and the poor girl, who did not know how to escape from her underground hiding place, feared she would die of inanition, when she suddenly saw a snowy dove creep through the fissure and drop a piece of bread at her feet. Fed thus, like Elijah in the desert, the maiden lingered there, vainly waiting for her father, who had fallen in the last encounter. She was finally discovered and rescued by some peasants, who had watched the dove fly into the crevice with bread pilfered from their tables, and soon issue without it, thereby greatly exciting their curiosity.

As the enemy had departed, after leaving the castle in ruins, the maiden had nothing more to fear. She was soon comforted for her father's loss by the love of a young nobleman of the neighborhood, who married her and remained faithful to her as long as he lived.

NEUENAHR.

A Father's Legacy.

THE old lord of Neuenahr lay upon his deathbed. He had already taken leave of all his weeping retainers, but the most trying ordeal yet remained, for he had to say farewell to his two sons, who stood broken-hearted beside him.

Laying a hand upon either bowed head in solemn blessing, the old father bade them remember his teachings, live in peace together, deal honorably with all men, and then, calling for his sword and plow, he suddenly added:

"To you, my eldest born, who delight in warfare, I bequeath my trusty sword,—which has never been drawn to uphold an unjust or unworthy cause,—together with my ancient castle, the cradle of our race. But you, my youngest son, who prefer the peaceful avocations of the husbandman and shepherd, shall have this plow, the emblem of all agricultural pursuits, and may use it to till my broad acres, which are henceforth your own."

Having spoken thus, and breathed a last prayer, the old lord of Neuenahr passed away, and his sons succeeded him. But while the sword bequeathed to the elder has long been covered with rust, and the old Neuenahr castle has fallen into ruins, the plow still furrows the rich lands of the younger son's inheritance, which continue to bear fine harvests and support a happy and thrifty race.

ALTENAHR.

The Brave Knight and the Craven.

WHERE the rocks tower highest above the German Ahr, a tributary of the Rhine, there once rose the castle of Altenahr, which withstood many a long siege. On one occasion an old lord defended it bravely month after month, year after year, until all his family and retainers had perished, either from the wounds received, or from the terrible privations of a protracted siege.

The lord of Altenahr finally remained alone, and feeling that he could not prevent the enemy from entering the stronghold now that his garrison was dead, he donned his armor for the last time, mounted his war horse, and riding up on the ramparts he blew a defiant peal upon his bugle. The enemy, who suspected that the garrison was greatly weakened by famine, called aloud to the old lord, imploring him to surrender, and promising not to take the life of any of his men. But the old knight grimly informed them that his men, being dead, had escaped their tyranny forever, and that he too would die free.

Then, with a farewell wave of his hand, he plunged his

spurs in his steed, urged him at full gallop along the rampart, and leaping the parapet, which rose sheer above the rushing river, he and his steed plunged down into the water, which closed over them forever.

The castle which this grim old knight defended so bravely was again besieged by the French in 1690, but instead of a hero it was a craven who now had charge of the garrison. Summoned to surrender, he immediately signified his readiness to do so, imploring the French, however, to fire upon the castle thrice, so that he might save his honor by declaring he had surrendered only after braving the enemy's fire.

This request was complied with, but when the faithless officer, who had been allowed to depart free, presented himself before his superiors, they angrily demanded how he had dared surrender before a shot had been fired. The officer vainly tried to defend himself by alleging that he had resisted an attack, but as the story of the three shots had reached the general's ear, he was sentenced to die by the same number of shots for which he had betrayed his trust.

SINZIG.

Constantine's Cross.

In the year 311, early in the morning, just after matins were over, Constantine, the first Christian emperor, riding forth to meet his rival Maxentius, suddenly saw in the skies overhead a resplendent cross, on which was inscribed the comforting assurance *In hoc signo vinces* (By this sign thou shalt conquer). The emperor and all the men in his legions immediately bent the knee before this vision, and in silence they watched the miraculous sign gradually fade away, until the skies were as blue as usual. Then, strong in the promise they had received, they hastened on, and meeting the enemy completely defeated him.

Countless places claim the honor of this miracle, among others Mainz and Rome, but the people of Sinzig invariably assure the traveler that it occurred in their town, and in proof of their statement point out an ancient painting, representing this miracle, which is the chief treasure of a quaint and interesting thirteenth century church.

NÜRBURG.

God's Mercy.

ULRICH, count of Nürburg, was about to die. As he had no wife or children to smooth his dying pillow, his only brother Conrad, archbishop of Cologne, whose record was far from blameless, hastened to his bedside and tearfully exclaimed :

"Alas, my brother! had you, like me, served God all the days of your life, instead of fighting, you would now be sure of forgiveness, and I, at least, would know you were enjoying bliss in Paradise."

In answer to this lament the lord of Nürburg calmly replied that as he had loved the Lord, had always acted like a true knight, and had fought only to defend the feeble and oppressed, he fully expected forgiveness for his sins and admission into the heavenly realm. Then, seeing a very incredulous expression on the archbishop's face, he bade Conrad hang his shield upon a nail, and declared that three days after his death he would send him a sign to prove that his trust in God's mercy was not misplaced.

Three days after Ulrich's death, while the archbishop was anxiously staring at the shield, he suddenly saw its bright disk touched by the dazzling light of a sunbeam, which played for a moment over its polished surface and then disappeared as the shield suddenly fell down to the floor.

An old servant, who had overheard the brothers' last conversation, and who had seen the promised sign, now drew near to the astonished prelate, tendering the keys of the castle, and gravely said :

"God grant that your life may be such that, when your last hour has come and your crozier hangs upon yonder nail, you may be vouchsafed as signal a token that the Lord has forgiven your sins, and received you into his glory."

DATTENBURG.

The Specter Wedding.

KURT VON STEIN was galloping wildly along the rocky road in a gorge not far from the Rhine, seeking a place where he might take shelter for the night, for the storm was raging and darkness was coming on rapidly. All at once he saw a light ahead of him, and coming nearer he perceived the ruins of the ancient castle of Dattenburg. He roused the echoes by calling for a servant to come and take his horse. As no one answered his call, he soon dismounted, and felt his way up the narrow winding stairs, which led to the top of the tower, where a light was shining brightly. When he came to the last step he perceived an open door, and through it he saw a beautiful lady sitting by a table all alone.

In answer to his courteous request for shelter, the lady silently motioned him to enter, and the table, bare a moment before, was soon covered with all manner of viands, of which she invited him by signs to partake. Somewhat awed by the maiden's beauty and silence, the knight obeyed, glancing about him from time to time, and taking particular note of two portraits on the wall. He conjectured these must represent the young lady's parents, as there was a great resemblance between them, in spite of the antiquated garb, which would seem to indicate that they had lived several centuries before.

After having finished his meal, Kurt von Stein ventured an interrogation, "Your parents, I suppose?" Receiving a gracious affirmative gesture, he concluded the fair lady was mute, and continuing his conversation on the same system, soon discovered that she was an orphan and alone, the last of her race. Excited by her beauty, he finally began to make love to her, and before many hours had passed, he was kneeling at her feet, entreating her to be his bride. Then, having won her consent, he saw her crown herself with a wreath of rosemary, and obeying her gesture, followed her down the stairs and into the castle chapel.

There he was surprised to see a numerous assembly of persons in antiquated garb steal from behind pillar and tomb and silently take their places in the empty church. A moment later a mitered bishop stepped down from the tomb on which he had been lying with folded hands, and marching gravely up to the altar began the service.

Kurt von Stein, sobered now, and quailing with fear, vainly tried to speak the necessary answer to the priest's demand, whether he accepted that lady for wife, but, before he could recover the power of speech, the twelve solemn strokes from the convent of St. Helena reached his ear.

"God have mercy upon me!" he suddenly exclaimed, and sank fainting to the ground. When he recovered from his swoon, the sun was shining above him, the phantoms had disappeared, and he was alone in the ruined Dattenburg chapel, his steed close beside him.

Kurt von Stein hastened home, but as long as he lived he vividly remembered the night he had spent in those ruins, and often gave thanks for having been saved from a marriage with the dead, for he instinctively felt that the lady could have been nothing but a ghost.

RHEINECK.

Desecrated Tombs.

THE tower of the old castle of Rheineck (which has recently been rebuilt) was erected in the twelfth century and once belonged to a spendthrift lord named Ulrich, who, having squandered all his money, ardently longed for more. One day, while he was trying to devise some plan to obtain gold, he saw an aged pilgrim draw near, and in answer to his appeal for food and shelter bade him enter his dismantled castle, whence the servants had all departed, and where nothing but bread and water could be procured.

The pilgrim, amazed at this state of affairs, inquired whether there was not a drop of wine left in the castle cellar, and when the knight replied that all his casks were dry, begged him to go down and inspect them once more. Ulrich and the pilgrim were soon wandering through the great cellar, where, in a remote corner, the latter finally discovered a well concealed cask of rich old wine. He and his host then indulged in sundry liberal potations, which soon loosened Ulrich's tongue, and induced him to confide to his guest his intense longing for wealth.

When he had ended, the pilgrim told him that his desire for gold could easily be satisfied, for not far off lay an immense treasure, which could readily be obtained. He then proceeded to inform the knight that the treasure was under the special protection of the witches, but that as they were all on their way to the Brocken for their yearly Walpurgisnacht dance, he could easily secure it by entering the castle chapel at midnight, breaking open his ancestors' tombs, and removing their bones, under which the hoard had been placed for safe keeping.

Ulrich was at first greatly shocked by this proposal, but soon the greed for gold overcame all his scruples, and he did

RHEINECK CASTLE.

as the pilgrim advised. One by one he carried the moldering bodies out of the chapel and laid them on the grass at midnight. As he was bending over the last coffin, which contained the remains of a brother who had died in infancy, he was startled by perceiving a rosy child rise up at his touch who exclaimed:

"Brother—quick—quick! Bring back the dead to their resting place, ere it is too late!"

A moment after the child was gone, and only a few crumbling bones were to be seen. Filled with nameless dread, Ulrich now rushed out of the chapel to fulfill the mandate he had received. As he stepped out of the sacred edifice he noticed that the pilgrim, whom he had left standing without, had assumed colossal proportions, and felt his claw-like fingers close over his arm, while he exclaimed in sinister tones: "Come, Ulrich, you are mine!"

But once more the rosy child appeared, crying loudly:

"Get thee behind us, Satan!" and the devil, for it was he, vanished at this command, with a hoarse cry of rage.

The knight, thus miraculously saved from an awful fate, piously replaced his ancestors' bones in their tombs, without pausing for a moment to search for the promised gold. On the morrow he began a pilgrimage to Rome, humbly praying at every shrine by the way for the forgiveness of his sins.

Some years later, the villagers saw an aged pilgrim toil slowly up the castle hill. Failing to see him come down again, they went in search of him, and found him dead in the chapel. They turned the body over, to view the face, hidden in the cowl, and suddenly recognized the emaciated but well-known features of their former lord.

Since then, when the moon is full, and the village bell tolls the midnight hour, a cowled figure is seen slowly wandering around the ruins, and the people declare it is the ghost of Ulrich, the desecrator of his parents' tombs, who, in spite of pilgrimage and penance, cannot yet find any rest.

HAMMERSTEIN.

The Emperor's Friend.

On the right bank of the Rhine, very near the river, but perched high up on a huge rock of gray freestone, rise the ruins of the ancient castle of Hammerstein.

This castle was occupied in the eleventh century by Otto, count of Hammerstein, who was unfortunate enough to enter into a quarrel with Erkenbold, the powerful archbishop of Mainz. But, while Otto carried on an open warfare, the wily priest continually tried to outwit him by underhand dealings, and ardently hoped that his opponent would infringe some ecclesiastical decree, so that he could have the satisfaction of excommunicating him.

The opportunity soon occurred. Otto married his beautiful cousin, without remembering to secure the sanction of the Pope, which was indispensable in marriages between blood relations. The archbishop, hearing of it, immediately excommunicated his hated rival, and declared his intention of denouncing him to the emperor at the general assembly at Cologne.

Otto, fearing lest he would be forced to relinquish his wife, whom he loved dearly, vainly tried to capture the priest on his way down the Rhine. He only succeeded in further increasing his enmity, for as soon as Erkenbold arrived in Cologne, he prevailed upon the emperor to declare war against Otto, and even besiege the castle of Hammerstein. During this siege, both Otto and his wife were wounded, still he bravely held out against the imperial forces, until Henry IV., weary of waiting, declared that after all the Lord of Hammerstein's offense was not so heinous that it could not be condoned, and, by dint of persuasion and commands, reconciled Erkenbold to his enemy.

Otto, who loved to live in peace with his neighbors, was

very grateful indeed for all the emperor's good offices in his behalf, and showed his gratitude by fighting valiantly with him for many a long year. But, when at last his arm grew too feeble to wield the sword with its former vigor and efficacy, he withdrew to his fortress of Hammerstein, where the tidings soon reached him that the emperor had been deposed and imprisoned by his favorite son.

Helpless to deliver him, Otto mourned his age and weakness, and often declared that he wished his daughters were sons, so that they might go out and do battle in his stead. While he was bewailing his master's fate one evening, several years after these tidings had reached him, the old emperor appeared before him, disguised as a pilgrim, told him how he had effected his escape with the aid of the jailor, and implored his protection and support.

Otto welcomed him warmly, and began to seek as many supporters as possible for him, so that he might wrench the imperial power from his unnatural son; but, before the forces were fully assembled, before the first blow had been struck, the aged emperor, worn out by suffering, died peacefully in his old friend's arms. He forgave his son and left the crown and seal in Otto's keeping, until they were claimed by his heir.

The castle of Hammerstein, which was besieged many times after this, was completely destroyed by the French in 1660.

LAACH.

The Sunken Castle.

THE deep Lake of Laach, near Andernach on the Rhine, fed by a thousand living springs and with no visible outlet, has not always existed, for tradition relates that a great hill once rose on this identical spot.

On the topmost peak of this elevation was once perched

a mighty castle, the home of a wicked robber knight, the terror of all the country f. r many a mile around.

One day, this cruel lord of Laach partook of a certain dish, which his cook declared was composed of nothing but stewed eels, but which, in reality, was a species of water snake. No sooner had he tasted it, than he became aware he could understand the language of beasts and birds, and wishing to keep this knowledge for himself alone, he ate up all there was in the dish.

It happened, however, that the waiter had tasted the stew in the pantry, before he set it on his master's table, and so was just as wise as he.

Although the lord of Laach now understood the language of all living creatures, he was none the happier, for he constantly heard them revile him for his cruelty, and learned bitter truths about himself. These had only the effect of making him more disagreeable than ever, instead of influencing him to amendment.

One day, however, he overheard the conversation of two hens, and learned that ere sundown his castle would sink down deep into the earth. Hurrying to his stable, for it was nearly time for sunset, the Lord of Laach hastily saddled his own steed, calling to his servant to bring his valuables as quickly as possible. But, when the man clung to his bridle, frantically imploring him not to leave him behind,—for he too had understood the fowls' conversation and was afraid to die,—the cruel master struck him to the ground with his gauntleted fist.

Before he could ride out of the castle gate, however, the sun set, and with a sudden rumbling noise the whole hill sank down into the bosom of the earth, with the Lord of Laach and all his servants. When the astonished peasants visited the spot on the morrow, they found a lake rippling in the sunlight, a lake said to be bottomless, for the wicked knight is reported to have sunk down to the nethermost hell, where he is slowly roasting in punishment for his many crimes.

Many years after this terrible judgment, a little castle was erected on an island in the center of the lake, by order of another Lord of Laach, a poet and musician, who took pleasure in dwelling there. The fairies, who are said to haunt the lake in great numbers, were so fond of this knight's entrancing music that one night, while he was sleeping, they gently drew island, castle, and master down into the crystal depths of the lake, where, on quiet evenings, the soft sound of his lovely music can still be heard.

Not far from the lake is a monastery which these fairies have also taken under their special protection, and whenever a monk is about to die, they warn him of coming dissolution by placing a snow-white lily in his stall in the chancel at midnight. The monk, finding this token in his place at early mass on the morrow, then prepares for death, which invariably comes exactly three days after the fairies' warning.

ANDERNACH.

The Prophecy.

THE little fortified city of Andernach, whose ramparts are still in a fair state of preservation, was one of the fifty strongholds founded by Drusus, who posted a legion here to restrain the constant invasions of the northern barbarians into the more civilized portions of the realm.

Chilpéric, son of Merovig who gave his name to the first dynasty of French kings, dwelt in this little town, and the legends record that while he was on the tower with his wife Basina, a druidess, she once bade him look toward the northeastern horizon and tell her what he saw.

The king obeyed, but soon shrank back in terror, exclaiming that he saw lions, tigers, leopards, and other wild beasts, which seemed coming to devour him. Quieting his fears, his wife bade him look again, and he reported that bears, wolves, and hyenas had fallen upon the wild beasts he had first noticed, and devoured them all. Next he saw dogs, cats, and mice devour the bears and wolves, falling a prey in their turn to smaller animals still, who suddenly vanished, leaving the scene as deserted as in the beginning.

Turning to his wife Basina, who could interpret all manner of dreams and omens, Chilpéric asked of her an explanation of what he had seen, and learned that his immediate descendants would resemble lions, tigers, and leopards, and would rule a hundred years. The wolves, bears, and hyenas were symbolical of the rulers who would hold the land during the next century, but they, with their uncouth appearance and rough manners, were destined to be followed by a timid, treacherous race, typified by the dogs, cats, and mice, which would finally be destroyed by the smallest of their vassals.

This prediction was duly verified, for while the first Merovingians were strong and brave, their successors were cruel and cunning. Then came the sluggard kings, whose effeminacy might well be compared to the cat's sensuous ways, and they were, as Basina had predicted, entirely supplanted by Pépin the Short, the smallest man in the kingdom, but founder of the great Carlovingian dynasty.

The Baker Boys.

DURING the Middle Ages, the inhabitants of Linz and Andernach could never agree and were continually at war, each hoping to obtain the supremacy and utterly destroy the other city. As the towns were only a short distance apart they could often pounce upon each other unawares, and the inhabitants of Linz, knowing the people of Andernach were sound sleepers, and took special pleasure in prolonging their morning nap, once resolved to attack them at dawn of day.

ANDERNACH.
Watch Tower.

In silence the enemy stole up under the city wall, which they prepared to scale. Their attempt would probably have proved successful had it not been for the greediness of two baker lads, who had crept up into the tower to steal honey from the hives which the watchman kept up there.

Hearing a slight noise, and fearing the approach of the watchman, the youths cautiously peered over the wall, and thus became aware of the enemy's proximity. A moment later, having thrown the hives down upon the foe, the boys rushing to the bell loudly rang the alarm.

The Andernachers, springing out of bed, hurriedly donned their armor, seized their weapons, and rushed out, but their interference was no longer necessary, as the infuriated bees had already routed the enemy.

In commemoration of this event, the statues of the two baker lads have been placed just within the Andernach gates. There they can still be seen, exact effigies of the boys who crept up the tower to steal honey, and saved the town.

The Legend of St. Genevieve.

THE most celebrated church in Andernach is dedicated to St. Genevieve, who dwelt here in the eighth century. She was the daughter of the Duke of Brabant, and the wife of Siegfried, ruler of Austrasia, who had established his capital at Andernach.

As Genevieve was as good as she was beautiful, her husband was very proud of her, and very reluctantly parted from her when the Saracens threatened to invade the southern part of his kingdom. To make sure his beloved wife would be perfectly safe, Siegfried entrusted her to the care of his friend, Golo of Drachenfels, who, unfortunately, was not as virtuous as he appeared, and soon began to persecute Genevieve with unwelcome attentions, trying to persuade her to break faith with her husband and elope with him.

As she was far too virtuous to listen to his infamous proposals, Golo became so angry against her that he falsely accused her of base crimes, and locked her up in a damp prison, where she languished for several weeks. Then, learning that Siegfried was on his way home, and fearing lest he should discover the fraud, Golo hurried out to meet him, and pretending extravagant sorrow, told him that Genevieve had broken her marriage vow, and had stooped to a low intrigue with Draco, her cook.

Siegfried, upon hearing these accusations, flew into a passion, declared he would not enter the city as long as such a base criminal lived, and bade Golo ride ahead and have her immediately executed, for she had deserved death. Hard-hearted as he was, Golo could not bear to witness the death of the beautiful Genevieve, so he summoned the executioner, bade him lead her out into the forest, and not return until he had duly beheaded her.

This man, touched by the young creature's beauty and tears, could not take her life, but let her go, after obtaining a solemn promise that she would hide in the depths of the woods, and never appear in Andernach again. Genevieve, alone and quite destitute, now withdrew into a cave, where a white hind supplied the milk necessary for her sustenance, and here, in the forest solitude, she gave birth to Siegfried's little son, whom she called by his father's beloved name.

The child was strong and beautiful, and Genevieve spent all her time in caring for him, in gathering berries, herbs, and roots for food, and in ceaseless prayer, for, in spite of her trials, she had not lost her faith in God, whom she served as devoutly as ever.

Several years thus were spent in comparative peace by Genevieve and her child, while Siegfried knew no rest, and was sorely troubled by remorse. During the long sleepless nights and companionless days, he continually thought of the beautiful Genevieve, and bitterly regretted having condemned her unheard, for now that his first anger was passed, he could not believe such a pure, virtuous woman guilty of any heinous crime.

To divert his mind from this constant thought, Siegfried rode out of Andernach one day, and went into the forest accompanied by a large and merry hunting party. In the course of the day he became separated from his suite and hotly pursued a snow-white hind. To his surprise, it took refuge in a cave, behind a beautiful woman, who, garmentless, but completely veiled in her long golden hair, was caressing a lovely child.

As soon as he glanced at the face turned in sudden terror toward him, Siegfried recognized his long lost wife, and clasping her in his arms passionately entreated her to forgive him for the cruel suspicions, which he was sure she in no wise deserved. An explanation ensued, and when Siegfried knew all, he wrapped his wife and child in the ample folds of his cloak, and winding his hunting horn soon roused the echoes of the dim old forest. His attendants, rushing to answer his summons, improvised a litter upon which they bore Genevieve back to Andernach in triumph. Golo then confessed his crimes, and would have been put to death had not Genevieve interceded in his behalf. The people of Andernach, touched by the story of Genevieve's sufferings, and by her simple faith in the love and goodness of God, honored her as long as she lived, and canonized and worshiped her as a saint after her death.

SAYN.

An Interrupted Wedding.

FREDERICK of Sayn, founder of the ruined castle near the new building of the same name, after fighting for years in Spain against the Moors, returned home and married a beautiful wife with whom he was perfectly happy. But, a short time after his marriage an angel of the Lord appeared to him in a dream, and bade him leave castle and wife, and hasten off to Palestine to defend the Holy Sepulcher from the infidels. Almost broken-hearted at the thought of parting from his beloved, newly won wife, the Knight of Sayn nevertheless obeyed the summons, and after seven long years spent in constant warfare the same angel appeared to him again, bidding him return to the Rhine, as his wife had need of him. With the same unquestioning faith as before, Frederick left all and returned home, entering his castle gates disguised as a pilgrim, only to learn that his wife, believing him dead, was even then in the chapel plighting her troth to his dearest friend, to whose care he had committed her when he departed.

Maintaining his incognito, the pilgrim hastened into the chapel, where, concealed behind one of the great stone pillars, he softly began a peculiar little love song. At this sound the bride, standing at the altar, fainted away, for she recognized an air which she had composed during her honeymoon, and which was known only to her husband and to herself.

The marriage ceremony, thus interrupted, was postponed to the following day, and the guests invited to take part in the banquet, at which the fair châtelaine presided with her usual grace as soon as she had recovered from her swoon. She paid no heed to the pilgrim, who was seated with the servants at the end of the board.

The pilgrim, however, had been watching her attentively, and toward the end of the meal took a cup which he filled with wine, and after secretly dropped something into it, he bade a servant carry it to the Countess of Sayn, asking her to pledge a poor pilgrim for the Lord's sake.

The lady received the cup, bowed to the sender without looking closely at him, drank the wine, and then, perceiving the signet ring at the bottom and recognizing it, she started from her seat, ran to the pilgrim, threw herself in his arms sobbing for joy and crying, "My husband! my beloved husband!"

An explanation ensued, and the pilgrim, learning that a lying rumor had proclaimed him dead shortly after his departure, and that no tidings had been received from him since, freely forgave his friend and the wife who had never ceased to mourn for him, and who had been drawn together by their common affection for him.

NIEDERWERTH.

The Divine Pilgrim.

On the long and beautiful island of Niederwerth, almost on the spot where the village of the same name now stands, there once rose a small convent, which was inhabited by an abbess and twelve nuns, remarkably holy women, who spent all their time in prayer.

The sisters, who lived there in perfect peace, were greatly terrified when they heard that Attila, the Scourge of God, was drawing near, with his wild bands of Huns, who, being heathens, had no respect for their vows and treated all women with the most revolting cruelty. As there were no means of defense, and as their convent was remote from any settlement, the poor nuns could rely on no human aid, and prayed more fervently than ever that Christ would have mercy upon them, and deliver them from the hands of their oppressors. One evening when the midnight prayers were ended, the poor nuns were greatly startled by a noise at the door; but when they discovered that it was only a poor pilgrim, they bade him welcome in the Lord's name, tenderly washed his weary feet, and compassionately gave him food and drink.

When he was somewhat rested and refreshed, the pilgrim inquired why the nuns were thus prolonging their vigils, and when he heard of the threatened invasion he exclaimed:

"You have helped me, now let me advise you. Prepare thirteen coffins within the chapel, and when the foe approaches let each sister commend her soul and body to God, and lie down in her coffin. I will be responsible for the rest."

The nuns, finding the advice good, immediately prepared their coffins, and on the morrow, when the wild Huns appeared on the river bank, they withdrew to the chapel, recited the prescribed prayer, and calmly crossing their hands on their breasts, lay down in their biers. As the outer doors fell in under the assailants ruthless blows, the aged pilgrim suddenly appeared in their midst, and stretched out his hands in blessing over them. Their eyes closed, they assumed a livid, corpse-like hue, and soon appeared wan and shrunken like persons long dead.

Two angels then came, lighted all the candles on the altar, and when the Huns burst into the chapel they drew back appalled at the sight of the angelic host, attending our Lord, who, under the guise of an aged pilgrim, had come to defend the helpless nuns who had put all their trust in him.

Filled with nameless dread, the Huns immediately re-embarked in their frail skiffs, and were overtaken by a storm, in which so many perished that the Rhine is said to have rolled corpses for many a day. When the Hun's army had swept onward, some of the people visiting the island to find how the nuns had fared, found dormitory, refectory, and chapel empty. Passing through the little churchyard, they found thirteen new graves within it, each bearing the name of one of the nuns, and the same date of decease. But "how they died, who carried them there, and who buried them" remains a complete mystery to this day.

COBLENTZ.

St. Ritza.

Louis I., the Débonnaire, the unworthy son of Charlemagne, is said to have lived in Coblentz where his fair daughter Ritza was born and brought up. This maiden from early youth spent almost all her time in prayer. As soon as she was old enough to leave home, she obtained her father's permission to retire to a little hermitage on the other side of the Rhine, on the spot where the Ehrenbreitstein fortress now stands. To attend church, Ritza daily crossed the river, and as her faith was as pure as that of St. Peter, she fearlessly walked across the waters, using no support except a slender little willow twig, which she generally carried. Of course, the rumor of this daily repeated miracle soon attracted great attention. The holy hermit was daily watched on her passage to and fro across the river by a breathless multitude, who, when the journey was safely accomplished, loudly extolled her virtues and called her the saint.

The church bells were ringing loudly one stormy day, and every wave was crested with a line of foam, when Ritza came down to the shore as usual. For the first time the loud wind and dashing spray daunted her, and seeing a heavy staff lying near, the maiden took it, instead of her willow wand, which appeared too slender to offer any support in the face of such a terrible gale.

Somewhat hesitatingly she now began her journey, and when she reached the middle of the river, frightened by the threatening appearance of the white-capped waves, she leaned heavily upon her staff, and immediately began to sink. A moment later faith conquered; she flung the treacherous prop aside, then clasped her hands, and uttering a fervent prayer found herself able to stand upright once more in the midst of the heaving and tossing billows, through which she safely made her way to the opposite shore.

In gratitude for the timely aid she had received, Ritza declared her resolution to place all her reliance from henceforth in God alone, and daily crossed the tide without either wand or staff. When she died, the people reverently bore her to St. Castor's church. There her tomb can still be seen; the people continue to revere her as a saint, and the Roman Catholics still lay offerings upon her shrine, imploring her aid in all cases of dire need.

Noble Deaths.

THE legends relate that Napoleon, closely pursued by the Cossacks, was once sorely defeated at Coblentz on the Rhine, where, surrounded by the enemy, he would have been made prisoner had he not been saved by the presence of mind of Corporal Spohn.

Seeing at a glance that there was no other means of escape, the corporal implored the emperor to exchange hats and steeds with him. The change was effected ere the battle smoke had rolled away, and while Napoleon mounted on an inferior steed, and with the corporal's hat on his head, was allowed to escape unhindered, the Cossacks pressed closely around the pretended Napoleon, whom they made prisoner, and proudly conducted to the Russian general.

There, the fraud was soon discovered, and the Cossacks, enraged at being deceived, slew the brave corporal, who thus lost his life to save his master. According to the Coblentz legend, Napoleon, in remembrance of his narrow escape and Corporal Spohn's brave self-sacrifice, preferred the uniform of a corporal to any other, and wore it so frequently that all the army were wont to speak of him with affectionate familiarity as *Le petit Caporal*.

Another historical souvenir connected with this city, is

the death of the brave young General Marceau, who lies buried here, and whose grave is mentioned by Byron in "Childe Harold's Pilgrimage," thus:

> "By Coblentz, on a rise of gentle ground,
> There is a small and simple pyramid,
> Crowning the summit of the verdant mound;
> Beneath its base are heroes' ashes hid
> Our enemy's—but let not that forbid!
> Honor to Marceau! o'er whose early tomb
> Tears, big tears, gushed from the rough soldier's lid,
> Lamenting and yet envying such a doom,
> Falling for France, whose rights he battled to resume.
>
> Brief, brave, and glorious was his young career,—
> His mourners were two hosts, his friends and foes;
> And fitly may the stranger, lingering here,
> Pray for his gallant spirit's bright repose;
> For he was Freedom's champion, one of those,
> The few in number, who had not o'erstept
> The charter to chastise which she bestows
> On such as wield her weapons; he had kept,
> The whiteness of his soul, and thus men o'er him wept.
>
> —*Byron.*

The Lovers.

HEINRICH and Bertha were lovers. They were separated by the swift Moselle, flowing into the Rhine, as well as by their cruel parents, who did not favor an alliance between them. Heinrich often took up his post on the Moselle bridge to obtain a glimpse of the fair face of his beloved, and gazed with eager eyes at the little house she inhabited, wishing that he might visit her once more.

One spring morning, while he was thus musing, paying no heed to the sullen waters beneath him which were seething and hissing as they wildly rushed along, he saw Bertha leave her dwelling and step into the ferryboat to cross to Coblentz. His fixed gaze must have had magnetic powers, for the girl looked up, and, perceiving her lover, uttered an exclamation of pleasure, as she sprang up and stretched out her longing arms toward him.

Startled by the sudden movement and exclamation, the ferryman dropped his oars, and the vessel, no longer guided, was whirled rapidly along by the current and dashed to pieces against one of the stone piers. When Heinrich saw his beloved Bertha in danger of drowning, he immediately sprang into the water, and, after almost incredible efforts, succeeded in saving her from a watery grave.

The respective parents, only too glad to recover their children alive, no longer refused to sanction the wedding. It was witnessed by all the inhabitants of Coblentz, who accompanied the newly married couple to their home, shouting for joy, and wishing them all manner of happiness and prosperity.

THE MOSELLE VALLEY.

St. Peter's Thirst.

THE valley of the Moselle, along whose winding course are dotted many mediæval castles, is the scene of many of the same legends told of places along the Rhine, and also of two Christian traditions which we will recount here.

Discouraged by the lack of faith shown by the Jews, Christ is said to have often wandered away among the Gentiles, who gladly received the good tidings He bore. On one occasion He came to the banks of the Moselle, where, weary with His efforts, and panting with the heat, He sat down by the roadside with His disciples, bidding St. Peter hasten on to the neighboring city of Coblentz and purchase a measure of wine for their refreshment.

Peter hurried to the city, bought the wine, which was handed to him in a deep wooden measure such as they use in that part of the country, and immediately set out to return.

He had not gone far, however, ere the wine began to run down over the sides of the vessel, which had been generously filled to the brim.

"Oh, dear!" exclaimed St. Peter, "this will never, never do. It is a pity to lose any of this good wine. I had better drink a little, so I can carry the measure without spilling any of its contents."

Peter, therefore, began to drink; but as he was hot and very thirsty, he took more than the sip he intended, and when he raised his head, he perceived with dismay that the measure no longer seemed full. Fearing lest he should be reproved for helping himself first, he quickly drew his knife out of his pocket and pared off a piece of the rim, so that the measure appeared as full as before; then he resumed his walk.

But soon the wine again began to overflow. He took another sip, which, being also too prolonged, forced him to have recourse to his knife for a second time. Sipping and whittling, Peter thus continued his way, and when he at last came to the place where the Master and disciples were waiting for him, the measure, greatly reduced, contained barely enough wine to moisten their lips.

Silently the Master gazed upon Peter and then remarked: "Peter, next time you drink wine, be sure and wipe the drops away from your beard. But tell me, don't you think the people of this country must be very mean to sell their vintage in such miserable little things as these?" and He tapped the little wooden measure.

Peter hung his head and did not reply, but ever since then the wine measures along the Moselle, which are very small indeed, have been known as "Miseräbelchen" or miserable little things.

COCHEM.

St. Christopher.

On the banks of the Moselle rises the recently restored castle of Cochem, where is found a notable old mosaic representation of St. Christopher, whose legend is a favorite among the neighboring peasantry, and is as follows:

There was once a giant by the name of Offero, who had proudly vowed to serve the mightiest monarch, and no one else. With that purpose in view he journeyed about until he reached the court of a king, whom all designated as the most powerful sovereign on earth. This ruler gladly accepted Offero's proffered services and for a while the giant was very happy indeed.

But one day a courtier mentioned Satan's name, and the king, seated upon his throne, shuddered. Surprised at this demonstration, Offero questioned his master, and learned that Satan was king of the Infernal Regions.

"Is he more powerful than you, oh, king?" thundered the giant.

"Alas! yes," replied the king.

"Then I shall leave your service, and go in search of him, for I have vowed to use my prodigious strength only for the greatest of all monarchs."

Offero departed; he had not gone far before he began to inquire his way, and was delighted to find that everyone he met could indicate an easy mode to "go to the devil."

This being the case, you can readily imagine that it did not take him long to get there. He tendered his services to Satan, who gladly accepted him, and found plenty of work for him to do. One day Satan bade the giant accompany him to the surface of the earth, where there was enough to occupy them both, and as they passed along a highway, Offero saw his dauntless master tremble and gaze fearfully

ST. CHRISTOPHER.
Tintoretto.

to the right and left. In answer to Offero's blunt question, why he acted thus, Satan timorously confessed that he was afraid.

"Afraid," exclaimed the giant, "and of what, pray?"

"Of that," said Satan, pointing to a rude wooden cross, erected by the roadside.

The giant's surprise increased, but when Satan gradually proceeded to inform him that he was so afraid only because Christ had died on a similar cross, he imperiously demanded who Christ might be, and insisted upon knowing whether He was more powerful than the master he served.

Satan shuffled, hesitated, and finally replied that Christ was king of Heaven, and reluctantly admitted that none was as powerful as He.

"Very well," exclaimed Offero, "as I have sworn to serve the mightiest only, I will go and seek Christ," and he then and there left Satan, and started out in search of the new Master, who was not as easy to find as the one he had just left.

After much journeying to and fro, Offero was finally told to seek a holy hermit, who would be sure to point out the best way to find Christ, and after questioning this man concerning the power and importance of the Lord he acknowledged, he inquired how he might best serve him:

"Do as I do," replied the hermit, "fast and pray without ceasing, mortify your flesh, and you will serve Him."

"What! I, a giant, spend my time in praying," exclaimed Offero; "that would be absurd. Were I to fast, I would soon lose the great strength which is my proudest boast, and that would never do. As you say there are many ways of serving Him, I will try and find another."

Once more Offero started out upon his travels, and ere long fell in with a band of pilgrims, all bound for the heavenly land. Joining them, he learned that Christ's Kingdom was on the other side of a deep river, which none could cross until invited to do so by one of the King's white-winged messengers. Ere long the little band came to the banks of this stream, and all gazed with awe at the dark rushing tide which was spanned by no bridge, crossed by no boat, and over which each traveler was forced to make his way as best he could.

While they were standing there, a white-winged messenger suddenly appeared in their midst, to inform an aged and feeble woman that the Lord required her presence on the other side. The poor old woman, who had longed for the summons, went bravely down to the river brink, but when she saw the rushing tide, and felt the coldness of its waters, she recoiled wailing, for she was afraid to venture further in. Offero, hearing this pitiful cry, then strode boldly forward, raised her in his powderful arms, and bade her have no fear, for he would bear her safely to the other side.

True to his promise, he carefully carried her across the river, and as he set her gently down on the bank, he bade her tell Christ that Offero, the giant, was anxious to serve Him, and that until he was summoned he would make use of his strength to help poor travelers over the river. Then he turned round and went back. Day by day, he now helped the pilgrims over, often marveling at the different ways in which the Lord's summons were received, for while some heard them with joy, others lingered, as if they would fain have waited a little longer.

In order to be near at hand night and day, the giant took up his abode in a little hut by the river's edge. One night, when a fierce storm was raging, and the darkness was almost impenetrable, he was greatly surprised to hear a plantive call. He went out with staff and lantern, and soon found a little child, who declared he must pass over the river that very night. The compassionate giant immediately lifted the little creature upon his shoulder, and, staff in hand, stepped unhesitatingly down into the cold and stormy waters.

In spite of all his strength, his stout oaken staff, and the small size of his burden, Offero stumbled, struggled, and almost fell. At every step the child seemed to grow heavier and heavier, until he could scarcely stand up beneath its weight, and was forced to use every effort to reach the opposite shore, where he thankfully set his burden down.

Then he looked up to examine the heavy child more closely, and suddenly saw, instead of an infant, a tall and gracious figure before him, and heard a gentle voice address him saying:

"Offero, I am the Christ, whom thou hast borne over the river of death this stormy night. Marvel not that thou didst stumble and almost fall beneath my weight, for I have taken upon me all the sins of the world. Thou hast served me well; and henceforth thou shalt be known as Christoffero, the Christ bearer. Enter thou into the joy of thy Lord."

Because of this beautiful legend, St. Christopher is always invoked in time of death to lend a helping hand to struggling mortals, whose favorite saint he is said to be.

THURANT.

A Carousing Army.

THE ruins of the ancient fortress of Thurant, which was first built in 1200, tower above the Moselle, and serve to remind travelers of the many sieges which the castle endured during the Middle Ages.

On one occasion, the united forces of the bishops of Trier and Cologne surrounded the stronghold, which was nobly defended by its owner. He and his brave garrison suffered much from hunger and thirst, while his foes drank their fill of Moselle wine, declaring they hoped the castle would hold out until they had emptied barrels enough to erect as imposing a building as the one they besieged.

This was before the days of gunpowder. Arrows and swords were of no avail when it was a question of seizing a well-defended castle, perched upon such almost inaccessible heights, where battering rams and other ponderous war engines could not be used.

To beguile the time, therefore, the hosts of Trier and Cologne drank morning, noon, and night, sang jolly songs, and kept up a perpetual carousal. This greatly exasperated the garrison at Thurant, who, however, held out bravely for two whole years, during which time the enemy drained no less than three thousand casks of Moselle wine. The gate-keeper, weary of this long siege, and longing to join in the noisy orgies which he daily saw and heard, finally made secret arrangements to open the castle gates, and deliver it into the enemy's hands. His treachery was discovered, however, and, in punishment, his master ordered him to be tossed in a blanket from the top of the castle tower into the midst of the enemy's camp, where he was so anxious to be. Strange to relate, the gate-keeper landed unharmed in the midst of his foes, drank a long draught of wine, and in gratitude for his narrow escape built the chapel on the Bleidenberg, from whence such a beautiful view can be obtained.

CARDEN.

The Rescued Knight.

A CRUSADER once fell into the hands of Saracens. They chained him fast in a tower near the sea, where, through the bars of his prison, he could see the white-sailed ships passing to and fro. The sight of these vessels only made his captivity harder to bear, and he often prayed that he might fly, like those white-winged vessels, to the western shores, and again be permitted to see his native land.

One night, while sleeping on the hard stones of his prison floor, the knight suddenly heard the flutter of wings, saw his prison door open, and heard a divine voice bidding him arise and depart. A moment later he was out of the dungeon, and, still obeying divine commands, he sprang on the back of a waiting swan, which, spreading its broad pinions, bore him rapidly over land and sea. When it began to sink he gazed downward, and recognized his native place on the banks of the Moselle.

A moment later, the knight awoke, and feeling hard stones beneath him, turned over in despair, thinking he had again been deluded by a tantalizing dream.

The perfume of flowers and the ripple of water made him suddenly open his eyes, however, and then he saw with rapture that he was lying on the hillside, near his old home, and humbly returned thanks for his escape from captivity.

In gratitude for his miraculous deliverance, the knight founded the lately restored church still known as the Swan Church, which is yearly visited by many pilgrims.

NIEDERLAHNSTEIN.

The Unhappy Twins.

A TRAGIC story is connected with the stretch of land near the junction of the Lahn and Rhine. This ground was set apart as the burial place of unrepentant sinners, and malefactors of every kind.

Near this spot there once dwelt a noble couple who rejoiced greatly at the birth of beautiful twin children, a boy and girl. These little ones were carefully guarded during their infancy by their tender mother. Her heart was therefore torn with anguish, when called upon to leave them for a short time to go and nurse her husband, who had been mortally wounded in war. The servants received strict instructions to watch over the children night and day, but, although the nurse at first faithfully discharged her duties, she soon allowed herself to be enticed to forsake her little charges while they slept, and take part in the merriment in which the other servants indulged, now that they were left to their own devices.

One evening some gypsies entered the castle court, and the servants soon began to dance to the merry tunes they played. The nurse, attracted by the alluring tones, soon joined them, leaving the children asleep in their room. In her excitement she entirely forgot the flight of time, and it was only when the gypsies had gone, and the fun had been duly talked over, that she hastened back to the nursery. There she found everything turned topsy-turvy, and no trace of the little girl. Her shrieks of distress soon brought the other servants, who discovered that while they were in the court dancing, someone had entered the room and had stolen the child and many objects of considerable value.

All search for the little girl proved fruitless, and when the widowed lady returned from her husband's death-bed, it was only to learn that one of her treasures had disappeared. The other child was safe only because his presence had not been noticed as he had slipped entirely under the bedclothes in his sleep.

Many years passed by. The boy became a man, and wooed and married the adopted daughter of a noble widowed lady farther up the Rhine. As soon as the wedding ceremony was ended, the youthful bridegroom hurried his beautiful wife home, where his mother was waiting to receive them and gently led her new daughter to her room.

There she lingered with her for a while, questioning the bride about her parentage, and inquiring whether there was no mark on her body by which she might have been recognized.

The newly wedded wife immediately revealed that she bore on her bosom a tiny birthmark like a rose, and the elder woman, clasping her joyfully to her heart, declared she was her long lost daughter, for whom she had mourned so deeply.

The little bride gladly responded to all her caresses, but,

when she suddenly realized that she had just plighted her troth to her only brother, she fell down upon the floor dead. The bridegroom entering the apartment at that moment, also learned the truth, rushed out of the house like a madman, and never returned. On the morrow, his body was found cold and dead on the hillside, and as there were no marks of violence upon it none ever knew how he had perished.

The twins who had slept together in one cradle, were now laid to rest in the same grave, but as they had, although unconsciously, infringed the laws of the church, the priest would not allow them to be buried in holy ground, but had them laid near Niederlahnstein, among the outcasts.

> "But why with their kind
> Rest they not? Say, the grave is surely blind—
> And the dark mold which covers corpses in
> Presents a front impenetrable to sin.
> Alas! alas! the virtuous of our race
> Had thrust them rudely from their resting place.
> In yonder churchyard—consecrated earth—
> As though one clay to all did not give birth.
> Oh, hypocrites! and to this shying shore
> Consigned their cold remains for ever, ever more."
>
> —*Snowe.*

LAHNECK.

The Last of the Templars.

NEAR the spot where the Lahn flows into the Rhine, rises the now restored castle of Lahneck, which was probably first built in the tenth century. This fortress was the last refuge of the Knights Templar in Germany, for their leader was then the aged and white-haired Count of Lahneck. Pope Clement V. and Philip IV. of France, coveting the vast wealth which the order of the Templars had amassed during many years of warfare, accused the knights of fraud. Next they condemned Jacques Molay, Great Master of the order, to death, and confiscated all the Templar property.

Peter, archbishop of Mayence, also instigated by the Pope, then tried to secure the wealth of the German Templars and to force them to dissolve their order, but threats and decrees were alike unavailing, as far as the old Lord of Lahneck and twelve of his bravest companions were concerned.

Resolved to remain true to their vows at any cost, and to defend the property of their order as long as strength endured, this handful of men entrenched themselves in the castle of Lahneck, where they fought so bravely that they succeeded in holding a force of two thousand men at bay for several months.

Finally, however, the heavy battering rams broke down the castle ramparts. The enemy, forcing their way through the breach and scaling the walls on all sides at once, poured into the fortress, bidding the knights surrender. The old Count of Lahneck, who now had only four companions left, beat a retreat toward the inner fortress, sternly declaring that he would never yield, but would sell his life dearly.

Step by step he and his little band retreated, but ere they reached the drawbridge all had fallen except the Count of Lahneck. He grimly hewed right and left, calling out: "Honor and Right" at every blow, and answering all the summons to surrender by an unflinching "Never!"

The young and brave leader of the opposite party, wishing to end the fray, suddenly threw aside his weapon. He darted forward, caught the old man in his strong arms, and vainly tried to drag him away from his dangerous position.

"Surrender," he cried once more, as he made a desperate effort to pull him off the drawbridge.

"Never!" reiterated the old lord. Then, finding he could no longer resist the strong grasp laid upon him, he suddenly flung himself over the drawbridge, dragging his captor with him. Both fell upon the jagged rocks below, where they were dashed to pieces. It was thus that the last of the Knights Templar in Germany fell, having kept to the end his vow to remain true to his order.

This castle, which was destroyed by the French, and long left in a sad state of ruin, was eventually purchased by an Englishman who intended to restore it. One morning his only daughter, Bessie, went alone to the top of the ruined tower. She had no sooner climbed up there than the stone staircase fell into ruin, with a crash which shook the whole tower. The poor girl fainted in terror, and remained unconscious during several hours, while her father vainly sought her, calling her name repeatedly yet receiving no response.

The bereaved father left the place in despair. Several years later the maiden's body was found by some of her countrymen, who had purchased the ruins and climbed to the top of the ruined tower by means of a ladder. The lost girl lay under a stone bench, still clutching in her dead hand a fragment of paper upon which her last words could plainly be seen.

STOLZENFELS.

The Pet Raven.

THE beautiful castle of Stolzenfels, which is now entirely restored, was founded in the middle of the thirteenth century by Arnold von Isenbourg, the archbishop of Cleves. It was once inhabited by Othmar and Willeswind, a brother and sister, who, having lost their parents, were devoted to each other, and to the care of their numerous retainers, who idolized them both.

The brother and sister were always together, so Willeswind grieved sorely when her brother was obliged to go off to war. He took all the able-bodied men with him, and left none but the old men, women, and children at home. As there were many lawless robber-knights along the Rhine in those days, Willeswind prudently ordered that the castle gates should remain constantly closed, and only sallied forth at midday, to visit a few of her pensioners in the village, and carry them the alms she was wont to bestow.

One evening, while she was sitting in the hall with all her retainers, keeping the women busily at work spinning and watching the men as they burnished their arms, the warder suddenly came to announce the presence of a pilgrim, begging for shelter. Willeswind immediately gave orders that he should be admitted; but, in spite of his worn garments, he inspired her with a vague feeling of fear, for his face was cunning and cruel, and his roving glances seemed to take note of the castle defenses, and of the small number of her aged retainers.

Her suspicions, which were shared by the warder, were only too soon justified, for although the pilgrim departed peaceably on the morrow, he came back three days later, in full armor, coolly demanding her hand in marriage, and threatening to take her by force if she did not consent to his proposal within three days' time.

Willeswind, knowing it would be impossible for her aged retainers to hold out against the robber knight's well-appointed forces until her brother, to whom she dispatched a message, could come to her rescue, finally decided to take the warder's advice and withdraw into a neighboring convent.

On her way thither with a small escort, she fell into an ambush laid by the treacherous knight. He soon overcame her retainers' brave but feeble resistance, made her captive, and carried her off with her maid to a lonely tower in the woods. There he locked them both in, declaring he would come in three days' time to receive a favorable answer to his suit.

As soon as he had departed, Willeswind and her maid began to inspect the premises, but could devise no means of

STOBZENFELS CASTLE.

escape, for the walls were thick, doors and windows heavily barred, and, in spite of careful search, they could find neither water nor food. While the unhappy captives were peering anxiously through the barred windows, and convincing themselves that the tower lay in the wilderness where no passer-by would come to lend them aid, Willeswind suddenly perceived her pet raven, which she whistled to her side.

She and Othmar had trained this bird to bring them berries at a sign, and she now resolved to make good use of the faithful raven. It journeyed busily to and fro, bringing so many luscious berries that Willeswind and her maid did not suffer acutely from either hunger or thirst. Three days later the robber knight appeared, seemed greatly surprised when Willeswind rejected his addresses as haughtily as ever, and departed, declaring he would return in three days, when she would probably prove more amenable. Time passed very slowly in that gloomy prison. In spite of the faithful raven's incessant visits, the girls were very faint and weak, and on the sixth day, while eagerly watching for the bird's return, Willeswind suddenly saw a knight emerge from the thicket and ride by. Judging by his horse and armor that it could not be her ravisher, she called aloud for aid, and wildly waved her handkerchief through the bars.

A moment later the knight had turned, and Willeswind with a cry of rapture recognized Othmar, who, to reach home sooner, was riding through the forest. Before he could take any measures to deliver her, however, the robber knight came riding up the overgrown path, and seeing him, challenged him to fight. Othmar, furious at the man's insolent behavior, and at the treatment he had made poor Willeswind endure, fought so bravely that he soon stretched his antagonist lifeless on the ground. Then he seized the keys at his belt, and freed the captives who had languished in the lonely tower six days.

As he and Willeswind slowly rode away, the raven, returning with a host of its companions, swooped down upon the robber knight's corpse and pecked out its eyes. Willeswind, safe home once more in her beloved Stolzenfels, now recounted all her adventures to her brother, who ordered an effigy of the raven to be placed above the gateway, to commemorate the fidelity of the pet bird whose exertions had preserved two human lives.

The Alchemist.

THIS same castle of Stolzenfels, which commands such a magnificent view of the Rhine, was the scene of another romantic story. One of the lords of the castle once left home, intrusting all his wealth and the administration of his property to a steward whose fidelity he had often tested.

Unfortunately, however, this man began the study of alchemy, and practicing daily in a turret chamber which he had fitted up as a laboratory, he became convinced that he could discover the secret which would transmute all base metals into gold. In the vain hope of discovering the process, he used up all his own slender store, and, borrowing gold, piece by piece, from his master's strong box, he used that too. At last, hearing his master would return in a few days' time, he examined the treasury and found it nearly empty.

Terrified at the account he would have to render, the steward was brooding gloomily over his situation one evening, when a pilgrim, who had taken shelter in the castle, wrung from him a confession of the cause of his despondency. This confession was overheard by the steward's lovely young daughter Mina. Horrified at the thought that her father had robbed his master, she stole sadly off to bed, wondering how she might save his honor. She little suspected that the pretended pilgrim was the alchemist Maso, who, by promises of unlimited wealth, was inducing her unhappy father to furnish him with all the gold left in the house, and to lend him his retorts and alembics.

The pilgrim, having obtained all he required, worked indefatigably all the next day. But when the steward entered the tower toward evening, he declared that he had missed the exact combination only because the stars were not in the right position, and that he was sure of discovering the secret on the morrow, when the planets would be in conjunction, if the steward would only procure him a little more gold.

Mina, who had stolen silently up into the tower, and was standing behind the door, heard her father declare there was not a particle of gold left. Then the pilgrim gradually revealed the fact that a pure maiden's blood was an excellent substitute for gold, and that if he would only sacrifice his daughter, his honor would be saved. The maiden heard her father indignantly refuse, and saw him rush away in despair. Prompted by filial affection and the spirit of self-sacrifice, she entered the laboratory, where she offered to die to save her beloved father from disgrace. This generous proposal was unhesitatingly accepted by the pilgrim, who bade her come at midnight, on the morrow, when the favorable hour would have struck.

At eventide on the morrow, the lord of Stolzenfels rode into his castle, attended by many followers, one of whom no sooner beheld the fair Mina, than he fell desperately in love with her. Standing at his bedroom window that night, this young man sentimentally watched the light in her casement, and near midnight was surprised to see her take up the candle and leave the room.

By the sudden illumination of sundry windows, he soon discovered that she was coming toward his side of the house. then, listening intently, he heard her pass his door, and creeping noiselessly after her, he mounted the winding turret stairs, and hid behind the door after she had passed into the laboratory.

In the deep silence he heard her tearfully inquire whether

nothing else could save her father from disgrace on the morrow, heard the pilgrim assure her that the sacrifice must take place, and through a crack in the door saw the glittering dagger raised to strike her to the heart.

One bound brought the young man to her rescue, and a moment later the pretended pilgrim, flung aside by a strong arm, fell among the retorts and alembics with a crash which awakened the whole household, and brought them in haste upon the scene. There an explanation took place, the guilty steward confessed his crime, and the lord of Stolzenfels, touched by his repentance as well as by Mina's devotion, freely forgave him. As for the noble youth, he soon won Mina's affections, and she became his wife, all the people of Stolzenfels dancing merrily at the wedding, and wishing the newly married couple a long life of unbroken prosperity.

RHENSE.

An Exchange.

On a wooded height, very near Rhense on the Rhine; stands the peculiar little octagon building known as the Königsstuhl, or seat of the king. Erected in 1376 by the Emperor Charles IV., on the spot where the boundaries of the four great electorates meet, it became the trysting place of the seven influential princes, who there discussed matters of state and elected the rulers of Germany.

These noblemen caused seven stone seats to be placed upon the flat roof of the little building. It fell into decay at the end of the last century, but is now exactly restored. The legend relates that when Wenceslaus was emperor of Germany, finding the cares of state too burdensome to endure, he often came here to forget them in drinking the delicious Rhine wines.

On one occasion he is reported to have openly declared that he would gladly exchange his crown for a generous yearly supply of the best Bacharach vintage. Prince Rupert of the Rhine, who coveted the imperial power, immediately declared his readiness to furnish Wenceslaus with four butts of wine every year, in exchange for which he received all the imperial insignia.

Wencelaus, it is said, never regretted his bargain, but the time came when Rupert understood that the cares of state far outweigh the pleasures and honors which may accrue from being sovereign of the whole land.

BREY.

The Water Nymphs.

THE villagers were all dancing merrily on the green, to celebrate the harvest home, when they suddenly became aware of the presence of three beautiful young damsels, clad in flowing white garments, and crowned with garlands of peculiar waxy-looking flowers. Although the maidens were total strangers, three village youths soon stepped forward to invite them to dance, and they heartily entered into the spirit of the merry-making.

When the night was already pretty far advanced, and the silvery moonbeams flooded the landscape, the maidens prepared to depart, refusing the escort of the enamoured youths, who followed them as closely as they dared, hoping to discover where the beautiful maidens lived.

Imagine their surprise, however, when they saw the girls step unconcernedly down from the bank into the river, and trip lightly from one silvery-tipped wave to another. When they reached the center of the stream, the maidens suddenly paused, and holding out their lily-white arms, called to the youths to join them.

Bewitched by their beauty and alluring gestures, the three

youths, forgetful of all danger, rushed blindly forward, but instead of embracing the maidens, who suddenly disappeared, they sank down into the moonlit river forever. At the first stroke of midnight, three crimson, blood-like streaks were seen stretching from the shore to the center of the river. These appeared for many centuries, on the anniversary of the youths' death, and after showing vividly for a short time, always vanished as suddenly and mysteriously as they had come.

The Nixie.

On the left bank of the Rhine, almost smothered by the luxuriant shade of fruit trees, is the little village of Brey, celebrated because it was one of the favorite haunts of the Nixie, a water nymph of the Rhine. Many stories are therefore told about her, and the villagers still declare that she has been seen at a distance.

Two young huntsmen once started out from Brey at dawn, and entering a skiff, proceeded to cross the Rhine. While one diligently plied the oars, the other gazed fixedly down in the flood, and suddenly exclaimed that he saw the Nixie combing out her golden hair. A moment later he seized his gun, and aiming at the water sprite in wanton mischief, he pulled the trigger and shot, ere his companion could hinder him from doing so.

Before they reached the opposite shore, however, a strange look had come into his eyes, and his companion rowed faster and faster, nervously gazing at him from time to time. All at once he muttered that the beautiful white-armed Nixie was beckoning to him and plunged down into the river.

Three days later his body was washed ashore, and the people gathering about their former companion in awe-stricken silence, noticed that his gun was still clasped close to his breast. But, as a beautiful smile hovered over his rigid lips, they all whispered that the Nixie had evidently forgiven him for his attempt to injure her.

MARKSBURG.

The Murdered Wife.

THE fortress of Marksburg, which is the only old fortress along the Rhine which has remained in a perfect state of preservation to our day, is almost impregnable, and has long been used as a state prison.

This castle once belonged to Ludwig the Cruel, Lord of Braubach, who married a young and beautiful, but weak-minded woman, called Maria. As she found it impossible to love her husband, this faithless wife began a flirtation with a steward called Henry, who was passionately in love with her.

The husband, however, soon discovered this state of affairs, and being obliged to leave home suddenly, bade the steward accompany him, taking sundry precautions to prevent any clandestine correspondence. But, in spite of all his vigilance, Maria and Henry managed to exchange many a letter, and they would have escaped detection, had not Maria once made the mistake of directing the letter intended for her lover to her husband.

Ludwig the Cruel, finding he had been outwitted, was so furious that he rode straight home, where he was not expected, and flung the maid who had acted as go-between out of the window on the rocks beneath the castle. Then, accompanied by two executioners, he entered unexpectedly into his wife's room and had her beheaded without further ado.

This summary mode of avenging his wrongs was greatly resented by his people, who would doubtless have punished him for his cruelty had they not been afraid of him. But although avenged, Ludwig was far from happy. He was soon tormented by such keen remorse, that he did penance for his sins, and founded a nunnery which was named in honor of the wife whom he had so mercilessly slain.

DINKHOLD FOUNTAIN.

The Spectral Foot.

In a little valley, not far from Braubach, are the mineral springs known as the Dinkhold, the favorite haunt of a maid named Ægle, daughter of old Father Rhine.

Many years ago a young knight lived at the head of this little valley, and daily rode down it with his mounted train on his way to the Rhine or to the chase. On one occasion he was detained, and sending his followers ahead of him, he presently rode down the familiar valley alone. He started with surprise when he saw a limpid fountain, in a spot which had hitherto been dry and arid. His surprise was further increased at the sight of a beautiful ethereal creature, bending gracefully over the fountain. This creature proved so attractive that he immediately dismounted, and going to her, began to converse with her. He soon learned who she was, declared the love which had been kindled at the first sight of her, and was overjoyed when she confessed that she had long loved him, and had only waited for him to pass by alone to reveal herself to him.

Ægle, the beautiful nymph, in spite of her protestations of affection was very shy indeed, and ere long told her lover she must depart, bade him meet her there on the morrow, and vanished before he could utter a protest or try to detain her.

The knight was, of course, faithful to his appointment on the morrow, but when he would fain have embraced the timid Ægle, she shrank back, exclaiming that she would again meet him on the morrow, but that if by that time he had not learned to behave as a true and loyal knight, she would never see him again. As she vanished as soon as this speech was ended, the knight cudgeled his brain to find out what her mysterious words might mean, and it was only after several hours' reflection that he remembered that while he had uttered countless words of love, he had never mentioned the subject of marriage.

His first words on the morrow therefore were to ask Ægle when she would become his wife, and to persuade her to meet him in his castle chapel that evening and plight her troth to him there at the altar. Ægle, whose beautiful face grew radiant at these words, promised to do so, warning him, however, that a marriage with a nymph was rather dangerous, as he would lose his life should he ever prove faithless. But the knight, sure of his love, led her to the altar, and lived seven years with the beautiful Ægle, who was a devoted wife and bore him several lovely children.

The happiness of this married couple, which was simply ideal, was troubled at last by rumors of war, and Ægle shed her first tears when her husband was obliged to join the imperial army. Then she clung to him imploring him not to forget her for a moment, as faithlessness would be punished by death. They parted beside the fountain where they had first met, and Ægle returned home to watch for her beloved's return.

After many months of warfare, peace was concluded, and the Emperor Henry, wishing to reward the knight for his bravery, summoned him into his presence and proposed to give him the hand of his beautiful niece, Agnes, who had long loved him in secret. The knight, with much dignity, declared the honor was far too great for so humble a subject as he, and added that being already married, he could moreover enter into no other alliance.

Angry and disappointed at this refusal, Henry questioned him closely. When he heard that he had married a nymph, he crossed himself, summoned the bishop of Bamberg, implored him to convince the knight of the sin of loving a demon, and tried to prevail upon him to annul the unholy contract by an immediate marriage with his niece.

The bishop of Bamberg, who was a subtle reasoner, argued with the knight, and so bewildered him that he finally prevailed upon him to consent to an immediate marriage with the fair Agnes. But, when the ceremony was over, and the wedding guests were seated around the festal board, the knight's eyes suddenly dilated with horror, for there, before him, appeared a small, white, naked foot, which, in the presence of all the guests, spurned him ere it vanished.

With a cry of "Ægle!" the knight fell down unconscious, and after vainly trying to restore him, the bishop of Bamberg, who was versed in magic, declared he must be carried over the Rhine, as the evil spirits would not relinquish their hold upon him until he had passed over running water.

The attendants immediately bore him down to a boat, where many of the guests followed him, but when they reached the middle of the river, a great wave swept suddenly down upon them and dashing over the vessel carried off the knight's body, which was never seen again. One of the boatmen, however, declared that he saw a little white foot thrusting it down under the waters, and heard the unhappy knight again cry "Ægle."

The emperor's niece Agnes, having lost her bridegroom, withdrew to a neighboring convent, where she spent the remainder of her life as a nun, but on the very day when the knight perished, Ægle and her children vanished. At the same time the waters of the Dinkhold fountain suddenly turned bitter to the taste, and have never again been sweet as at first, although they are considered a sure cure for every complaint except a broken heart.

BOPPART.

The Emperor's Ducking.

Rudolf of Hapsburg came to the little town of Boppart, in the year 1288, to hold an imperial diet, for he was very anxious to obtain subsidies to continue the war in which he was engaged. As was his custom, he strolled about the streets alone early in the morning, and entering a bakery, asked the old woman who kept it for permission to warm himself by her fire.

No sooner did the old woman perceive his uniform, however, than she became very abusive, declaring she hated all soldiers, for the emperor had quartered so many upon her that she was reduced to want. She finally grew so excited over her wrongs, that she took a pailful of water and flung it angrily over her visitor, as he was anxiously beating a retreat.

Rudolf, having returned home unseen, quickly changed his wet garments and met his councilors. But, when they proposed as usual to tax the people to obtain money to supply his demand, he utterly refused to take their advice. To prove how bitterly the people resented taxation he summoned the old woman, who, at his bidding, repeated her assertions and accusations as fearlessly as in her own little shop.

When she had finished all she had to say, the emperor left the hall, bidding her await his return, and soon reappeared in the garments he had worn in the morning. When the old woman caught sight of him she again began to abuse him, to the councilors' speechless horror, for they immediately recognized him.

As her victim paid no heed to her angry vituperation, the old woman then threatened a second dousing; but when she suddenly became aware of her mistake she was sorely frightened, and humbly begged the emperor's pardon.

Rudolf, who was a magnanimous ruler, did not at all resent her conduct, but dismissed her with a generous sum of money, and then, turning to his advisors, remarked that it was seldom that princes thus heard the voice of the people.

The old woman's speech had been so convincing, that never again did the councilors venture to suggest an increase of the burdens which already rested so heavily upon the shoulders of the common people, and devised other means to raise the necessary funds for the maintenance of the army.

The Deserted Wife.

CONRAD, one of the lords of Boppart, once courted and secretly married a poor but beautiful lady, of whom he grew very weary after they had lived together a few years. As all the witnesses of their marriage were dead, and she had no male relatives to defend her, he one day informed her that he was about to leave for Palestine to fight in the crusade. He also declared that his marriage was annulled, and that he would never recognize its validity. His poor wife, who could show no proof of her marriage, and could only oppose his word by hers, was almost broken-hearted at the thought of her unmerited disgrace, and vainly implored him to do her justice ere he went away. He would not listen, however, and she soon ceased pleading and let him depart.

As he was gayly riding along on the morrow, Conrad was overtaken by a young knight, fully armed, and with lowered vizor, who challenged him to fight. Such a challenge was never refused in that martial age, and Conrad, closing in with his opponent, soon dealt him a mortal blow.

While loosening the helmet to give the dying knight air, he suddenly became aware that he had slain his own deserted wife, who, having none to defend her rights, had preferred death at his hands to public disgrace. Tortured by remorse, now that it was too late, the knight tenderly laid her to rest, and in her honor founded the convent of Marienberg, which is now transformed into a much-frequented sanitarium.

He then proceeded to Acre, where he fought bravely, and when he fell at last, pierced by a Saracen arrow, he breathed a prayer that he might be forgiven, and permitted to meet his wronged wife in heaven.

LIEBENSTEIN AND STERRENBERG.

The Hostile Brothers.

THE two castles on the right bank of the Rhine, which owing to their similarity and proximity are always called the "Brothers," were founded in the beginning of the Middle Ages. They both belonged at one time to a noble lord named Dietrich, who, in dying, left a castle to each of his sons. He also bid them share his treasure with their only sister, who, unfortunately, was blind.

The youths, who were notoriously unscrupulous, immediately resolved to take advantage of their sister's infirmity to increase their own wealth, and leading her into the strong room, proceeded to divide the gold by the measureful. But, while they carefully kept the measure right side up when they were dealing out their own shares, they invariably turned it upside down when the turn of their blind sister came, and laying a single layer of coin on the upturned bottom, bade her ascertain by touch that her measure was full.

This unjust division ended, the poor girl took refuge in the neighboring convent of Bornhofen, for her fortune was not sufficient to enable her to dwell elsewhere, while the avaricious brothers each took possession of his own castle, and reveled in wealth.

The ill-gotten gold, however, did not long suffice to make them happy. They soon both fell in love with a lady who would not choose between them, so they determined to settle the affair in a duel. Meeting at midnight on one of the moonlit peaks of the mountain, they crossed swords, and after a fierce encounter both fell mortally wounded.

Ever since then, the ghosts of the hostile brothers—whose feud has been immortalized in one of Heine's poems—haunt the spot, and at midnight the clash of their swords can still be heard, for they are condemned ever to renew that fatal duel.

"Many a century has departed,
Many a race has found a tomb,
Yet from yonder rocky summits
From those moss-grown towers of gloom,

"And within the dreary valley,
Fearful sights are seen by night;
There, as midnight strikes, the brothers
Still renew the ghastly fight."

—*Heine.*

According to another version of the legend, the two brothers were sole survivors of their race and both fell in love with Laura, their father's ward. As she preferred Heinrich the younger, Conrad, a noble-minded man, immediately withdrew his suit and retired to his own castle, that the sight of his unhappiness should not trouble their bliss.

Unfortunately, however, the favored suitor was very fickle indeed, and before the marriage could take place, he suddenly decided to join a crusade and departed, intrusting his fair betrothed to his brother's care. Conrad honorably discharged this duty, carefully suppressing every sign of the love he could not overcome, but his heart was rent with anguish when he heard that his brother had broken his promise, and was about to return with a beautiful Greek bride.

Laura at first refused to believe the report, but when the newly-married pair actually arrived, she grew so pale

BOPPARD.
Sterrenberg and Liebenstein Castles.

and wan that Conrad began to fear for her life. One day he met his junior, whom he had carefully avoided, on the hillside, and could not refrain from administering a scathing rebuke. Heinrich, incensed, drew his sword and impetuously began to fight. While Conrad was warding off his fierce blows, and watching for an occasion to disarm him without doing him any harm, Laura suddenly came rushing between them, imploring them not to quarrel for her sake, and declaring that she intended to take the veil in Bornhofen convent, but could not depart until they promised to fight no more. Her prayers prevailed, but Conrad's sense of honor was too deep to forgive his brother right away, and he withdrew to his castle, erecting a heavy wall between them which was known throughout the land as "the wall of strife."

A few years later, Heinrich's Greek wife suddenly forsook him in favor of another lover more to her taste. Left alone, the deserted husband had ample opportunity to regret the lack of honesty which had deprived him of all his friends. Conrad, however, hearing he was forsaken by all, now nobly sought and forgave him, and became his truest friend, although he never forgot the pale nun, who was spending her life in penance and prayer within the somber walls of the Bornhofen convent.

RANKENBERG.

The Giants' Pot.

THREE huge giants once lived in a cave on the Rankenberg near the Rhine. Their appetites were fully as great as their size, and as they ate nothing but oatmeal, they bade a neighboring founder make them the biggest pot ever seen. After cooking their porridge for the first time in this colossal new pot, the giants sat round it, dipping their spoons with military precision into the center of the mass, drawing them out very full, opening their mouths, shutting their eyes, and gulping down each spoonful in concert. When the last spoonfuls had thus been disposed of, and no porridge remained in the bottom of the vessel, each giant carefully licked his spoon clean, and, running it through his belt, exclaimed that the pot was just the right size to satisfy his appetite.

Time passed on, but, although the pot remained unchanged, and the giants grew no larger, it seemed as if, little by little, they had less and less to eat, and they daily drew their belts tighter, to prevent their spoons from falling through. Finally, one of them declared he knew the the pot was bewitched, for every day his portion grew less. His brothers agreeing with him, they angrily invaded the founder's shop, threatening all manner of evil if he did not remove the baleful spell from their pot. The poor man, bewildered by their threats and accusations, vainly tried to defend himself, and to disarm their anger finally bade them bring the pot to him, so that he could carefully examine it and see where the fault lay.

The giants immediately went in search of their porridge vessel, and tipped it upon one side so the founder could walk in, for it was so large that he could not look over the brim when it stood upright on the floor. The giants gloomily watched him walk in, and were greatly surprised to hear him burst into prolonged peals of laughter. Then, setting aside their eager questions, he ran into his shop, came out again with a hoe, and in a very few moments had scraped out a great heap of dried porridge which had gradually formed a thick crust all around the edge.

His work finished, he turned to the astonished giants and coolly said: "Gentlemen, if you scrape your pot clean, you will find that it will always contain the same amount of porridge."

The giants took this advice to heart and taught their

descendants, and all the people around Rankenberg, that one of the most important maxims of life was, to "scrape their pots clean."

HIRZENACH.

The Innkeeper's Wine.

A TRAVELER once came to Hirzenach, entered the village inn, and bade the host bring him a jug of wine, that he might quench his ardent thirst. The innkeeper, Hans Teuerlich, a thrifty man, seized his crock, and marched down into his cellar where were two faucets. He turned the first very gingerly, indeed, and partly filled the jug with sour wine. Then, rushing to the other faucet, which was set in the wall, he turned it full cock, and allowed the water from the Rhine to flow freely until the jug was quite full.

Hans Teuerlich then marched upstairs again, and filled his guest's tumbler, declaring that nowhere would he find such good, unadulterated Rhine wine. The guest drank eagerly, but made somewhat of a face when he tasted the sour drink, and setting his empty tumbler down again asked whether the host were quite sure that no water had been mixed with the wine.

The innkeeper now swore more emphatically than ever that his wine was undiluted, and himself poured out a second glassful. But as he did so, three little fishes passed from the jug into the tumbler, where they swam merrily round and round, convicting the innkeeper of fraud. Of course the traveler saw the little fishes, made fun of the host, and duly advised him to use a strainer next time he attempted to make Rhine wine out of Rhine water. This piece of advice Hans Teuerlich took to heart, and faithfully impressed upon his numerous descendants, who are *all* innkeepers along the Rhine, and who still occasionally eke out their wine with plenty of water.

EHRENTHAL.

The Steward's Shroud.

THE Ehrenthal with its rich mines was the property of the lords of Thurnberg, who, loving war, were seldom at home, and left the care of their serfs and estates to an able steward. One of these men was noted for his cruelty and tyranny, for he forced the miners to work incessantly, gave them remarkably small wages, and ill treated even the castle servants, who were ill clad and ill fed.

The foreman of the mine, a young man by the name of Benno, had fallen deeply in love with one of the castle maids, Clara, and the young people were very anxious indeed to marry. But, as they were serfs, they could not do so without the consent of their master, who was absent, or at least the sanction of his steward, to whom he had temporarily delegated all his authority. They therefore tremblingly ventured into the surly man's presence to ask his permission to marry.

After considering the matter for a moment, the steward maliciously declared that they might be united as soon as Clara had woven a bridal garment for herself, and a shroud for him, out of thread taken from nettles which she must sow upon her parents' graves. He added that the garments must be ready in three weeks' time, and that she must be very careful not to have a bit of thread left over. The steward departed, laughing at the young people's utter dismay, and bade them go to work. Clara and Benno tearfully parted, the former pausing for a moment to weep over her parents' grave, ere she returned to the castle. While she knelt there, in tears, she suddenly felt a little hand laid upon her shoulder, and looking up beheld a tiny female gnome. She bade her be comforted, for she would help her to fulfill all the cruel steward's conditions. Then the gnome waved her staff over the grave, bade the maiden meet her here at sundown on the morrow, and vanished. Comforted by the assurance the tiny creature had given her, Clara resumed her work, and at sundown on the next day hastened to her parents' graves, which she found covered with tall stalks of nettles. These she hastily pulled up and bound into sheaves, as the gnome bade her, for she could not bear to see the noxious weeds growing over the remains of those she loved.

When the last stalk had been bound into the sheaves, the little old woman took charge of the nettles, and departed, promising that the girl would see her again ere the three weeks were ended. She withdrew to the entrance of an abandoned mine, and there began to prepare the nettles exactly as if they had been flax.

A few days later the steward, passing near there, became aware of her presence, and grimly asked what she was spinning. "A bride's garment for Clara and a shroud for you, wretch!" replied the old woman, with such utter conviction of the truth of her assertion, that the cruel steward could not help shuddering with fear.

When the three weeks were ended, Clara appeared before the steward with the bridal garment and shroud, both woven from nettles grown on her parents' grave, and the steward was obliged to consent to her immediate union with Benno. But as soon as the merry marriage peal was ended which proclaimed that Benno and Clara were happily united, the village church bells began to toll loudly, for the cruel steward had died suddenly, and the people openly rejoiced to hear that he would trouble them no more, and that his shroud had been ready just in time.

WERLAU.

The Bewitched Mine.

DAGOBERT, the ancient and renowned Merovingian king, was said to derive his almost fabulous wealth from a very productive silver mine, situated in the mountains back of Werlau. All at once, however, the revenue from the mine ceased, and the directors reported that the work could not be continued, as invisible hands caught and cruelly buffeted any man who attempted to go down the shaft.

Seized by superstitious dread, the miners finally refused to make any further attempt to descend, and Dagobert, finding his coffers empty, resolved to visit Werlau, and see what could be done to induce the miners to resume their wonted labors. Accompanied by St. Eloi, his prime minister, his fair daughter Beatrix, and a goodly retinue, the king rode out of Andernach and soon came to Werlau. There the royal cavalcade was joined by a handsome youth, who declared he too would fain visit the mine, but whose chief interest seemed to be centered on the fair princess.

Dagobert, arriving at the shaft, dismounted, and would have descended himself, had not his courtiers restrained him, and his daughter implored him to desist. His proffers of reward to the man who would venture down into the mine were not taken up. He was about to try some other means, when the stranger suddenly sprang forward, volunteering to descend, not to obtain the reward, but to please the fair princess who seemed so anxious about her father. A moment later he had sprung into the bucket, and was rapidly lowered into the shaft, but although the spectators watched eagerly for any signs or sounds, they heard and saw nothing, and the youth did not reappear. When half an hour had elapsed and the bucket came up empty, one of the courtiers declared the youth must be dead, and at these words the princess fainted away.

While all were bending over her, trying to restore her, a little dwarf appeared in their midst, and touched the princess, who immediately opened her eyes.

Before he could vanish, the king seized him and inquired what he wanted, and as he refused to answer, ordered him flung headlong into the shaft of the mine. The men were about to carry out this order, when Beatrix, falling upon her knees before the king, interceded so eloquently for the little creature's life that it was granted to her.

As soon as the gnome was released he vowed that the princess should never repent having helped him, snatched the golden necklace from her neck, and springing into the empty bucket, dropped down the shaft like a stone. The people, in breathless wonder, were still gazing at the shaft where he had disappeared, when they suddenly saw the bucket reappear, and in it lay the gallant youth, bound and unconscious.

Dagobert gave orders that he should be lifted out and released, and, as he still gave no signs of returning consciousness, had him carried into the royal tent. There Beatrix, bending solicitously over him, discovered that he wore her necklace, over which his fingers were so convulsively clasped that she could not remove it. All day long she watched over him, and when night came on, and she was left alone with him, the gnome appeared before her, telling her he could restore the youth to life providing someone were willing to die to save him.

As Beatrix heard these words, she realized for the first time that she loved the unconscious youth dearly enough to die for him, and straightway informed the gnome of the fact. To test the truth of her assertion, which he appeared to doubt, the dwarf produced two delicate little flowers, which he told her bloomed simultaneously, with the birth of a new love. He laid one on her breast, saying that if her love were pure, the flower would fall into ashes at her seventh heart-beat.

Fearlessly Beatrix submitted to the test, and at the seventh heartbeat the flowers fell into ashes and she dropped asleep.

As in a trance, however, she saw the gnome take the second flower and lay it on the youth's breast, where it also fell into ashes, touch his eyes with them, and recall him to life. The dwarf then vanished, and the doctors entering just then, awakened Beatrix and announced that her patient was restored to consciousness and perfectly well once more.

Early the next morning the youth, wandering alone in the forest, met the tiny dwarf, who promised to help him secure the princess' hand in marriage if he would only act a passive part. A moment later the youth saw a royal train appear. An old servant paused before him, called him duke, bade him mount, and led him back to Dagobert's court, where he announced him as the young Duke of Suabia, who had come to marry Beatrix.

Dagobert, pleased with this alliance, immediately gave orders that all should be prepared for a speedy marriage. All would have taken place as the dwarf had planned, had not the youth been too honest to take advantage of the king's credulity and revealed the fraud.

Incensed at his presumption, Dagobert now ordered that the stranger should be beheaded early the next day, and all Beatrix' tears and entreaties could not move him. In despair the princess then rushed off to the shaft, and called aloud for the friendly gnome, whose help she implored, bathing his hands with tears.

These drops were immediately changed into sparkling jewels, and the gnome joyfully exclaimed: "Fair princess, weep no more. I will save your beloved, for you have released me from a cruel spell, which banished me from my kingdom until I could produce the priceless gems which I now hold."

The gnome then explained to the princess that in his rage at being exiled he had cursed the mine, but that he would remove the curse if she were given in marriage to the youth.

These tidings, skillfully conveyed to Dagobert, made him consent to the marriage, which was celebrated on the morrow with all due pomp. After the festivities were ended, the miners returned unmolested to their work, and continued to dig silver enough to supply the king with all the money he needed for many a year.

ST. GOAR.

Miracles and Shrine.

THE little town of St. Goar is situated on the very spot once occupied by the hermitage of the saint whose name it bears. This holy man came thither as a missionary, and took up his abode near the whirlpool and sandbank, intending not only to preach the gospel to the barbarians, but also to lend a helping hand to all those who came to grief on their way either up or down the river.

As he rescued them from danger, he invariably inquired whether they were Christians or heathens. If they denied the Redeemer he plunged them back into the tide, holding them under the water until they changed their faith. Then, having forcibly baptized them, he bore them off to his cell and duly fed and dried them.

The rumor of St. Goar's good works finally came to the ears of the Austrasian Prince Sigebert, who summoned him to court, and offered him the bishopric of Treves. But the good man humbly refused this honor. To amuse the king, and show him that he had won God's approval, he hung his mantle on a sunbeam, as on a peg, and leaving it there until he was ready to resume it, won permission to hasten back to his chosen abode.

After founding a monastery there, and attaining extreme

old age, St. Goar died and was buried in the monastery church. There his tombstone can still be seen, bearing his name and the date of his decease, which occurred in 611. His tomb very soon became the favorite resort of the lame, deaf, and blind, who were perfectly cured after a pilgrimage to his shrine, and gradually enriched it by their grateful offerings.

This saint also became the special patron of the Rhine boatmen, who were sure to escape all danger, providing they paused to pray at his shrine on their way up and down the river. If they failed to pay him the customary respect, however, misfortune, and sometimes shipwreck, was sure to be their lot.

Charlemagne, on his way from Ingelheim to Cologne, once passed the town without disembarking, but no sooner had he done so than a terrible storm overtook him, threatening his boat with destruction and greatly alarming the boatmen, who declared they had grievously offended St. Goar.

The emperor hearing this, immediately vowed to return and pray at the shrine, so the storm abated as suddenly as it had arisen, to permit him to keep his promise without delay. In gratitude for this narrow escape, Charlemagne gave the monastery a grant of land and a butt of wine, which the saint evidently took under his special protection, for it was soon discovered that it possessed the admirable property of always remaining full.

Trusting to this miracle, the cellarman once carelessly left the faucet open, thus allowing the precious wine to escape. St. Goar, who was evidently very thrifty, must have immediately become aware of this oversight, for it is said he sent a spider, which so quickly wove a thick web across the opening that very little wine was lost.

Charlemagne also gave the town of St. Goar the famous silver collar, which was fastened to the toll house, and which, until the days of steam navigation, was secured around the neck of every boatman and traveler on his first visit to the place. To obtain release the victim was obliged to select between the wine and water baptism offered him. If he declared his preference for the former, he was set free after drinking a brimming beaker of Rhine wine, but, in case he selected the latter, he was dismissed only after a great pailful of cold water had been emptied over his head.

Thanks to all the offerings made by pilgrims and travelers, the monastery of St. Goar soon became very rich indeed, and on sundry occasions this excited the cupidity of the bold robber knights of the Rhine, who ventured to attack it to secure this vast wealth. After defending the convent bravely on one occasion, the abbot, seeing he would soon be forced to yield, but hoping to awe the assailants, held a crucifix up at the window, loudly commanding the assailants to forbear.

His commands were received with derision, however, and one robber knight, drawing his cross-bow, sent an arrow, which pierced the image on the cross. To the amazement of monks and soldiers, who were horrified at this sacrilege, the blood suddenly began to flow from the sacred emblem.

This miracle so terrified the besiegers that they fled in haste, and never dared return, while the monks gave hearty thanks for the preservation of their property and lives. The robber knight who had shot the arrow was converted by what he had seen, and in atonement for his sins he hastened off to Palestine, where he fought bravely and fell gloriously defending the Holy Sepulcher against the Saracens.

KATZENELLENBOGEN.

The Assassin Priest.

THE castle of Katzenellenbogen, which is generally known as the Cat, was built in the fourteenth century. It was once occupied by a very popular lord and his equally unpopular wife, who was greatly disliked on account of her irascible temper.

Worn out by her constant recriminations, her husband finally obtained a divorce, and as he had no children to inherit his vast possessions, he soon married again, choosing this time a lady as lovable, gentle, and good as she was pretty. In the course of his wedding journey he led his bride to his castle of Rheinfels, where a priest, hired by his divorced wife to kill her hated rival, administered a subtle poison to her in the communion cup.

The countess, noticing the powder on the wine, called the priest's attention to it, but he bade her drink without fear, as it was nothing but a little dust which had fallen from the ceiling. The young bride obeyed, but was soon seized with convulsions, and although she did not die, her health was permanently impaired.

Soon after, the Count of Katzenellenbogen also became mysteriously ill, and died, leaving all his possessions to the noble house of Hesse, for he had no direct heir.

The priest's crimes were, however, eventually discovered, and after a public ceremony, in which all the emblems of his sacred office were solemnly taken from him, he was deposed from the priestly office, and hanged, amid the loud execrations of the assembled people.

THURNBERG.

The Haunted Castle.

THE ruins of the ancient castle of Thurnberg tower above the little village of Welmich, not very far from St. Goar. This castle was contemptuously called the Mouse by the haughty lords of Katzenellenbogen, for their stronghold was known as the Katze (Cat), and they openly boasted far and wide that their cat would soon devour the mouse. But for all their boasting, it never did so, and the little mouse ever kept them at bay.

Above the ruins lurid lights are often seen after sunset.

The people declare they are the reflections of the fire in which a former owner, an unbeliever, is slowly burning in the Infernal Regions. Tradition further relates that, irritated by the ringing of the village church bell beneath him, which on Sunday mornings always roused him from his prolonged nap, this arbitrary nobleman once coolly confiscated it. When the priest came to claim it, and expostulated about his impious conduct, the Lord of Thurnberg had the bell bound firmly round his neck, and ordered him flung into a very deep well in his courtyard.

The clang of the bell was not silenced, however, by this crime, for the deeper it fell the louder it pealed, waking all the echoes with its deafening sound. In vain the lord of the castle had the well filled up, the bell rang loudly night and day, driving him mad and causing him to die at last of insomnia. But the moment he had breathed his last, the bell suddenly ceased ringing, and since then it has been heard for a few moments only, at midnight, on the 18th of January, the anniversary of the wicked Lord of Thurnberg's death.

The ruins are further said to be haunted also by a lovely maiden, all dressed in white. She once appeared to bring a drink to a young nobleman, who had thrown himself down near the ruins to rest and mockingly called for a beaker of wine. This rash youth, who had thus ventured to summon a spirit from the tomb, was sorely punished, for he fell in love with the lady, and remained there, pining for her return until he died from inanition. The legend tells, however, that as he passed away, she appeared once more, and bending to kiss him, claimed him for her own. This legend resembles the story of the lady of Vindeck, versified by Chamisso and translated by Byrant, and which ends as follows:

"And ever from that moment
He haunted the ruins there,
A sleepless, restless wanderer,
A watcher with despair.

"Ghost-like and pale he wandered,
With a dreamy, haggard eye;
He seemed not one of the living,
And yet he could not die.

"'Tis said that the lady met him
When many years had passed,
And, kissing his lips, released him
From the burden of life at last."

REICHENBERG.

Barbarossa's Beard.

FREDERICK BARBAROSSA, emperor of Germany, was the owner of a magnificent, fiery red beard. This the devil coveted sorely, as he fancied such an ornament would be particularly becoming to a gentleman of his complexion, and delicately suggestive of his avocation.

As he could grow no beard of his own, he finally resolved to steal the emperor's, and as he did not understand the art of shaving, he proceeded to the little town of Bacharach, and engaged the service of one of the numerous barbers living there. It was duly agreed between them that, for a certain consideration, the barber would shave off the imperial beard, providing Satan conveyed him safely to and from the palace, and caused such a deep sleep to fall upon the victim that he would never discover the delinquent.

A Wisperthal fairy, overhearing this plot, and knowing that Frederick would visit the town a few days later, wished to protect him, for he had once done her a good turn. So she went in search of a giant, and coaxed him to lend her his great bag. The giant, seeing her diminutive size, and fearing lest she should be crushed by the sack's weight, gallantly offered to carry it for her wherever she wished, and walking beside her came to the entrance of Bacharach, just as the town clocks were striking twelve. The fairy bade him sit down on a stone and await her return, then cleverly caught all the barbers while they were asleep, and without waking them, spirited them into the bag, which she then fastened securely.

She next awoke the giant, who had fallen into a doze, and bade him carry the bag far away, and dump its contents into the river at early dawn. Good-naturedly, the giant shouldered his burden and tramped off. The barbers, awakened by the jolting, kicked and struggled to get out, frightening their bearer to such an extent that he began to run, and with one leap cleared the castle of Reichenberg. At that selfsame moment one of the barbers, quicker-witted than the rest, ripped open the bag with his sharp razor, and he and his companions rolled down into the castle moat, where they were all drowned.

Frederick Barbarossa came to Bacharach on the morrow, but the devil failed to secure his fiery red beard, for there was not a single barber left in town to do his bidding.

LORELEI.

The Unhappy Beauty.

THE bed of the Rhine grows suddenly narrow and almost fathomless after St. Goar, while great masses of rock shut out the pleasant light of the sun. On the right bank, a huge basaltic cliff towers above the Rhine. This is the famous Loreleiberg, noted for its magnificent prospect and sevenfold echo, no less than for the numerous romantic legends connected with it.

A maiden of wondrous beauty, called Lorelei, dwelt at Bacharach on the Rhine, in the beginning of the eleventh century. Suitors without end came to woo her, and as she was as tender-hearted as she was beautiful, she regretfully saw the misery her loveliness inflicted, and would gladly have consented to lose all her charms could she have saved anyone from pain.

Ill-natured people, however, vowed that she was quite heartless, a statement which was soon refuted by her acceptance of and response to the suit of a handsome young knight of the neighborhood. As the young people had always met in secret, no one at first knew of their love, but a short time after they were betrothed the knight went off to war, declaring he would win honor and glory before he claimed the beautiful Lorelei as his bride. Vainly she entreated him to remain by her side; vainly she pictured the dangers and possible death which awaited him, he refused to listen to aught but the promptings of his ambition and departed.

Lorelei, bathed in tears, and oppressed by nameless fears, no longer took any pleasure in life. In spite of her openly announced engagement, new suitors constantly crowded around her, trying to win her from her allegiance to her absent lover. But, although no tidings of the rover reached her, and she feared he had either perished or turned faithless, Lorelei still refused to console herself with the love of another. Every day some new suitor appeared, and every day the village gossips whispered that some rejected lover had drowned himself in the Rhine, pined to death, or left the country to find an honorable end on the battlefield. Only a few youths were now left in the country, and everyone knew they were well and happy only because they had never seen the beautiful Lorelei, and that as soon as their eyes rested upon her they too would fall victims to her charms. Mothers with marriageable daughters were specially anxious to get rid of Lorelei, and, little by little, spread the dark report that it was not only the maiden's beauty which won the hearts of men, but her magic arts, spells, and incantations. The rumor, as rumors will, spread so rapidly that Lorelei was finally summoned to appear before the criminal court of the archbishop of Cologne.

There, in spite of all accusations made by virulent gossips, judge and jury alike agreed that such a beautiful, innocent face could not belong to a guilty person, and acquitted her. Lorelei, feeling that life had no charms for her, and weary of persecution, now flung herself at the archbishop's feet crying:

"I'm not a witch, but let me die. I'm so unhappy. My lover has forsaken me, and his silence has lasted so long that I am sure he is either faithless or dead. Life is a burden to me, for the young men of the neighborhood constantly annoy me by pleading for a love which I cannot give, as my heart is in my lover's keeping. Let me die!"

The aged prelate kindly raised the tearful supplicant and said:

"My child, I see no cause to credit the accusations brought against you of practicing magic arts, but perceive only too plainly the natural charms which have done so much harm. I cannot let you die; but, if you wish to mourn in peace, you may enter a convent, where none will ever again molest you."

Lorelei accepted this proposal with joy. Two old knights were summoned to escort her to her future home, and the little cavalcade wended its way along the Rhine, and crossed it at St. Goar. Soon after they drew near a huge mass of basaltic rock, which Lorelei expressed a desire to climb, that she might from thence view her home once more.

The old knights immediately acceded to this innocent request, and the maiden, bounding lightly ahead, climbed until she reached the highest point and stood directly above the dark stream. Her tearful eyes rested for a moment upon her native town, then upon the towers of her lover's home, and lastly fell upon a bark slowly floating down the stream. At the sight of a mailed figure standing at the helm, she suddenly uttered a loud cry of joy, for she recognized the lover whom she had long believed dead. Her sudden exclamation, rousing the echoes, attracted the attention of the knight, who, still faithful, forgot all else at the sight of his beloved standing far above him with outstretched arms.

The little boat, no longer guided by the helm, was seized by the current, whirled against the dangerous rock, and dashed to pieces. Lorelei, seeing her lover's danger, made an impetuous motion, as if to save him, lost her balance, and fell over the precipice into the Rhine, where she perished by his side, at the foot of the rock which still bears her name.

The Fisherman.

ANOTHER tradition of the Lorelei which, although equally tragical, differs widely in many points from the first, has inspired Heine's immortal song, and is generally told as follows:

Long years ago, whenever the moonlight flooded mountains and river, a beautiful maiden was seen seated upon the top of the Lorelei rock. There she sang sweet and entrancing melodies, while she combed her long golden hair with a jeweled comb, her pure white draperies fluttering in the night winds as she made her toilet under the blue vault of heaven and by the witching light of the moon.

"And yonder sits a maiden,
The fairest of the fair;
With gold in her garment glittering,
And she combs the golden hair:
With a golden comb she combs it;
And a wild song singeth she,
That meets the heart with a wondrous
And powerful melody."

—*Heine.*

This fair creature, whom all called Lorelei, was an immortal, a water nymph, daughter of old Father Rhine. During the day she lingered in the cool depths of the river bed, but late at night she sat aloft where travelers and boat-

LORELEI ROCK.

men could easily see her. But woe unto them if the evening breeze wafte l the notes of her song to their ears, for the entrancing melody made them forget time and place, until their vessels, no longer guided along the dangerous pass, were whirled against the rocks, where they were dashed to pieces, and all on board perished. One person only is said to have been favored with a near view of the charming Lorelei, a handsome young fisherman from Oberwesel, who climbed the rocks every evening to spend a few delightful hours, his head pillowed in the nymph's lap, his eyes drinking in her beauty, while his ears were charmed by the melody of her song.

Tradition further relates that ere they parted the Lorelei invariably pointed out the places where he was to cast his nets on the morrow, and as he always implicitly carried out her instructions he never came home with an empty creel.

One moonlight night the fisherman was seen as usual boldly scaling the rocks to keep his tryst, but he never came down the cliff again. The river was dragged, the rock was searched, but no trace of him was found, so the peasants of the neighorhood invariably declare that Lorelei dragged him down into her crystal palace beneath the flood to enjoy his society undisturbed forever.*

A Magic Spell.

COUNT LUDWIG, the only son of the Prince Palatine, once left his father's castle at Stahleck to sail down the Rhine, hoping to catch a glimpse of the Siren Lorelei, of whom he had often heard such marvelous tales. It was evening—the stars were twinkling softly overhead, and the bark slowly drifted down the river. Darker and darker grew the waters as the bed of the Rhine grew narrower, but the young count

* See "Myths of Northern Lands," by the author.

paid no heed to that; his eyes were fixed on the rocks far above, where he hoped to see the beautiful nymph.

Suddenly he perceived a glimmer of white drapery and golden hair, and heard the faint, sweet sound of an alluring song. As he drew nearer, the melody became more distinct, and the moonbeams, falling upon the maiden, seemed to enhance her marvelous beauty, as she bent over the rocky ledge beckoning to him to draw near. The count and boatmen, spellbound by the vision above them, paid no heed to their vessel, which, striking suddenly against the rocks, sunk with all on board, one man only escaping to tell of the young count's cruel fate.

The bereaved father, thirsting for revenge, issued immediate orders for the capture of the siren who had caused so much woe, and a few tried warriors set out at the head of an armed band, which they posted all around the rock, with strict orders not to let the nymph escape.

Then, climbing noiselessly up the moonlit cliff, the captain and three of his men suddenly presented themselves before the matchless Lorelei. She was, as usual, combing her hair and crooning her song. The men hemmed her in so securely that no mode of escape remained except by the precipitous descent to the river. Then they loudly bade her surrender. Quite unmoved, however, the nymph gracefully waved her white hands, and the grim old warriors suddenly felt as if rooted to the spot, and were utterly incapable of moving hand or foot or of uttering the slightest sound.

With dilated eyes fixed upon the Lorelei, they saw her divest herself of her jewels, which she dropped one by one into the Rhine at her feet, then whirl about in mystic dance, muttering some strange spell, wherein they could only distinguish some words about white-maned steeds and pearl shell chariots. When dance and song were ended, the waters of the Rhine suddenly began to bubble and seethe, and rose higher and higher, until they reached the top of the cliff, and the petrified warriors felt the cold tide surge about their feet. Suddenly they saw a great white-crested wave rolling rapidly toward them, and in its green depths they beheld a chariot, drawn by white-maned steeds. Lorelei sprang into this car, and quickly vanished over the edge of the cliff, into the river.

A few moments later the angry waters had subsided to their wonted level, the men recovered the power of motion, and, when they bent down over the cliff, no trace of the sudden rise could be seen, except the water drops along the face of the cliff, shining in the moonlight like diamonds.

The next morning Count Ludwig's body was found washed ashore near the Pfalz, "whither it had come contrary to the course of the current," doubtless borne thither by the Lorelei, who has never since then reappeared on the cliff, although boatmen and belated travelers have often heard the faint sweet echo of her alluring song, wafted toward them on the summer breeze at midnight.

The Devil's Imprint.

THE Devil one day made up his mind to take a trip along the Rhine, and, to be fashionable, he thought he would go up, rather than down the stream. He enjoyed his journey pretty well until he came to the great rock, which barred the course of the river, causing it to make a sudden bend, and seeing that the cliff impressed strangers, and made them marvel at the power of God, he angrily resolved to move it away.

The Devil had just sunk his claws into the stone, and was about to lift and throw it aside, when the Lorelei's marvelous tone fell upon his ear. While leaning spellbound against the stone, he heard her sing of deathless love, of the charms of her crystal palace, of rippling waves and silvery moonlight, and, realizing that they all helped to make the charm of the spot complete, he relinquished his plan of removing the rock, and hastened away. His red-hot body had, however, softened the stone against which he leaned, and ever since then the fishermen have pointed out his effigy in the rock when they relate his attempt to remove it.

OBERWESEL.

The Little Martyr.

In the thirteenth century, one of the burghers of the little town of Oberwesel incurred the wrath of a wicked old woman, who in revenge stole his only son and sold him to the Jews. This people had endured so many cruel persecutions at the Christians' hands, that they were much embittered, and now sought to avenge themselves by mercilessly torturing the innocent little lad.

But in spite of all persecutions, the brave child persistently refused to deny Christ, and patiently allowed himself to be scourged and finally crucified. When he was quite dead and they could no longer torture him, the Jews cast his corpse into the river, where early the next morning a fisherman found it, the little dead hand pointing fixedly up the river, and the body remaining motionless in spite of the strong current.

Frightened by this phenomenon, the fisherman hastened to summon all his companions, and while they were all gazing upon the poor little mutilated corpse, it began to move slowly up the river. It finally ran ashore at the very feet of the wicked old woman, who had come to see what was the cause of the general excitement. As the little dead hand pointed fixedly at her, she was suddenly seized by remorse, and with many tears confessed how she had kidnapped him and sold him to the Jews. The marks on the child's body revealed only too plainly all he had endured, so the people of Oberwesel, wishing to discover the real perpetrators of the crime, forced all the Israelites to appear and lay their hands upon the corpse. At the mere contact of one of the criminals' hands the wounds began to bleed afresh, and the guilty men, after confessing all their cruelty, were immediately sentenced to death and summarily hung.*

As for the poor child, whose name was Werner, he was duly canonized for his faith and martyrdom, and a church was erected at Bacharach over his remains. In this building the people have carefully preserved the pillar to which he was bound when scourged, ere the Jews finally put him to death, in the same manner as they had slain his Redeemer so many years before.

SCHÖNBERG.

The Seven Sisters.

In the castle of Schönberg, whose ruins tower above the little town of Oberwesel, there once dwelt seven beautiful girls. They were sisters, and as they had no living relatives they exercised full control over their persons, lands, and fortunes.

As these young ladies were so very attractive, they were wooed by knights of every degree, but although they delighted in receiving attention, they would never consent to bind themselves by any vows. They favored a suitor for a short time, merely for the pleasure of watching his impotent wrath when discarded to make room for a rival. One knight after another thus left the castle in despair, but for one who departed discouraged, two arrived full of hope, confident in their powers to please and hold the capricious fair. One day a Minnesinger arrived at Schönberg, and fell desperately in love with Adelgunde, the youngest sister, for whom he composed his sweetest lays, which he sang to his own accompaniment on the guitar. Day after day the maiden

* See Note 14 in Appendix.

led him on, making him believe her heart was all his own, but in reality caring nothing for him, and taking mental note of all his passionate speeches merely to report them to her sisters and make fun of the enamored youth.

Anxious to witness one of the love scenes she described so vividly, the six other sisters once concealed themselves in various parts of the apartment, leaving Adelgunde apparently alone. A few moments later the Minnesinger appeared, and, finding his lady love alone, fell upon his knees before her and eloquently declared his love.

While he was still in this position, pleading with eager eyes and trembling lips for the love he had a right to think he had won, the sisters simultaneously rushed out of their hiding places. They then all began to mimic him, while Adelgunde, whom he had fancied so gentle, noble, and refined, laughed louder than all the rest at his discomfiture.

Enraged at this heartless treatment, the Minnesinger rushed out of the castle, sprang on his horse, galloped madly down the steep hill, and, beside himself with grief, plunged into the Rhine. There tradition relates that the water nymphs laid him on a soft couch in their crystal palace, and bade him confide all his sorrows to their queen, the matchless golden-haired Lorelei.

When he had told her the whole story of his love and despair, she exclaimed: "Many are the complaints which have reached me about those cold-hearted maidens, and the just punishment for their crimes will soon overtake them. As for you, sweet minstrel, sorrow and care shall never again approach your poetic soul. Tune your guitar and forget you were once unhappy."

The Lorelei then gently waved her fairy wand. At the same moment the pain in the Minnesinger's heart vanished, his sorrows were forgotten, his eye beamed with happiness, and his guitar awoke to a joyful lay beneath the touch of his inspired fingers. When she saw him happy once more, with a bliss which would never cease, the Lorelei left her crystal palace and went in search of the cruel ladies of Schönberg, whom she had resolved to punish.

It was evening, one of those matchless summer evenings along the Rhine, and the sisters were idly drifting down the stream, talking and laughing incessantly. While they were as usual recounting their heartless triumphs, and mimicking their unfortunate suitors, the Lorelei suddenly rose out of the waves before them and solemnly warned them their end was near.

In vain the frivolous sisters pleaded for mercy, in vain they proffered their richest gifts, the Lorelei insisted that as they had shown no compassion for the sufferings of others they need expect no reprieve, and while she was still speaking the vessel suddenly sank with all its living freight.

On the morrow, seven rocks rose out of the river in a spot where none had previously stood, and the superstitious peasants aver that these are the bodies of the seven sisters, which have become as hard as their hearts, and that on stormy evenings their drowning shrieks still rise above the sound of the wind and waves.

GUTENFELS.

The Emperor's Wooing.

ABOVE the ancient little town of Caub rises the castle of Gutenfels, which was occupied in the middle of the thirteenth century by Philip, count of Falkenstein, and his only sister Guda. The young people, who were orphans, lived together in perfect amity, and if Philip sometimes urged his sister to make a choice among her numerous suitors, it was only because he was very anxious to secure her happiness.

On one occasion the brother and sister attended a brilliant tournament at Cologne, where Guda's beauty attracted the attention of a strange knight, who had won all the prizes. He was known only to the bishop, who vouched for his birth and general good character.

The stranger's manners and address were so polished, his conversation so interesting, and his pleasure in Lord Falkenstein's society so very evident, that the latter invited him to visit him at Gutenfels. This invitation the knight gladly accepted, as soon as he saw that his presence would be welcome to Guda also.

Of course he was courteously received and duly entertained. Day by day his love for the beautiful young châtelaine increased and he often said he would fain linger there forever. This could not be, however, for just then all Germany was in a turmoil. Conrad IV. had died leaving no heir, and the throne was disputed by Adolf of Holland, Richard of Cornwall, brother of the English king, Henry III., and Alfonso X. of Castile.

The seven electors supported Richard, and as most of the noblemen followed their example, Philip of Falkenstein soon left the castle of Gutenfels to go and fight in his behalf. His guest promised to follow and fight by his side, as soon as he had received a certain message for which he had been waiting.

Two days later the message came, and the knight took leave of Guda, after winning her promise to love him and await his return without making any attempt to learn his name or station. Left alone in the castle of Gutenfels, Guda spent hours in thinking of her absent lover and in longing for his return, but when the war was ended and her brother came home she began to grow anxious, as she had received no tidings from the strange knight.

A few weeks of suspense robbed her of all her pretty color, and she withdrew weeping to her chamber, for she felt sure that her betrothed was dead. She did not even wish to be present when the new emperor arrived at the castle as he had sent word he was about to do.

Richard of Cornwall had no sooner entered the castle, however, than he inquired for the fair châtelaine. He said that he had often heard her beauty extolled by his courtiers, and that his purpose was to sue honorably for her hand. Philip, overjoyed at the prospect of such a brilliant marriage for his only sister, withdrew to lay the emperor's proposal before her, after again vainly entreating his imperial guest to lay aside the heavy armor which he wore, or at least to raise his vizor.

In a very short time he returned. In stammering accents and greatly embarrassed, he now replied that his sister could not accept the monarch's proposal, as she had already plighted her troth to some man, whom, until then, she had obstinately refused to name.

The emperor calmly listened to these excuses, and, when they were ended, bade Philip lead him into the presence of the lady, that he might press his suit in person, and, if possible, obtain a more favorable reply. With lowered vizor, and in muffled tones, he inquired of the trembling Guda why she refused to forget a lover who was either dead or faithless. The maiden replied that she would remain true to her lover, living or dead, and again refused the proffered crown. Then the emperor suddenly threw up his vizor, clasped her in his arms, and rapturously claimed her as his bride.

Guda immediately recognized her lover, now that he spoke in his natural tones. She no longer refused to listen to his suit, and shortly after married Richard of Cornwall, the strange knight, and became empress of Germany in 1269.

CAUB.

Story of St. Theonest.

THEONEST, the holy missionary, had been put to death in Mayence. In derision the unbelievers thrust his remains in a tub and set them afloat upon the river which he had admired so openly, and along which he had hoped to secure so many converts.

The tub, bobbing up and down on the waters, was carried on by the swift current until it finally ran aground at Caub, where the saint, miraculously restored to life, stepped serenely ashore, and taught the gospel to the heathen. While he was converting them to Christianity, he initiated them also in the cultivation of the vine and the making of wine, using the tub in which he had drifted down the stream as his first wine press.

Ever since then the inhabitants of Caub have held his name sacred, and in the month of October they never fail to celebrate his festival with dance and song, drinking many a hearty toast to the saint who first taught them how to make the wine for which their town is famous.

PFALZ.

A Secret Marriage.

IN the middle of the Rhine, almost directly opposite Caub, is a quaint little castle known as the Pfalz, or Pfalzgrafenstein. Its numerous turrets, central dungeon, ramparts, and eight towers, adorned with the Palatine arms, all conspire to add to the picturesque appearance of this building, which was erected in the fourteenth century.

History claims that the Pfalz was built to serve as toll house that the nobles might levy a certain tax upon the numerous vessels constantly sailing up and down the Rhine,

CAUB.

Pfalz and Gutenburg Castles.

but tradition ascribes its foundation to a far more romantic cause. The principality of the Pfalz was given by the emperor of Germany, Frederick Barbarossa, to Conrad of Staufen, when his half brother died leaving no heirs. This new elector had only one daughter, the fair young Agnes, who dwelt with her mother at Stahleck, and as she was a beauty as well as an heiress, she soon had plenty of suitors. Prince, knight-errant, and minstrel seemed equally anxious to secure her favor, but she dismissed them all gently, for her heart was quite free until Henry, duke of Brunswick, appeared.

Favored by the young lady's mother, the lovers spent many a happy hour together, talking of the day when Conrad, returning from war, would give his consent to their speedy marriage. What was their dismay, therefore, when a messenger suddenly appeared, saying that Conrad had promised his only daughter's hand to a member of the imperial family, and would soon appear with the bridegroom he had chosen, to celebrate the wedding.

Agnes wept, Henry fumed, but knowing the arbitrary character of Conrad they both realized that he would insist upon having his own way, and that neither tears nor remonstrances would be of any avail. The young people were in despair, until the mother suggested a secret marriage. Then Henry and Agnes were hurriedly made husband and wife.

Shortly after their marriage Conrad appeared, and when he heard that his daughter had plighted her troth he angrily declared the marriage invalid, locked her up in her apartments, and drove Henry of Brunswick ignominiously away. Then, fearing lest the young people should manage to communicate in spite of all his watchfulness, he hastened the completion of the castle he was building in the middle of the Rhine, and transferred Agnes thither. There he declared that she should remain a prisoner until she consented to marry the husband he had chosen for her, refusing to see or speak to her until she submitted to his will.

One day, however, several months after Agnes had been locked up in the Pfalz, he heard that she had given birth to a little son. He bitterly regretted that he had refused to recognize the marriage, and hastened to court to inform the emperor, for the first time, that the marriage they had projected could now never take place. The emperor, who had been very anxious to secure the fair Agnes and her fortune for his own family, was very angry indeed, and vowed that the child which she had just borne would never be recognized as heir to the Palatinate, unless every formality had been observed at her marriage, and he saw the contract was correctly drawn up.

Conrad then sadly returned home, for he felt sure that a love-sick youth and two women would have overlooked a marriage contract, but when he saw the great parchment, and ascertained that every legal formality had been duly observed, he joyfully hastened back to court.

The young couple were forgiven, Henry was again allowed to visit his wife, and the little babe born in the Pfalz lived to grow up and inherit all their property. Ever since then, it has been customary for the Princess Palatine to await her first confinement in this little fortress, and the birth chamber is still shown to the inquisitive public.

They are also allowed to gaze upon the exact spot in the turret where Blücher took up his post on New Year's Day, 1814, to watch his army cross the Rhine, for he was then on the way to encounter Napoleon, and finally defeat him a few months later at Waterloo.

BACHARACH.
Old House.

BACHARACH.

The Altar of Bacchus.

THE picturesque little town of Bacharach was once visited by Bacchus, in whose honor it is named, who is said to have planted the vines which produce a vintage which has won a world-wide reputation.

> "At Klingenberg on the Main,
> At Würzburg by the Stein,
> At Bacharach on the Rhine,
> There grows the best of wine"
>
> —*Old Rhyme.*

The Romans, who had a military post here, erected a great stone altar in honor of the god of wine, on an island in the river. This island has now sunk and only one stone of the ponderous altar is at times visible. The people use this stone as an omen, for when it is visible at a certain epoch of the year they declare the vintage will be good, but if it remains submerged they always predict a bad year. The imposing ruins of Stahleck castle rise directly above the village, and now belong to the Prince of Prussia, while in the center of the town is the church of St. Werner, erected over the mortal remains of the child-martyr of Oberwesel, who was so cruelly murdered by the Jews.

FÜRSTENBERG.

The Tender Mother.

IN the thirteenth century the castle of Fürstenberg was occupied by Franz von Fürst, who, after a youth of reckless dissipation, fell suddenly and dangerously ill. Terrified by his condition, he vowed that in case he recovered he would lead an exemplary life, and, rising from his sick bed shortly after, married the beautiful Cunigunde of Flörsheim, with whom he lived very happily indeed.

She was so sweet and virtuous that for a while she succeeded in interesting him in doing good, but just as this quiet life was beginning to pall upon him, his wife's cousin, Amina, a handsome but utterly unprincipled girl, came to visit them. She soon began a lively flirtation with Franz, which was easily carried on while Cunigunde was occupied in watching over her infant son Hugo.

Little by little the flirtation ripened into passion, and soon the guilty couple began to wish that Cunigunde were out of the way, so that they might marry. Prompted by Amina, Franz finally poisoned his lovely wife. No one suspected the cause of the young countess' death, although many people commented upon the heartlessness of a husband who could contract a second alliance a week after his wife's death, and soon the matter seemed forgotten. Poor little Hugo alone seemed to miss his dead mother, for he had been intrusted to the care of a selfish old woman who neglected him sorely. She awoke one night to hear the child moaning as if in pain, and angrily turned over and tried to go to sleep, for she did not wish to be disturbed by the cries of a sickly babe.

All at once, however, it seemed to her as if someone had entered the room ; the cradle began to rock, and soon the infant's cries ceased. Looking in the direction of her little charge, the careless nurse started in terror, for there in the silvery moonlight stood the wraith of her dead mistress, tenderly stooping over her ailing child.

A few moments later, the child having fallen asleep, the ghost noiselessly glided from the room, and as soon as day dawned and she dared venture to creep out of the protecting bedclothes, the nurse rushed off to the countess' apartments to report the spectral visitation.

Amina first laughed her to scorn, but finally said she

would spend the next night in the room herself, for she suddenly thought that perhaps the poison had not been effective enough, and that the dead woman had risen from a trance, and must be more surely disposed of if she would remain in her present place.

That night the child again proved very restless, and as Amina paid no heed to its cries, the dead countess, urged by true mother love, again returned to earth to soothe it to sleep. Springing from the bed, Amina plunged her dagger again and again into the spectral form, but as her blows met with no resistance, she suddenly became aware that she had to deal with a spirit, and fainted away in terror.

When she recovered consciousness toward morning, the nightly vision was gone, and all seemed as before. Amina, urged by acute remorse, then sought her husband's presence and announced her decision to retire into a convent, to spend the rest of her life there in doing penance for her sins.

Franz also repented, and after having committed little Hugo to the watchful care of the priest of Rheindiebach, he withdrew into an hermitage, where he, too, incessantly implored divine forgiveness.

Cunigunde's spirit now ceased to haunt little Hugo's bedside, for he was tended by a gentle, motherly woman, who watched over him as lovingly as if he had been her own. But she often told him of his mother in heaven, who had left the celestial mansion merely to still his infant cries, and enable him to sleep in peace.

LORCH.

Delusive Whispers.

On the right bank of the Rhine, near the entrance of the little valley known as the Wisperthal (the whispering valley), stands the little town of Lorch, one of the most ancient places along the river. Three young men, stopping at the inn, once asked their host whether there were any places of interest to visit in the neighborhood, and hearing that the Wisperthal was haunted, immediately resolved to explore it.

They had not gone very far before their attention was attracted by soft, sibilant sounds, and looking in the direction whence they came they beheld a huge rock-like wall, which they had first taken for the side of a precipice. It was evidently a castle, for near the top were three small windows, whence protruded three beautiful female heads.

The sibilant sounds were made by the ladies, who were thus trying to attract the young men's attention, and who now invitingly beckoned to them to come up and join them. The impressionable youths immediately sought some mode cf ingress. After groping their way through the underbrush, they reached a door, which opened at their touch, and led them into a mirror-lined hall, magnificently illumined, where the three lovely ladies graciously advanced to receive them.

But, when the dazzled youths would fain have kissed the beautiful hands stretched out in welcome, they found themselves stopped by a wall of glass, and discovered that what they had taken for a reality was nothing but a reflection. Bewildered they turned around, only to be again deluded, and as every mirror in the hall reflected the same gracious figures, they soon stood still in amazement.

Their embarrassment was soon dispelled, however, by the appearance of a peculiar-looking old man, who said the fair maidens were his own daughters. He promised to give them in marriage to the youths, with dowries of a thousand gold pieces each. Then he led them to the maidens, allowed them to kiss their hands, and, under pretext of testing their complaisance, bade them go in search of his daughters' pets, who had escaped that very morn.

These pets were a raven, which sang a song; a riddle-repeating starling, and a story-telling magpie. The old man further assured them that the birds would be found on the same tree as they never parted company. Anxious to prove their devotion, the three young men rushed out of the hall, and after seeking in the thicket, finally descried the three pets. They recognized them readily, for the raven sang his song, the starling propounded his riddle, and the magpie told his story. The youths, having each secured one of the birds, retraced their steps, and, opening the door in the rocky wall, were surprised to find themselves in a damp and ruined hall, instead of in the resplendent mirror-lined apartment which they had left a short time before. Instead of three beautiful damsels, three toothless and palsied hags now came to meet them, clasped them in their bony arms, and claimed them as bridegrooms.

Disgusted, dismayed, and wofully disappointed, the youths finally yielded to their invitation, sat down to the well-spread board, but no sooner had they tasted the wine which the old women offered them than they sank unconscious on the floor. When they recovered their senses, they found themselves lying on the marshy ground in a dense thicket, the fair maidens, mysterious birds, and old hags had all vanished, and springing to their feet they hurried away.

In spite of the repetition of the sibilant sounds which had once deluded them, they rushed out of the valley, and solemnly vowed they would never return there again, lest worse adventures should befall them.

HEIMBURG.

A Cruel Father.

THE recently restored castle of Heimburg, or Hoheneck, situated above Niederheimbach, is built on the site of an old Frankish keep, often visited by Pharamond the first of the Merovingian kings, who often rode thither from Worms. The attraction was Ida, daughter of Sueno the castle owner. Sueno was utterly unconscious of the king's love for his daughter, and fancied that Pharamond hastened thither only to enjoy the beautiful situation and the pleasures of the chase, for even when he was absent the king sometimes came to Heimburg.

After a prolonged absence, Sueno once returned to find his daughter the mother of a beautiful babe, and when he angrily demanded who had made her forget her duty, she wept and told him that she was married, but had promised not to reveal her husband's name. As entreaties were of no avail, Sueno ordered that Ida should be scourged, and persisted in his cruel treatment of her until she died.

Two days after she had breathed her last, Pharamond, the king, came to Heimburg, and as he entered the castle he asked for Ida, his wife. Then he heard how she had perished.

A few minutes later he rode down the hill again, bearing his infant son in his arms, and leaving Sueno lifeless in the castle, for, upon hearing how cruelly he had treated poor Ida, the barbarian king had drawn his sword and laid him dead at his feet!

SONNECK.

The Ghost Feast.

THE castle of Sonneck, with its tall tower, was first built in 1015, and was the ancestral home of a noble family of the same name. All the men of this race was remarkably fond of hunting in their wide forests, and the castle eventually fell into the hands of Prince Heinrich, who loved the chase so dearly that it absorbed all his time and thoughts.

To be perfectly free to indulge in his favorite pastime, the young lord of Sonneck intrusted all his business to the care of a steward. This man sorely oppressed all the poor people, but Heinrich always exclaimed that he had no time to hear their complaints, as he must go out into the woods and hunt.

One day, however; he could start no game. So he gayly proposed that he and his companions should separate and scour the forest in different directions, returning at nightfall to a trysting spot, which he indicated. This plan was immediately acted upon, and Prince Heinrich soon started a stag which he hotly pursued, only to see it vanish mysteriously after a long run.

Then only he looked about him to find his bearings, and was greatly surprised to find himself in a strange place. Although he repeatedly blew his horn, no answering sound was heard. He was about to ride on, when he suddenly saw a gaunt, cadaverous-looking form rise before him, and heard a voice command him, in sepulchral tones, to follow.

Involuntarily Prince Heinrich obeyed, and as he passed on he noticed with awe that the garments of his guide seemed covered with mold, and that he exhaled an ancient and earth-like smell. A few moments later they came before a building which Heinrich had never seen, and, still implicitly obeying his guide, he dismounted and entered the hall in silence.

There he saw a long table, on either side of which were seated many ghastly-looking guests, who silently devoured the rich food set before them. They seemed to swallow it with contortions of pain. When he had gazed for several minutes upon this strange feast, the guide made Heinrich a sign to leave the hall and remount, and led him back to the place where he had first seen him.

There the cadaverous man paused for a moment, ere he informed Heinrich that the silent guests were his ancestors, condemned to eat the rich food which, in spite of its inviting appearance, was as bitter as the apples of Sodom. This was the punishment inflicted upon them for their selfish absorption in their own pleasures.

"Be warned, therefore, oh, prince," he concluded, "for our life is unbearable and our hearts constantly burn hot within us."

With these words, the specter pushed aside the damp folds of his moldy garments, and there, between his whitening ribs, the count perceived a glowing ball of fire. A moment later the apparition had vanished, and Heinrich, looking in the direction of the palace, saw only a raging sea of flames, which slowly sank down to the earth, while heart-rending cries and groans fairly made his hair stand up on end with horror.

When the count of Sonneck arrived home that evening, his servants were surprised to find that his coal black hair and beard were as white as snow. He was as much altered in character as in appearance, and his first care ever after was to discharge every duty with the utmost conscientiousness, and to use only his leisure moments to indulge in his favorite pastime, the chase.

SONNECK CASTLE.

RHEINSTEIN.

The Gadfly.

THE castles of the Rheinstein and Reichenstein, which rise on neighboring hills, were once inhabited by a youth and maiden. Having grown up together, these young people learned to love each other so dearly that when they reached maturity they were very anxious indeed to marry. Kuno, the young lord of Reichenstein, daily visited his beloved Gerda, and on her birthday offered her a magnificent steed, which he had carefully trained for her use. Then, longing to possess her, he begged her permission to reveal their mutual affection to her grim and avaricious old father, and win his consent to a speedy union.

As a suitor in those days seldom approached the father of his beloved on such a subject, and generally made his proposals through an older person, Kuno sought a bachelor uncle and entreated him to bear his message. The uncle immediately departed, presented himself before the lord of Rheinstein, made known his nephew's wishes, and after casually mentioning that as he was unmarried the youth would also inherit his vast estates, he obtained a favorable reply.

These preliminaries settled, the uncle, who was a baron, requested permission to see his future niece, whom he complimented greatly, making no mention of his errand, however, and carefully avoiding his nephew's name. When she had left the apartment, the baron suddenly turned to her father and declared that if he would give his daughter to him instead of to his nephew, he would accept her without dowry, and even, if necessary, give him a large sum of money in exchange.

As the Lord of Rheinstein was very avaricious indeed, he joyfully acceded to this new proposal, promising that the marriage should take place on the morrow, in the little chapel of St. Clement, which stood in the valley between the two castles. Delighted with the success of this interview, for he secretly hated his nephew, the baron rode away, and when Kuno met him he took grim pleasure in telling him how he had won the promise of Gerda's hand.

Poor Kuno, almost mad with rage and despair, rode home and made a bold plan to carry Gerda off by night. But alas! this plan was never carried out, for the Lord of Rheinstein, mistrusting the lovers, guarded his daughter so carefully that her suitor was driven away by a force of armed men.

Day dawned and gentle Gerda, who dared not openly resist her father's authority, was arrayed in bridal finery, and placed upon her handsome steed. Then escorted by her father, the baron, and all their retainers she slowly rode down the hill to St. Clement's Chapel, in full view of Kuno, who, from the top of his turret, sadly watched the girl he loved.

The procession halted at the church door, and all dismounted except Gerda, who sat passively upon her steed imploring St. Clement to deliver her from a hated marriage. At that moment a gadfly stung her horse, and he, goaded to madness, rushed off, galloping madly up the road which led to his former home at Reichenstein.

Gerda clung helplessly to the saddle, and heard her father and bridegroom loudly calling to her to draw rein, while they prepared to pursue her. But as death seemed preferable to a hated marriage, she did not obey. A sudden cry of joy above her made her raise her head, however, and she soon descried Kuno making frantic signs to her to hurry, while he lowered the drawbridge which led into his yard. This sight immediately gave the almost fainting maiden courage, and she urged her steed on faster and faster. She was closely pursued by the baron, who, better mounted than she, overtook her, and was about to seize the bridle of her steed when his horse stumbled and fell, throwing and killing him instantly.

RHEINSTEIN CASTLE.

Without pausing to see what had happened, Gerda rode rapidly on and crossed the drawbridge, which was immediately drawn up behind her. Then she was lifted from her panting steed by the triumphant Kuno, who rapturously pressed her to his heart. Their raptures were interrupted at last by the angry father without, so Kuno led the fair maiden upon the rampart, where they stood in full view of the wedding company below. There he flatly refused to let Gerda go, but proclaimed that his own chaplain should marry them in presence of the whole assembly.

Before this plan could be carried out, however, the baron's retainers came to report their master's death, and to pay their respects to Kuno, who, as heir at law, was now owner of all his uncle's vast wealth. The lord of Rheinstein, hearing this, loudly declared he would no longer oppose his daughter's wishes, and implored the young people to come down and be married in St. Clement's Chapel, where all was ready for the wedding. At a whispered word from Gerda, Kuno consented, and a few moments later a bridal cavalcade passed slowly down the hill, and again paused at the church door. This time, however, the bride uttered no frantic prayer to be saved from the marriage, the steed did not run away, and all passed off as merrily as the traditional wedding bells, for no one cared for the old baron, who was entirely forgotten.

FALKENBURG.

The Specter Bride.

THE ruins of the castle of Falkenburg, which is also know as Reichenstein, are picturesquely situated near the chapel dedicated to St. Clement, and are connected with another very romantic mediæval legend. This states that

Liba, daughter of the Lord of Falkenburg, plighted her troth to Guntram, a brave and handsome young knight.

The young people were obliged to defer their marriage for six months, however, as the emperor had selected the youth for an important mission. So the lovers parted with many repeated vows that they would think incessantly of each other, and that nothing would ever make them forget the promises they had exchanged.

His mission safely accomplished, Guntram prepared to return to Falkenburg, and finding the pace too slow, soon left his suite behind him and impatiently urged his steed onward. He was overtaken by a storm toward nightfall, and took refuge in an old castle, which appeared in a sad state of ruin and decay. The castle servants, who seemed as decrepit as the building, led him into a hall, where they bade him await their master's coming, and to beguile the time Guntram examined the antique paintings on the wall. He soon noticed that a curtain hung over one of these pictures, and absently pushing it aside, was startled by the sight of the portrait of a beautiful woman, seated beside an open grave.

A few moments later, the old master of the castle appeared and made him welcome. When bedtime came, an old servant led him along dismantled halls and cobwebby corridors to a wing of the castle where, he explained, the only inhabitable apartment was to be found. Then they entered a chamber which had apparently once belonged to a lady, and the servant bade Guntram good-night, warning him to say his prayers and pay no heed if he heard mysterious sounds during the night, for, although the castle was haunted, no harm befell those who had a clear conscience.

Somewhat excited by this warning, Guntram did not fall asleep as readily as usual, and when midnight struck he heard a noise in the adjoining chamber. Through the half open door he now beheld the lady whose veiled portrait had attracted his attention in the great hall, and heard her softly singing to herself. The maiden was so beautiful, that Guntram would fain have spoken to her, but the thought of the waiting Liba restrained him from holding any intercourse with this strangely fascinating person, whom he in no wise took for a ghost, but for a *bona fide* girl, whose presence the aged servant had cleverly tried to keep secret.

Guntram slept, and when he awoke the girl had vanished and the sun was high in the heavens. When he joined his host he was courteously invited to tarry a few days, so he forgot his haste to join his beloved and resolved, if possible, to find out who the fair lady might be. He wandered idly about the ruins during the afternoon, came to the chapel, and amused himself by reading the inscriptions on the tombs, on one of which stood the words: "Pray for me, but beware of my glances."

But, in spite of diligent search, he caught no glimpse of the maiden who had so excited his curiosity. It was only when he had returned to his room, and midnight had again struck, that a light shone in the adjoining chamber and he again saw the golden-haired lady sitting before the table crooning her song.

This time Guntram approached and addressed her, marveling because she answered him only by gestures, but in a few moments a lively pantomime flirtation was begun. The young man, forgetting Liba, and allured by the beautiful maiden's glances, finally threw his arms around the girl her and kissed her.

To his surprise she then drew a ring from her finger, placed it on his, returned his kiss, and then suddenly vanished, leaving him bewildered and alone. When morning dawned, Guntram, ashamed of his conduct, took leave of his host, and rode away. He paused only at the foot of the hill to ask a peasant why the castle was all in ruins and the people so old and sad.

In answer to this inquiry the peasant informed him that

the castle had once been strong and handsome, the favorite resort of many knights, who came to woo Etelinda, the fair young châtelaine. She, however, was coquettish and capricious, and wearied them all by her exactions, until at last a youth presented himself vowing he was ready to stand every test, providing she would honor him with her love.

Etelinda laughingly bade this suitor stand unarmed at the crossroads on Walpürgisnacht, and report what he saw; but, although he fearlessly started out to do her bidding, he never returned, and his body was found torn to pieces either by the angry witches or by ravenous wolves. The youth's mother, inconsolable at his loss, cursed Etelinda, who sickened and died nine days after, and whose body mysteriously disappeared just as it was about to be consigned to the tomb.

Since then her spirit haunted the ruins, and would only be allowed to rest when someone had withstood her glances, all the rest being forced to die nine days after they had seen her. When Guntram heard this, he shuddered with fear, and rode on. As he arrived near Falkenburg, he fancied he saw men carrying a coffin over the drawbridge, and knew no rest until he had clasped Liba in his arms and ascertained that she was safe.

A few days later, Guntram and Liba stood side by side in the chapel to be married, but when Guntram would fain have claimed his bride, he felt an icy hand in his, and saw that Etelinda had placed herself beside him, and considered him as her own. The sight of this specter and the touch of her cold hand made him faint with terror, and when he came to his senses again he had only time to confess his sins and receive absolution before he died.

Liba, broken-hearted at his loss, died nine days after, and was laid, at her own request, in the same grave as her lover, whom she forgave for his temporary forgetfulness, and loved as long as she lived.

CLEMENSKAPELLE.

The Robber Knight.

THE knight of Rheinstein, one of the most unscrupulous robbers along the Rhine, fell in love with the noble maid of the Wisperthal, and when she scorned to listen to his proposal, he angrily vowed to win her by fair means or by foul. The former having soon been exhausted, in his opinion, he had recourse to the latter, and one day, while the maiden was gathering flowers, his attendants seized and gagged her, and rapidly carried her down to the boat where their wicked master was waiting for them.

When they reached the center of the stream, the robber knight removed the bandage from the fair maiden's face; but when she piteously implored him to let her go, he smilingly curled his mustache and cried:

"Blow ye winds from the Wisperthal, and ripple faster ye waves, that my bride and I may the sooner reach my castle, where I shall jealously guard my own!"

The noble maiden, seeing her entreaties were vain, then fell upon her knees and began to pray, vowing she would build a chapel in honor of her favorite St. Clement, if he would only intercede in her behalf, and save her from becoming the wife of the dishonorable knight who had kidnaped her.

As she prayed, the Wisperthal winds began to rise with a vengeance, the waves tumbled and tossed, and the thunder crashed. While the knight and his men were frantically trying to row ashore, and keep the vessel from sinking, St. Clement came calmly walking over the waves, stretched out his hand to the maiden, and led her safely ashore, allowing the boat and all on board to perish.

The maiden, thankful for her rescue from double danger, built a chapel in honor of her favorite saint on the left shore of the Rhine, where its ruins still remind the traveler of the fair maid of Wisperthal, and of her miraculous deliverance from the cruel hands of the robber knight of Rheinstein.

EHRENFELS.

The Bishop's Treachery.

Opposite the Mausethurm or Rat Tower, on the right bank of the Rhine, are the picturesque ruins of the old castle of Ehrenfels, which was founded in the beginning of the ninth century, and was demolished by the French in 1689.

In the days when Louis, the last of the Carlovingians, was reigning over Germany, the lord of Ehrenfels, Adalbert, seized and imprisoned his brother Conrad. In vain the emperor summoned him to relinquish the captive; in vain he besieged the fortress, Adalbert remained firm, until, in disgust, the emperor withdrew with his troops to Mainz.

The bishop Hatto, hearing of the emperor's disappointment, sought his presence, and volunteered to deliver the rebel knight into his hands. This offer was gladly seized by Louis, who bade him bring the prisoner to Ingelheim, where he was about to take up his abode. Hatto presented himself at Ehrenfels, with a very small retinue, was admitted, and told Adalbert that the emperor longed for a truce to all hostilities and had commissioned him to negotiate a reconciliation.

Adalbert, very glad to end the strife, immediately expressed his readiness to suspend all hostilities, and even declared he would go and seek the emperor, were he but certain no treachery were intended and that he would return home safe and sound.

Hearing these words, Hatto laid his hand upon the crucifix and swore a solemn oath to the effect that he would bring Adelbert back to the castle of Ehrenfels, without his having been molested in any way.

THE ROBBER KNIGHT. *Schuch.*

Thus reassured, the knight mounted his steed, and, riding beside the bishop, started out for the court at Ingelheim. They had not gone very far, however, before the bishop complained that he was weary, and playfully reproached Adalbert for having forgotten to offer him the usual refreshments. Shocked at his lack of hospitality, the knight of Ehrenfels implored the bishop to turn around once more, and after a little persuasion the cavalcade re-entered the castle of Ehrenfels where refreshments were served, and where the bishop and his followers were richly entertained.

When the feast was ended, and Hatto duly rested, they again set forth, and entered Ingelheim. There, to his utter surprise, Adalbert was made prisoner and dragged in chains to the foot of the imperial throne, where he was sentenced to death. In vain he protested against this cruel decree, and finally fell at the bishop's feet imploring him to remember his oath to take him back to Ehrenfels in safety. The bishop turned carelessly aside, saying: "I did take you back to Ehrenfels safely. Why did you not exact a pledge the second time we started out, if you wished me to interfere in your behalf."

Realizing too late that he was the victim of a preconcerted plot, Adalbert started to his feet and tried to cut his way out, but in spite of all of his courage he was soon overpowered and led away to the scaffold, where he was treacherously beheaded.

BINGEN.

The Rat Tower.

In the year 914, when Hatto was bishop of Mainz, a protracted rain entirely ruined the harvest, occasioning a terrible famine from which the poor people suffered sorely. As they were perishing with hunger, they finally applied to the bishop, whose granaries were filled to overflowing with the produce of former, more favorable, years.

But Hatto was cruel and hard-hearted and utterly refused to listen to them, until at last they so wearied him by their constant importunity, that he bade them assemble in an empty barn, where he promised to meet them on a certain day and hour to quiet all their demands.

Almost beside themselves with joy at this promise, the people hastened to the appointed spot, gathering there in such numbers that the empty barn was soon quite full. Anxiously they watched for the bishop, whom they greeted with loud cries of joy as soon as he appeared. These acclamations however, were soon changed into blood-curdling cries of distress, for the cruel prelate, after bidding his servants fasten doors and windows so that none could escape, set fire to the moldering building and burned them all, declaring they were like rats and should perish in the same way.

This wholesale massacre ended, the bishop returned home, sat down before his lavishly-spread table, and ate with as healthy an appetite as usual. When he entered the dining room on the morrow, however, he stood still in dismay, for during the night the rats had gnawed his recently-finished portrait out of the frame, and it now lay, an unseemly heap, upon the floor. While he was standing over it, his heart filled with sudden nameless terror, for he fancied it was a bad omen, a servant came rushing into the room, bidding him fly for his life, as a whole army of hungry, fierce looking rats were coming that way.

Without waiting for his usual escort, the bishop flung himself upon the messenger's steed and rode rapidly away. From time to time he nervously turned his head to mark the gradual approach of a dark line, formed by thousands of rats, animated by the revengeful spirits of the poor he had so cruelly burned.

Faster and faster Hatto urged his panting steed, but, in

spite of all his efforts, he had scarcely dismounted, entered a small skiff and rowed out into the Rhine, ere an army of rats fell upon his horse and devoured it. The bishop, shuddering with fear, rowed with all his might to his tower in the middle of the Rhine, where he quickly locked himself in, fancying he had escaped from his hungry foes.

But the voracious rats, having disposed of his steed, now boldly swam across the Bingerloch to the tower, and swarmed up its sides, seeking some crevice through which they could get at their foe. As they found none, they set their sharp teeth to work, and Hatto quailed with dread as he heard them gnawing busily on all sides.

In a very few moments the rats had made a thousand holes through which they rushed upon their victim.

Southey, who has versified this legend, which he calls "God's Judgment upon a Wicked Bishop," describes their entrance thus :

> " And in at the windows, and in at the door,
> And through the walls, helter skelter they pour,
> And down from the ceiling, and up through the floor,
> From the right and the left, from behind and before,
> From within and without, from above and below,
> And all at once to the bishop they go.
>
> " They have whetted their teeth against the stones,
> And now they pick the bishop's bones ;
> They gnaw'd the flesh from every limb,
> For they were sent to do judgment on him."

Ever since then, that building in the Rhine has been known as the Rat Tower. Tradition relates that the bishop's soul sank down to the nethermost hell, where it is ever burning in a fire far hotter than that he kindled around the starving poor. At sunset a peculiar red glow may be seen over the tower, and this, the people declare, is only a faint reflection of that infernal furnace, sent to warn all mankind against cruelty to God's poor.*

* See Note 15 in Appendix.

KREUZNACH.

The Freshet.

THE little town of Kreuznach is built on the banks of the Nahe, one of the principal tributaries of the Rhine, and is said to have been founded many centuries ago, when that part of Germany was still covered with the dense primeval forests. A missionary, penetrating into these wilds to preach the gospel, once erected a stone cross on a little island in the river, and, encouraged by this visible emblem of peace on earth, several poor fishermen built their huts close by the banks of the stream.

Here they lived peaceful and happy, during the fall and spring, but when the spring freshets came, the waters swept away their fragile huts and nought but the cross remained. The people then crowded around the missionary, imploring him to teach them how to build, so that their huts might stand as fast as his cross, so he led them to a spot near it and constructed solid stone dwellings, which no freshet could ever sweep away and which, standing "near the cross," became the nucleus of the present town of Kreuznach.

RHEINGRAFENSTEIN.

The Devil and the Donkey.

A NOBLEMAN, in search of a site for his castle, once saw the mighty porphyry rocks upon which Rheingrafenstein castle is now perched, and, thinking a fortress upon such an eyrie would be well-nigh impregnable, he made up his mind to build upon it. In answer to all objections, he declared that he would bespeak the devil's aid, if need be, to accomplish his purpose.

Satan, hearing himself called upon, promptly appeared before the nobleman, and promised he would build the castle for him in the course of a single night, if he would only give him as reward the first living creature which looked out of the new building's windows. The nobleman agreed and withdrew, and when he reappeared on the morrow, he found the castle completed. But, although he longed to take possession of it, he did not dare do so, lest the devil, perched upon the edge of the roof, should secure him if he ventured to look out of the window.

In his perplexity, the poor man confided his troubles to his wife, who, being "as wise as the serpent" as well as "gentle as the dove," declared she knew how she could circumvent the fiend. She therefore mounted her favorite donkey, and rode up into the new castle, bidding all the men follow her. Satan, well pleased, watched them file slowly into the building and kept a sharp lookout upon the windows, intending to swoop down from above upon the first creature which ventured to thrust its head out of the window, and, seizing it by the nape of the neck, carry it away without further ado. The countess, in the meanwhile, had brought the donkey into the hall, pinned a kerchief around its neck, bound a large frilled cap over its ears, and leading it to the window let it thrust its head out into the open air. The devil, catching a glimpse of cap, ribbons, and frills, immediately concluded he was about to secure the countess herself, and swooping down, caught and carried away his prey, discovering his mistake only when the struggling donkey gave vent to his feelings by a loud bray.

Satan was so disgusted at having thus been cheated that he dropped his prey on the rocks below, vanished in the midst of a horrible stench of brimstone and sulphur, and never again visited the banks of the Nahe, where he had been so cleverly deceived.

SPRENDLINGEN.

The Butcher.

A HERALD once galloped wildly into the little town of Kreuznach, summoning the people to arms. The enemy was threatening the neighboring town of Sponheim, which their valiant lord was vainly trying to save by engaging the van of the army in battle at Sprendlingen.

The people of Kreuznach rushed for their weapons and began to muster, but the butcher, Michel Mort, hearing his master was in danger, caught up his sharpest cleaver, rushed out of his shop, and hastened to Sprendlingen as fast as he could run. There he plunged into the very midst of the fray, hewing ruthlessly right and left, and shouted encouraging words to his master, who was entirely surrounded by the foe, and about to give up in despair.

In a few minutes' time butcher and knight stood side by side, and began their retreat, the man heroically shielding and defending his master. He succeeded in saving him, although at the cost of his life, for the enemy, furious at the havoc he had made in their ranks, rushed simultaneously upon him and pierced him through and through with their spears.

To commemorate this fight at Sprendlingen, and to honor the heroic butcher, a stone has been erected upon the very spot where he fell, while a carved lion on the Schlossberg near Kreuznach serves still further to testify to his bravery.

SPONHEIM.

The True Cross.

THE count of Vianden, who had led a wicked and lawless life, once fell in love with a noble lady. She told him she could not accept him until he had proved himself worthy of trust by performing a pilgrimage to the Holy Sepulcher, to obtain the forgiveness of his sins, bringing back a holy relic to bestow upon her as a wedding gift. This penance, however hard, seemed none to great for the knight, who immediately departed for the Holy Land, which he reached after encountering countless dangers. He then secured a span of the Holy Cross and placed it in a casket of gold, upon which was engraved the name of the lady he loved.

Slowly and painfully, for he was greatly weakened by privation and fatigue, the count now wended his way home, guarding the relic night and day, and finally embarked upon the Rhine, thinking all dangers were over, and the goal of his wishes very near. Unfortunately, however, the boat capsized, and when the count recovered his senses he found he had been saved by the devotion of the boatmen, but that the precious relic was lost.

His despair was terrible to behold, for he felt that as he now had no proof to show his lady-love that he had obeyed her and obtained the forgiveness of all former sins, she would again to refuse to listen to his pleadings. As he wished to see her once more before he withdrew into some monastery, he wended his way to her castle, and was quite overcome when she rushed out to meet him with happy tears coursing down her cheeks.

In broken, faltering accents he told his story, but when he would fain have left her, after telling her of the loss of the relic, she detained him, saying that a handsome youth had passed at the gate that very morning. He had given her a golden casket upon which her name was engraved and which contained a piece of wood.

As the angel had delivered the precious relic into the lady's hands she plighted her troth to the count of Vianden. After their marriage they founded the castle, church, and abbey of Sponheim, which was thus named because it became the home or resting place of a span of the True Cross, which miraculously reached its destination and turned the penitent count's sorrow into lasting happiness.

DHAUN.

The Monkey as Nurse.

ONE of the Rheingrafs once lived in the pretty castle of Dhaun, of which nothing but ruins now remain. He assigned the sunniest room for the nursery of his little heir, who, although motherless, was constantly watched and tended by a faithful old nurse. In the castle there was also a large-sized monkey, which was allowed to range about the place at will, and which often came into the nursery and gravely sat in a corner, watching the nurse handle the babe, and amusing it by its queer antics.

One day, after putting her little charge to sleep, the nurse sat down beside it, as usual, and, as usual also, was soon lost in slumbers as profound. When she awoke and glanced at the cradle she was terrified, for the babe was missing! The poor woman, conjecturing that he had been stolen by gypsies, and fearing her master's anger, ran and hid in the depths of the neighboring forest.

There she heard a peculiar sound, and gazing cautiously through the bushes, saw the babe seated on the moss, while the monkey amused him with red apples and gay flowers, imitating her gestures with the most absurd precision. In a few moments, however, the child began to cry, and the monkey, taking it up gently, began to dandle it, and swinging gently backward and forward soon put it to sleep. Then he laid it down on the soft moss and, still imitating the old woman closely, clasped his hands in his lap and fell asleep.

The nurse crept cautiously out of the thicket, recovered the babe, and hastened homeward. She found the whole castle in an uproar, for they had been missed, so she was obliged to confess all that had occurred.

In gratitude for the recovery of his child, the Rheingraf placed a carving above the gateway representing a monkey amusing a babe with an apple, and ever since then the monkey has figured on the escutcheon of that noble family.

OBERSTEIN.

A Lifelong Penance.

THE castle of Oberstein, on the Nahe, a tributary of the Rhine, belonged in the thirteenth century to an irascible lord who had a constitutional aversion to cats. One day his younger brother playfully slipped a kitten into his boot. The lord of Oberstein coming in contact with the beast, and discovering by his brother's merriment that he had been the perpetrator of the joke, flew into a violent rage, and, not knowing what he was doing, caught and flung the youth far over the parapet, down the rocky wall into the Nahe, where he was drowned. This terrible murder committed, the lord of Oberstein felt the most intense remorse, and assuming a pilgrim's garb he wended his way, alone and on foot, to Rome. He knelt at the Pope's feet, confessed his crime, and humbly craved forgiveness. But the Pope, shocked at his violence, told him that he must do penance if he would obtain forgiveness for his sin, and condemned him to relinquish castle and wealth, reserving nothing but a hammer and chisel. These he was to use to hew a chapel out of the rock over which he had flung his only brother, and when the chapel was finished and ready for consecration he was told he would obtain the forgiveness of his sins.

The poor pilgrim slowly wended his way back to the Nahe, disposed of castle and wealth, and with hammer and chisel painfully scrambled up the steep rock, where he began to hew at the hard stone. From early morning until late at night, the incessant tapping of his hammer was heard. Day after day, month after month, and year after year, the penitent lord of Oberstein labored on, advancing by almost imperceptible degrees, watering the hard stone with many a repentant tear, and persevering in spite of weakness and advancing age, in the hope of at last obtaining the forgiveness he craved.

When he was very old, when his beard was white as snow, when he could scarcely hold hammer and chisel any more, a tiny chapel and altar had been hewed out of the solid rock. The people, who had watched its progress, went in search of a priest to consecrate it, promising to return with him on the morrow. As they came toward the little chapel they were surprised not to see the well-known figure at the door, and hurrying in to discover what had become of him, they found the lord of Oberstein lying dead at the foot of the altar. A beautiful smile lingered upon the face, which, furrowed by repentant tears, had never smiled since the day when a violent outburst of anger had blasted all his life.

The peasants buried him at the foot of the altar, in the chapel he had hewed out of the rock in penance for his crime. This chapel, duly consecrated, was further enlarged in the fourteenth century, and is now the parish church of Oberstein. The traveler can still see the part which was hewn by the penitent lord.

RÜDESHEIM.

A Broken Vow.

A FISHERMAN once paused at Rüdesheim to pray at the shrine of St. Nicholas. For the first time in his life he was about to encounter the dangers of the Bingerloch, which his companions had described so vividly as to fill his simple heart with nameless fear.

"Oh, good St. Nicholas," he prayed, "if you will only guide me safely over, I will give you a taper as tall and thick as the mast of my vessel."

GERMANIA. *Niederwald.*
National Monument.

Strengthened by this prayer he re-entered his vessel, pushed away from the shore, trimmed his sail, and was soon gliding over the dreaded waters. But the Bingerloch was as smooth as the most placid lake. The boatman looked around him in wonder and then exclaimed:

"Fool that I was to believe my companions' tales of the Bingerloch, and to stop and pray at St. Nicholas' shrine! I won't give him the big taper I promised, but a two-penny dip!"

Scarcely had these words left his lips, however, than the smooth waters became rough, and the gentle breeze changed into a hurricane. The little bark, caught in the terrible eddy, was whirled about and suddenly sucked down into the vortex with the boatman and all his crew.

Since then the vows made at St. Nicholas' shrine have been scrupulously paid, for all the river boatmen are afraid of suffering the fate of their sacriligious companion.

Hans Broemser.

VERY near the city of Rüdesheim, which is principally renowned for its excellent wines, are the ruins of the castle of Niederburg. This place once belonged to Hans Broemser, who, won by the eloquence of St. Bernard, took part in the second crusade.

Broemser left his home and lovely daughter, and went forth to fight the Saracens. Once he was attacked by a terrible dragon, which guarded the only spring where water could be obtained to quench the burning thirst of the weary crusaders. Although many knights had already lost their lives in trying to slay this monster, Broemser attacked him boldly, and, after a fierce struggle, left him lifeless, and cut out his tongue as a memento of his victory.

As he was wending his way back to camp, however, he

was surprised by a band of Saracens, who chained him fast in a foul dungeon. There he lingered for several years, praying for deliverance, and vowing that he would build a convent, and make his only daughter take the veil, if he were only allowed to see his native land once more.

In answer to this prayer, the Christians soon took the town and delivered him. Broemser wended his way back to Germany, carrying his chains and the dragon's tongue, which he showed to his lovely daughter Gisella, as he recounted his adventures and escape.

"And now, my daughter," he added, "I must tell you the nature of my vow, for you are bound to fulfill it. I promised to build a convent, in which you would take the veil, and spend the remainder of your life in serving God."

Gisella heard this and grew pale with horror, for she loved a young knight of the neighborhood, who had only waited for her father's return to claim her as his wife. She now fell at Broemser's feet, imploring him not to sacrifice her and make her assume vows which would be so very distasteful. All these entreaties were, however, of no avail, and the maiden, hearing her father declare she must obey him, rushed wildly out of the room and flung herself over the castle ramparts into the rushing waters of the Rhine, where she perished.

Early on the morrow some fishermen found her body at the foot of the Rat Tower, and reverently carried it home for burial. But ever since then, the maiden's uneasy spirit is said to haunt the ruins, and every night, with a shriek of despair, her wraith rushes up to the tower, from whence she throws herself again into the Rhine.

It is said, however, that her tragic death did not produce much effect upon Hans Broemser, who soon forgot his vow and spent all his time in revelry. One night, however, the dragon again appeared before him, but as it opened its capacious jaws to devour him, Gisella's spirit drove it away. At the same moment Broemser was awakened by the clank of his chains which had fallen from the peg upon which they had long been hung.

While Hans was musing over his strange dream the next morning, one of his servants came to announce that the plowman, in tracing a furrow, had found an image of the Saviour, which had called aloud for help as the plow touched it. This miracle caused Broemser to remember his vow, and he immediately began the construction of the church and cloister of Noth Gottes, on the exact spot where the miraculous image was found.

The church and convent are still extant, and there, among many other curious relics, the traveler can see the dragon tongue, the chains which Hans Broemser brought back from Palestine, and the image which is considered particularly sacred.

JOHANNISBERG.

The Corkscrews.

THE beautiful castle of Johannisberg, now the property of Prince Metternich, stands in the midst of the most productive vineyards along the Rhine. This castle is built on the site of an old monastery or abbey dedicated to St. John, and if the legend is true, it is very evident that those ancient monks knew how to appreciate the product of their own vines.

One day the prior of the abbey invited all the brethren to accompany him on an inspection tour of the monastery vineyards. This invitation was accepted with very evident pleasure by all. After they had walked a long while along the sunny slopes, between the loaded vines, they reached a shady spot. The prior then proposed that they should all sit down, rest and refresh themselves morally and physically by reading the afternoon prayers and drinking a few bottles of delicious old wine which they had brought with them for this purpose.

Again the monks joyfully acquiesced, but when the prior asked for a breviary, they all hung their heads and shamefacedly confessed that they had forgotten to bring them along. The jovial prior good-naturedly remarked that since there was no prayer-book handy they would forego spiritual refreshment and proceed with the physical. He therefore took up one of the bottles and vainly attempted to remove the cork with his fingers. Suddenly turning to the assembled brothers, he asked whether any of them had thought of bringing a corkscrew.

Simultaneously the monks thrust their hands into their capacious pockets, and a moment later each eagerly tendered a corkscrew for the prelate's use. The prelate accepted one of them, uncorked one of the bottles, and as he was about to raise the goblet of sparkling wine to his thirsty lips, he dryly remarked with a merry twinkle in his eye: "Not a single breviary, but plenty of corkscrews. Is that a proof of your zeal in serving the Lord?"

The monks all hung their heads and quaffed the wine in silence, but their temporary embarrassment soon passed away, and ere long they were all drinking merrily, and showing their loyalty by repeatedly pledging their favorite saint John.

LANGE WINKEL.

The Silver Bridge.

OPPOSITE the hamlet of Kempten is the little village of Lange Winkel, which is said to have been so dear to Charlemagne, that his spirit haunts it still, as is set forth by Geibel's lovely verses:

THE SILVER BRIDGE.

On the Rhine,—the green Rhine—in the soft summer night,
The vineyards lie sleeping beneath the moon's light ;
But lo ! there's a shadow on green hill and glade,
Like the form of a king in grandeur arrayed.

Yes, yes ! 'tis the monarch that erst ruled this land,
It is old Charlemagne, with his sword in his hand,
And his crown on his head, and his scepter of gold,
And the purple imperial in many a rich fold.

Long ages have fled since he lived in this life,
Whole nations have perished by time or by strife
Since he swayed with a power never known from his birth;
What brings his great spirit to wander on earth ?

He hath come from his tomb that's in Aix-la-Chapelle.
He hath come to the stream which he once loved so well.
Not to ban nor to blight with his presence the scene,
But to bless the blithe vineyards by Luna's soft sheen.

The moonbeams they make a brave bridge o'er the Rhine,
From Winkel to Ingelheim brightly they shine.
Behold ! by this bridge the old monarch goes over,
And blesses the flood with the warmth of a lover.

He blesses each vineyard on plain and on hill ;
Each village, each cottage, his blessing doth fill ;
He blesses each spot, on the shore, on the river,
Which he loved in his life—which forget he can never.

And then from the house that he still loves so well,
He returns to his tomb that's in Aix-la-Chapelle,
There to slumber in peace till the old year is over,
And the vineyards once more woo him back like a lover.

—*Geibel. Translated by Snowe.*

Whenever the emperor's mighty shadow is thus seen to cross over the moon-light bridge, the vineyards are sure to be filled with rich clusters of grapes, and the wine is particularly mellow and sweet, but when he omits his yearly visit the vintage is sure to be very poor.

OESTRICH.

The Revengeful Ghost.

NEAR the village of Oestrich once rose the renowned convent of Gottesthal, where many a holy nun spent her life in penance and prayer.

The legends relate that a neighboring knight, falling desperately in love with one of the convent inmates, prevailed upon her to forget her vows and meet him every evening in the chapel. There he promised ever to be faithful to her, even if they could never be married, owing to her vows.

The knight was a rover, however, and soon forgot the pretty nun, who pined and grew pale when she heard he was courting another. The rumor of these doings was soon confirmed, and the perjured nun, mad with jealousy and despair, hired an assassin to slay the lover who had deceived and deserted her.

The knight's remains were duly interred in the Gottesthal chapel, where he had come so often to make love to the little nun, and when the midnight hour struck, the door opened, a closely-veiled figure stole to his tomb, opened it, and with muttered curses and shrieks of rage tore his base heart out of his body and trampled it wildly under foot.

The veiled figure was the nun, driven insane by remorse and grief, and many years after that her ghost returned at midnight, dragged the knight from his tomb, tore out his heart and trampled it, while her shrieks echoed through the ruins. Now no trace of convent or chapel remains, and the ghost is no longer seen, but her despairing cries of rage can still be heard from time to time, and the people of Oestrich declare she still hates her false lover.

> "Since then long time has passed but still,
> Old legends say that she
> Till cock crow tarries in that aisle,
> Aye shrieking fearfully.
> And that, when tolls the midnight bell,
> She seeks his monument ;
> And from it brings, with looks so fell,
> A heart with blood besprent."
> —*Legends of the Rhine.*

INGELHEIM.

Charlemagne and Elbegast.

CHARLEMAGNE had come to inspect his new palace near the Rhine. As he lay asleep in his room, the very first night, he was honored by the visit of an angel, who, standing at the foot of his bed, solemnly bade him arise, go forth and steal.

This command, coming from an angel, seemed so incongruous, that it had to be thrice repeated ere the emperor rose noiselessly from his couch. He stole unseen to the stable, saddled his horse, and rode out of the palace armed *cap-a-pie*, ready to attack any traveler along the highway and despoil him, as the angel had commanded. He had not gone very far, however, before he met a knight, apparently bound on the same errand, whom he challenged, fought against, and brought to the ground. There he held the point of his sword to the man's throat, demanding his name and standing, but when he heard it was Elbegast, a notorious robber knight whom he had long been trying to secure, he bade him rise and accompany him on a predatory excursion.

Nothing loath, Elbegast joined his conqueror, little suspecting it was the renowned Charlemagne, and hearing him declare that he had vowed not to return home until he had robbed someone, led him to the house of one of his ministers, where, thanks to his cunning, they soon effected an entrance. Bidding the emperor wait for him, Elbegast glided noiselessly into the minister's bedroom, and there, crouching in the darkness, overheard him confide to his wife a plot for Charlemagne's assassination on the morrow.

Elbegast returned to his waiting companion, and implored him to go and warn the emperor of the threatened danger. After they had secured a few worthless trifles, the chance companions parted, one returning to his stronghold, and the other wending his way back to the palace, which he re-entered unheard and unseen.

Thanks to the information gleaned during the night, Charlemagne cleverly outwitted and secured the conspirators, whom he generously pardoned upon their promise of future loyalty. Then having obtained an interview with Elbegast, he revealed to him that his conqueror and companion in theft was none other than Charlemagne, who owed his life to the angel's warning.

Elbegast was so amazed at these tidings, and so penetrated with admiration for the only man who had ever been able to disarm him, that he forsook his evil practices and became a devoted attendant of Charlemagne, who made good use of his sagacity and courage.

In commemoration of the angelic visit, received during his first sojourn in his new palace, Charlemagne called it Ingelheim, the angel's home. The place has borne this name ever since although the palace has long fallen into ruins, and the only fragments of it which now remain are the columns incorporated in a part of the picturesque castle of Heidelberg.

KEDRICH.

The Devil's Ladder.

Above Lorch, near the entrance of the Wisperthal, stand the ruins of the ancient castle of Nollich, which was once inhabited by a stern and tyrannous knight, Libo von Lorch. His heart was tender only toward Gerlinda, his little daughter. He was so grim and discourteous that he even refused to show common hospitality, and roughly dismissed the belated travelers who paused for food and shelter at his gates.

One stormy night the lord of Lorch turned a poor old man away, laughing scornfully when the trembling fist was shaken in wrath, and the cracked old voice warned him that he would have cause to repent of his cruelty, and would rue this refusal for many a day. This prediction was only too soon fulfilled, however, for early on the morrow Libo von Lorch learned that his fair little daughter had been carried away by a dwarf. He had conveyed her to the huge rock towering far above his castle. The father rushed toward the window, and looking eagerly up to the top of the rocky wall, saw that the tidings were true, for there stood Gerlinda, holding out her hands to him as if to implore him to come to her rescue.

In vain the frantic father made every effort to scale the rock, in vain he promised large rewards to anyone who would restore his daughter, the dwarf guarded her securely, and defeated the efforts of all who tried to reach her, by pelting them with stones. Several years passed by, and although Libo von Lorch knew his daughter was well,—for she appeared at the top of the rock for a moment morning and evening,—he could not obtain access to her.

The poor father was so grieved at her loss that he forgot his old imperious ways, entertained all travelers with lavish hospitality, prayed at all the neighboring shrines, and vowed to bestow rich gifts upon every saint in the calendar, if they would only help him to recover his child. One evening he entertained a returning crusader, Sir Ruthelm, who, hearing the cause of his grief, vowed to rescue the captive maiden or perish in the attempt. The impetuous knight called for his horse and immediately rode off to try and find some means of scaling the rocky wall. But all his search proved vain, and he was about to postpone further efforts until the morrow, when a dwarf suddenly stepped out of the crevice and mockingly promised him the hand of the fair Gerlinda if he would only scale the wall.

Before Sir Ruthelm could answer the dwarf had vanished. A moment later another appeared, gave him a silver bell, bade him hasten to the Wisperthal, summon the gnomes by ringing it there, and ask them to build a ladder up the Kedrich, as the rocky precipice was called, and have it ready before sunrise on the morrow.

Of course the knight implicitly carried out all these instructions, and, before sunrise on the morrow he found a ladder reaching to the very top of the wall. He quickly climbed up, and encountering the dwarf, bade him fulfill his promise and give him the fair Gerlinda as wife. The dwarf, well pleased at the young man's daring, bade him return by the way he had come, telling him Gerlinda would meet him at the foot of the rock. And as soon as Sir Ruthelm reached the bottom of the ladder the fair damsel stepped out of a crevice, placed her hand in his, and allowed him to conduct her to her father's castle where they were duly married and lived happy for many a year.

According to another legend, a knight of Nollich once left his newly-won bride to take part in a crusade, but overcome with the longing to see her once more he soon deserted the holy cause and rapidly made his way home. On arriving at Lorch, however, he heard that his lovely bride had been carried away by a robber knight, whose castle was perched on top of the Kedrich and was simply inaccessible to all.

The knight of Noll'ch, after vainly striving to scale the wall, knowing that God would no longer help a man who had deserted his holy cause, now wildly appealed to the devil. In exchange for the knight's soul Satan enabled him to ride straight up the rocky wall, where his horse's hoofprints can still be seen. Then he rode into the castle and rescued his lovely wife, who soon after died from the results of her long imprisonment.

Inconsolable for her loss, the knight, who could no longer hope to join her pure spirit in heaven, committed suicide, and the devil took charge of his soul. In proof of the truth of this tradition, the inhabitants of Lorch exhibit the saddle upon which the knight sat as he climbed the steep precipice, where they also point out the marks of his horse's hoofs.

ELFELD.

The Rope of Hair.

A RECKLESS knight called Ferdinand once dwelt at Elfeld on the Rhine. When he had duly squandered all his patrimony and found himself too poor to purchase an outfit to attend a tournament given in honor of the queen, he vowed life was no longer worth living, and rushed out of the castle to commit suicide.

He was about to cast himself headlong into the river, when Satan suddenly appeared before him and offered him a heavy purse of gold in exchange for a single hair. The knight accepted, the exchange was made, and the devil vanished, promising to return whenever the knight summoned him, and to furnish an equal sum of pure gold for every hair which he was allowed to pluck from Ferdinand's head.

The sum thus furnished by Satan was quite sufficient for the knight's present needs, so he spent it gayly. When it was exhausted he pronounced the formula taught him, and in exchange for another hair received another bagful of gold. Little by little, however, the knight grew more reckless, the devil's visits more frequent, and the knight's head soon became so very bald that it attracted much playful attention on the part of his friends.

Finally, after a long, dissipated life, the knight fell dangerously ill, and unwilling to bear the pain he suffered he would fain have committed suicide, but had no strength left to go in search of his sword to plunge it into his breast. While he was bemoaning his helplessness and loudly calling for someone to come and end his wretched existence, the devil suddenly appeared before him, gave him a rope fashioned entirely out of the hair plucked from his head, and told him that, forseeing the end, he had fashioned it into a noose so that he might hang himself.

When the doctors came to visit their patient on the morrow they found him dead, with a hair noose drawn tight around his neck, and an expression of fear upon his dead face, for the devil in departing had carried away his soul.

BIBERICH.

The Ghostly Interview.

NEAR the picturesque little towns of Biberich and Mosbach, which stand so close together that they form but one and the same place, is the pretty castle of the Duke of Nassau, surrounded by tasteful grounds, in which the ruins of the ancient palace of Louis, the German, can still be seen.

The legend relates that shortly after the completion of this castle the wife of the founder died. Her body was duly shrouded and laid in state in the castle hall, while fifty men of the duke's body guard marched to and fro around the castle and along the corridors, keeping watch over the mortuary chamber. They had been at their post since early morn, and the night was far advanced, when the silence was suddenly broken by the arrival of a coach. In it sat the principal lady of the bedchamber, who, closely veiled, stepped out, and gliding past the sentinels, would fain have entered the great hall where the dead duchess lay in state.

One of the sentinels challenged her, however, and it was only when she had told her name—and raising her veil had shown her pale and rigid countenance—that he allowed her to enter and close the door. As the man was not sure he had done right, however, and wondered what the principal lady of the bedchamber could still have to do with her mistress, he peeped through the keyhole. Suddenly he started back in amazement, calling for the captain, who, looking through the same aperture, beheld the dead duchess sitting up, and talking excitedly to the principal lady of the bedchamber.

Before he could utter a word, however, the duchess sank back in her former corpse-like rigidity, and the lady of the bedchamber, gliding out, remounted her chariot, and drove rapidly away. Captain and sentinel were so bewildered by what they had seen that they kept the adventure secret, but when they heard on the morrow that the principal lady of the bedchamber had died of grief on hearing of the duchess' decease, they concluded they had witnessed an interview between the dead, and told the story to silence some of their companions who asserted they did not believe in ghosts.

MAINZ.

The Golden Shoes.

Mainz, one of the oldest cities along the Rhine, is situated at the junction of the Main, and boasts of one of the oldest and finest cathedrals in Germany. The present sacred edifice, which was founded in the tenth century, has six times been a prey to the flames, and has repeatedly been desecrated by soldiers, who have used it as barracks, stable, and even as slaughter house.

The various ravages of time have been repaired as well as possible, however, and the cathedral of Mainz now stands as a monument of the various styles of architecture of bygone ages. Under its mighty roof are the tombs of Frastrada, wife of Charlemagne, and of the great Meistersinger Frauenlob. He was borne to his tomb by the ladies of the town, one of whom is represented bending over his grave, just as she stood when she died of grief at his loss.

The image of the Virgin in the cathedral is said to be a miracle-working statue. The old women of Mainz relate that a poor old musician, finding that no one would listen to his antiquated tunes, stole starving into the cathedral, and after praying fervently for aid, played an air upon his fiddle in honor of Heaven's queen.

The Virgin, touched by the old man's distress, daintily raised her jewel-incrusted robe, and deftly kicked one of her little golden slippers into the tattered hat, which the old fiddler had deposited on the pavement before her. Tremulous with gratitude at the unexpected charity, the old man fervently spoke his thanks, and hastening off to a neighboring goldsmith, tried to sell the little golden shoe to obtain bread.

The goldsmith questioned him, demurred, and finally arrested him. A few hours later the poor old man, accused of sacrilegious theft, was judged, sentenced to death, and hurried off to the place of execution, accompanied by a hooting populace. As he was dragged past the cathedral door he implored permission to say a last prayer at the Virgin's shrine, and was permitted to kneel before her, with his hat and fiddle beside him.

Tremulously the old fiddler implored Mary to open the Gates of Paradise for him, and when he had ended again played his little hymn, declaring the last music he ever made

would be in honor of the Blessed Virgin. While he was playing thus, his tearful eyes fixed upon the statue above him, the Virgin, in the presence of the assembled multitude, again lifted her robe, and deliberately kicked her second golden shoe down into the tattered hat.

This second miracle, which all had seen, convinced the people that the minstrel had been unjustly condemned, and the priest, coming forward, offered to redeem the shoes for a small pension which would give him food for the rest of his life. The fiddler accepted, and the priests, having recovered the precious shoes, carefully locked them up in the treasury, lest the Virgin should again be tempted to bestow them upon some penniless beggar who prayed for her aid.

The Street-Sweeper.

ONCE, when the French army occupied Mainz, and the country, devastated by war, was groaning under the harsh rule of the invader, the young ladies of Mainz, instigated by the beautiful young Countess of Stein, solemnly vowed that they would neither marry nor listen to a word of love from any man until their country was entirely free.

The Frenchmen, hearing of this league, and seeing that it stimulated the ardor of their foes to attack them with renewed courage, angrily resolved to make an example of the young Countess of Stein. They dragged her a prisoner into the city, publicly thrust a broom in her hand, and bade her sweep the principal street.

Instead of bursting into tears as they expected, the noble girl grasped her broom firmly, and gazing upward, prayed aloud: "God of my fatherland, bless my sweeping, and as I sweep the highway, grant that the enemy may be swept from our land." Then she set vigorously to work, sweeping very clean, and although the Frenchmen stood on either side the street, twisting their mustaches until they stood straight out like needles, and waiting to hear the people jeer, they saw nothing but uncovered heads and heard nothing but low and fervent ejaculation of: "God bless the sweeping!" Fired by the courage of the young countess the men now fought with a will, and succeeded at last in sweeping the enemy completely out of their land.

A Thief in Heaven.

AN old tenth century ballad, which has been preserved in the original words and meter, relates how a false prophet once came to Mainz, pretending he had visited both heaven and hell, and offering to teach a sure method of reaching either.

The archbishop of Mainz, afraid lest this loud-spoken man should exert an evil influence upon the credulous people, summoned him into his presence and bade him relate his visit to heaven. He added that while he could easily imagine horrors enough to stock the infernal regions, his fancy was utterly incapable of picturing the delights of the heavenly mansions. The false prophet, somewhat embarrassed at being questioned by the archbishop himself, now lamely began to tell how he had seen the Saviour and St. John, seated at a richly-spread board, eating and drinking, while Peter, with heated countenance, bent over the steaming pots and kettles in the kitchen.

The archbishop quietly remarked that he had always been told that St. Peter was heaven's porter and not heaven's cook, and abruptly inquired where the false prophet had sat to obtain such a good view of all that was going on.

"I!" exclaimed the impostor. "Why, I was in a corner, and while St. Peter was not looking I stole a bit of meat which was too delicious for words."

"Wretch!" cried the archbishop. "You were admitted

to heaven, and even there you dared indulge in your thievish propensities! Away with you, no punishment can be too severe for such a base pilferer!"

Then the archbishop gave orders that the man should be put in the stocks on the market place, near the fountain, where the people all collected to hear the herald read an account of his crime, and hooted and jeered at him until they were tired.

The Goldsmith.

HATTO, the treacherous bishop of Mainz, was very anxious indeed to get rid of Heinrich, duke of Saxony. As he preferred cunning to open warfare, he sent him a cordial invitation to come and visit him in Mainz, on a certain day, adding that he had a handsome gold chain which he wished to put around his neck with his own hands.

The duke of Saxony, suspecting no evil, accepted the invitation, and prepared to ride into Mainz on the appointed day, while the bishop sent seven marks of pure gold to the best goldsmith in town with orders to fashion them into a strong and handsome necklace. This order was duly executed, and when the messenger came to get the finished chain the goldsmith noticed with surprise that his hands were trembling, and that his eyes were dimmed with tears.

When he inquired the cause of these strange demonstrations, he learned with dismay that Hatto was planning to strangle his beloved master, under pretext of laying the chain around his neck. Instead of showing his feelings, however, the clever goldsmith said that he did not care what use the bishop made of the chain, but was only anxious to secure his pay for the work he had done.

Indignant with the man's apparent callousness, the messenger paid for the work and departed. Scarcely had he left than the goldsmith hastened out of town, and meeting

Heinrich, warned him of the treacherous reception awaiting him.

Heinrich turned to the bishop's messenger, who rode beside him, and bade him go back to his master and tell him that he had no wish to suffer Adalbert's fate, but preferred to do without the handsome golden necklace which the bishop had so kindly promised to give him. Then, while the bishop's servant returned alone to Mainz, Heinrich again withdrew into Saxony, taking with him the honest goldsmith who had so cleverly managed to warn him and had thus saved his life.

FLÖRSHEIM.

The Shepherd's Death.

In a pretty little castle which stood above the village of Flörsheim, on the banks of the Rhine, dwelt a most charming young lady, who, in spite of many noble suitors, fell in love with a poor young shepherd. He was wont to pipe his lays, gazing up admiringly at her, while he watched his sheep on the green slopes which led from the castle down to the river.

One day when the young shepherd lay under a tree sound asleep, the lady of Flörsheim, stealing softly through the bushes, bent down to gaze upon him, and in a sudden outburst of love bent over and kissed him. Her touch, however light, immediately awoke the young shepherd, who, seeing her blushing face near him, caught her in his arms and repaid her kiss by a fervent embrace.

After lingering beside him for some time the pretty lady of Flörsheim stole away, promising to visit him again some other day, and the shepherd resumed his happy day dreams and waited for her coming. On the morrow, when he was again lying under the selfsame tree, he suddenly heard a rustle in the bushes, and fancying it was his beloved, who might perchance again favor him with a kiss, he pretended to sleep. But, instead of the expected caress, he was suddenly bitten by a deadly snake, and a few moments later was cold in death. The lady of Flörsheim, stealing noiselessly through the bushes toward evening, fancied she had again caught her lover napping, but her kiss called forth no response, so she soon discovered he was dead.

In her despair she flung herself over an overhanging rock down into the river, and on the morrow, after vainly searching for her, her parents found her drowned at the foot of the rock upon which the young shepherd lay cold in death.

FALKENSTEIN.

The Gnomes' Road.

KUNO of Sayn, one of the noble family whose ruined castle still rises on one of the hills along the Rhine, once fell in love with the daughter of the surly lord of Falkenstein, and having won her consent, formally presented himself before her father to ask her hand in marriage.

He proceeded for this purpose to the castle of Falkenstein, which was perched on the heights above one of the tributaries of the Main. The youth made his proposal, which the grim old lord promised to consider, providing the suitor would subscribe to one condition. The impetuous lover immediately vowed to do so, without waiting to inquire what the condition might be. Imagine his chagrin and dismay, therefore, when the Lord of Falkenstein told him that he could wed his daughter, only if he built a convenient road from the castle to the valley, over the jagged rocks, and rode up thither on his war-steed before sunrise on the morrow.

Sadly Kuno von Sayn scrambled down the rocks again,

without having been able to catch a glimpse of the fair Irmengarde, his beloved. He sat down upon a rock in the valley and berated himself for his stupidity, for many workmen and many months of arduous labor would scarcely accomplish the task which had been appointed him. Suddenly, however, he was aroused from his abstraction by the sound of a little voice calling him by name. He looked up and beheld the king of the gnomes, who said there was no need for him to despair, as he and his subjects would gladly aid such a deserving knight. He bade Kuno hasten to the inn where he had left his steed, promising that the road would be ready before sunrise on the morrow. Then the king of the gnomes waved his hand and caused a mist to rise and shroud valley and hill with its dense vapor.

Thousands of dwarf-like creatures now crept out of the ground on all sides, and began using axes, hammers, and spades with great good will. All night long Kuno von Sayn heard the crashing of great forest trees, the breaking of stone and occasionally a long rumble like thunder. At dawn he emerged from his bedroom and was greeted by the innkeeper, who told him that, judging by the noise which had kept him awake, a terrible storm must have raged over the valley. Kuno did not pause to listen to the man's tales, but loudly called for his horse, and mounting, rode rapidly away to the foot of the eminence upon which rose the castle of Falkenstein. True to his promise, the king of the gnomes had built a broad and convenient road, and Kuno galloped boldly up, exchanging radiant smiles with the kindly dwarfs, who peered out at him from behind every rock and tree. As he thundered over the arched bridge they were just finishing, he gayly waved his hand to Irmengarde, who, blushing and happy, stood up on the castle ramparts. Then the dwarfs unanimously raised a glad shout of triumph.

The knight of Falkenstein, seeing his condition had duly been complied with, could no longer refuse his consent to his daughter's speedy marriage with Kuno von Sayn, and the first sunbeam, falling upon the castle, illuminated the golden hair and blushing cheeks of the maiden, who was joyfully clasped close to her lover's heart.

This legend has been a suggestive theme for several German poets and has also given rise to an English version, which concludes as follows:

> "And Kuno on his coal black steed
> Came riding gallantly,
> There was the finished road indeed,
> A miracle to see!
>
> "Up, up, and up he galloped gay,
> Till, at the portal grim,
> He saw the Ritter old and gray
> Come out to welcome him;
>
> "And by her white and slender hand
> He led his daughter fair:
> 'Take her,' he cried, 'you who command
> The powers of earth and air!'
>
> "And Kuno looked in her sweet eyes,
> And rapturously obeyed;
> And so he won his matchless prize,
> The snow and rose bloom maid."
>
> —*St. Nicholas Magazine.*

The Elopement.

THE castle of Falkenstein once belonged to a grim old lord, who arbitrarily decided that his only daughter must enter a convent, and with that purpose in view placed her under the exclusive care of some nuns. When her novitiate was ended, however, the priests refused to allow her to take the veil until she had, as was customary, seen the gay world and its attractions, and made her choice in an intelligent way.

Thus forced to bring his daughter home for a few weeks, the lord of Falkenstein received no visitors, and never went out, keeping her as strictly secluded as in a convent, in his fear that she should refuse to obey his wishes and take the veil. The only recreation permitted her was to walk alone in a little garden, where, unbeknown to her father, she met the young count of Helfenstein. He fell deeply in love with her at first sight, and lost no time in pressing his suit.

As soon as he discovered that his love was returned he proposed to ask her father's consent, and it was agreed between them that he should come on the next day, when her father would surely be ready to give an answer, as the young lady proposed enlightening him on the state of her wishes in the interim.

But, when the count of Helfenstein came to Falkenstein on the morrow, father and daughter had both gone, and the servants reported that their master was in a terrible rage when he gave the orders to prepare everything for his daughter's immediate return to the convent.

The disconsolate lover now set out for the convent too, and knowing he would be refused admittance, lingered outside the walls till midnight. Then, seeing only one light burning, he uttered the low, familiar whistle which had been wont to warn his beloved of his approach.

A moment later a fair form appeared at the convent casement, and rapidly signing to him to keep silence, intoned a church hymn, using the familiar air to convey this information to her lover:

"The convent wall is broken near the shore,
Climb quickly over there, my loving knight;
In the convent wall is an iron door,
Break through its bars with giant's might."

The lover, listening breathlessly to every word, signaled that he had understood as soon as she had finished, and carried out her directions so faithfully, that in a few minutes he clasped her in his arms. Together now they made their escape, but scarcely had they reached the other side of the wall when the lady's flight was discovered. The convent alarm bell pealed through the quiet night, and the sounds of close pursuit were heard. The count of Helfenstein, clasping his beloved closely, ran wildly along the banks of the Rhine, and was about to drop down exhausted when he saw a skiff moored to a tree. To place his treasure in the stern, cleave the rope with one blow of his sword, seize the oars, and propel the skiff out into the middle of the stream, was the work of but a moment. Favored by the darkness and the rapid current the young people evaded their pursuers, and safely reached the castle of Helfenstein, where they were married and lived happy ever after:

> "Rowed her o'er the rapid Rhine
> To his castle Helfenstein,
> Where, in wedlock's holy glow,
> Lived and loved they long ago."

FRANKFORT.

The Crossing of the Ford.

FRANKFORT-ON-THE-MAIN, the birthplace of Goethe, and the town where the coronation of many of the German emperors was celebrated with much pomp, is also noted for its ancient legends, to one of which it owes its name. Charlemagne, having penetrated far into the Teutonic forests to wage war against the Saxons, was once defeated and forced to beat a hasty retreat with his brave Franks.

The country was unknown to him, a heavy fog rested all over the land, and the fugitive army, coming to the banks of the Main, saw no means of escape. Knowing that his small force would soon be cut to pieces if he lingered here, yet not daring to attempt to ford the stream when he could scarcely see a few feet ahead of him, Charlemagne in despair had recourse to prayer.

A second later the heavy fog bank parted, and the emperor saw a doe fording the river, followed by her young. He called to his men to keep close beside him, took the same road, and brought his army safely over. The fog bank closed behind them and completely concealed them from the pursuing Saxons, who declared that if the Franks had attempted to pass, they must have perished in the waters of the Main.

In commemoration of his deliverance from the hand of the enemy, Charlemagne called the place where he had crossed Frankfort (the ford of the Franks), which name is borne by the city erected shortly after on the spot where the fugitive army passed over the Main.

The Devil and the Rooster.

THE beautiful red sand-stone bridge which spans the Main at Frankfort, and on which stands a fine statue of Charlemagne, was built in 1342. Previous to that date many architects had attempted to build a bridge there, but the winter ice and spring freshets invariably carried away their pillars. This prevented the completion of the work, and all would-be builders had given up the attempt with a muttered "Devil take the bridge."

Finally an architect, more worldly wise than his predecessors, fancied that the devil had probably taken them at their word. So he called upon his Satanic Majesty and asked his permission to begin the bridge, and bespoke his help in finishing it. Satan, well pleased at this request, gave full permission and promised his aid, upon condition that the first living creature which crossed it on the day it was opened to the public would be delivered up to his tender mercies.

Mentally resolving not to cross the bridge first on the

opening day, the architect subscribed to the devil's conditions. He immediately began the construction, which progressed favorably, and in due time was brought to a successful conclusion.

All the town magistrates then assembled to open the bridge, while the people of Frankfort, in gala attire, formed a long procession behind them. When he reached the head of the bridge the master of ceremonies paused, and called the architect, who was walking modestly in the rear. With a graceful gesture he then bade him pass first and open the march, as was his due.

Pale and stammering, the architect refused the honor, urging that he could not think of preceding the master of ceremonies, who, curled, perfumed, and as pompous as a drum major, really considered the honor belonged to him. He was about to ride forward, therefore, and be the first upon the bridge, when an old market woman, who had a live chicken in her basket, suddenly held up her hands in admiration at his fine appearance. The basket lid, no longer held down, opened with a bang, and a distracted rooster flew out with a squawk almost directly under the feet of the prancing steed. The fowl, as chickens will, instead of retreating to either side of the road began zigzagging wildly in front of the horse, and then fluttered upon the bridge, still uttering a frightened cackle. Suddenly, however, it disappeared, and the people standing near declared they saw a claw-like hand clutch it, heard some angry imprecations, and caught the fumes of an almost intolerable stench.

When the architect heard this report he frankly confessed the bargain he had made with the fiend, and the people were beside themselves with joy when they heard how nicely an old rooster had cheated the devil. As a memento of this occurrence they placed the golden effigy of a rooster upon the bridge, and they declare this miraculous bird crows loudly whenever he *sees* a Jew cross the bridge.

It is said, however, that either the numerous Jews who live at Frankfort avoid the bridge from fear of hearing the denouncing crow, or that the cock's eyesight must have failed him, for it is many a year since he has flapped his wings and uttered his shrill cry.

The Great Fire.

On the fourteenth of January, 1711, the whole quarter of the Jews in Frankfort was reduced to ashes. This memorable conflagration is ascribed to the magic of an old rabbi, who, under the pretext of showing his disciples the power of the cabala, banished the spirits of water and damp, and conjured up the spirits of fire and heat.

As often happens, however, the spirits he had called upon came suddenly and with a vengeance, setting fire to his house and garments, singeing his hair and beard. This frightened him so sorely that he entirely forgot the required cabalistic formula to recall the spirits of water and damp, and restrain the destructive energy of the heat and fire. The flames, spreading rapidly from house to house, soon invaded all the Jewish quarter. They would surely have consumed the Christian dwellings also, had it not been for the presence of mind of a priest. He suspected that there was magic at work, and called upon the fire to pause in the name of the Father, Son, and Holy Ghost, praying that water and damp might prevail over the fiendish flames. At his appeal the roaring flames paused in their advance, and not a single Christian dwelling was injured, while the Jews lost houses and all in the flames, and nothing but ashes remained in the part of the town which had been set aside for their use.

The Executioner Ennobled.

A GRAND masked ball was once given in the town hall of Frankfort, in honor of the king and queen, who, also disguised, mingled with their guests. Her Majesty even accepted partners in the dance, and twice trod a measure with a tall, distinguished-looking man, whose reserved but courtly manners greatly pleased her.

As none of her eager questions had elicited any answer which could enable her to discover who he might be, she resolved to watch him when he unmasked, and even gave the signal for it by removing her own disguise a whole hour earlier than usual. All the guests immediately imitated her with the exception of the stranger. Only when compelled to do so by the queen's explicit command, he tore the mask away from his face, and falling down upon his knees before her craved her pardon for having presumed to ask her to dance.

The queen, gazing down upon a beautiful and melancholy, but unknown, face, was about to ask who he was, when the people suddenly shrank back with a shudder, exclaiming: "The executioner of Bergen!"

"Yes," replied the stranger sorrowfully, "I am the executioner of Bergen, and because I do the king's will I am shunned and scorned by all. All flee from me and loath me as if I were not of their own kind. The longing to mingle with my fellow creatures once more as an equal drove me hither."

The king, hearing these words, was so indignant that he called for his guards, and angrily bade them lead the knave away, and behead him with his own axe in punishment for his audacity.

Before this order could be executed, however, the man exclaimed that even were he slain the queen would none the less have danced with the vilest of the commoners. Anyone could taunt her with that fact, and even blood would never efface the stain. With a groan the king acknowledged that this was true. Then the executioner declared himself ready to defend her against any man, and vowed he would even fight the greatest nobleman were he but a knight. So the king concluded to ennoble him, and seizing his sword gave him the wonted accolate and bade him rise, calling him the Knave of Bergen. The queen then bade her champion hold himself ready to defend her honor at any time, and do battle for her, and the executioner was thus respited from death and admitted among the nobility of the land.

The Weather Vane.

ONE of the weather vanes in Frankfort bears a number nine, neatly pricked on its surface by nine holes. The legend relates that a poacher, having been caught and imprisoned in the tower during nine weary days and nights, complained sorely of the creaking of this vane, which, he declared, had prevented him from finding a moment's oblivion in sleep.

"Were I only free," said he, "I would show the good people of Frankfort how accurately I can aim, by shooting as many holes in that accursed old weather vane as I have spent nights in this tower, and what is more, those nine holes would form the number nine."

The jailor reported this speech to the city councilors, who, anxious to see such a proof of skill, declared the poacher should be allowed to try and fulfill his vain boast. They added that if he succeeded in touching the vane nine times, and formed a number nine with the holes, they would set him free.

The poacher, brought before them, loaded his gun, aimed at the mobile vane, and shooting, punched a hole in it.

Nine times he shot, and each hole, round and near its fellow, helped to form the well-shaped number nine, which won him his freedom. Leaving the city, the poacher then swore he would never again return to town, where such creaking engines as weather vanes prevented a man from sleeping. Since that day, however, the weather vane has borne the number nine, and the people often point it out as a proof of his good marksmanship.

HANAU.

The Death of the Innocent.

AN executioner's cart was slowly wending its way through the crowded streets of Hanau. As it rumbled over the stones it drew many groans from the woman who sat within, bound hand and foot, and exposed to the jeers and insults of the assembled populace. She had been tried and duly sentenced to death for some heinous crime, although she had persistently asserted her innocence.

She gazed at her tormentors, who were hurrying her ruthlessly on to the gallows, raised her bound hands to heaven, and once more solemnly declared that she had committed no sin. "Heaven itself and the angels will have compassion upon me," she cried. "See, they shed tears for me."

As she spoke, in spite of the cloudless blue sky above great drops of rain suddenly began to fall. But, notwithstanding this evident miracle, the people hurried the poor woman on and put her to death.

A few weeks later the real criminal was discovered, judged, and executed, and the mobile populace execrated him loudly, bewailing the untimely fate of the poor woman who, in spite of the miracle worked in her behalf, had been the innocent victim of their cruelty and injustice.

DARMSTADT.

The Virgin's Victory.

WALTHER VON BIRBACH, a brave knight-errant, had vowed to serve the Virgin Mary only. In her honor he went about from place to place, challenging every knight, and forcing them all to recognize the supremacy of the Lady he served and to bend the knee at her name.

When he heard that a great tournament was about to take place at Darmstadt, he wended his way thither. On the road he encountered a beautiful woman, in whom he immediately recognized his holy patroness. She bade him dismount and give her his weapons and steed, which she promptly appropriated. A moment later, arrayed in his armor, the Virgin galloped away, and Walther of Birbach, bewildered by this sudden apparition, sat down by the roadside to collect his thoughts.

He had not entirely succeeded in doing so, however, ere the Virgin returned, gave him back his horse and armor, and bade him ride on. When he arrived in Darmstadt he learned that the tournament was over, and that all the honors of the day had been won by the Knight of Birbach. A few moments later he was surrounded by the enthusiastic multitude, who, recognizing the coat of arms on his shield, received him with loud applause.

A number of knights forced their way through the crowd and humbly proffered ransom, declaring he had conquered them in fair fight, and that they were ready to do him homage. Realizing then that his fair patroness had assumed his armor only to tilt in his behalf, and win a signal victory for him, Walther of Birbach humbly exclaimed:

"Do homage to Mary, the blessed Virgin, for it is owing to her that you have been disarmed. Lay your ransom before her shrine, serve her as long as you live, and be ready at all times to recognize her as the most blessed among women."

The knights obeyed these injunctions, and it is said that the Virgin never had more faithful servants than the knights she once disarmed in the Darmstadt tournament.

AUERBACH.

The Bewitched Lady.

THE ruined castle of Auerbach, from whence a beautiful view can be obtained, is said to be haunted by the spirit of a lovely maiden, upon whom a magician once laid a terrible spell. By mystic incantations he made her invisible to all, and declared that she would haunt the ruins until the castle was visited by a youth, rocked in infancy in a cradle made of the wood of a cherry tree beneath whose shade she had been wont to linger.

The magician had found her beneath this tree, and had spirited her away, declaring she would remain invisible to all until her deliverer came. He could release her from the spell only by pressing a kiss upon her lips, and would then become possessor of a large fortune and of a bride whom all his companions would envy him.

The deliverer has not yet come, however, and the maiden's restless spirit is still said to await him in the romantic ruins of Auerbach castle.

WORMS.

The Hoard of Gold.

THE city of Worms, so frequently mentioned in the legendary poems of the North, is the scene of Siegfried's wooing of Kriemhild, who here cultivated her beautiful roses, mourned for her husband, and lost the precious

Nibelungen hoard, which her uncle Hagen sank in the waters of the Rhine.

This treasure has often and vainly been sought. A poet once came to the Rhine, and hiring a skiff, plied around for many a day, reading over the poem to discover a clew to the exact spot where the hoard was sunk, and refreshing himself from time to time with draughts of delicious Rhine wine.

After many a day he relinquished his search, for he now felt convinced that the gold had melted in the Rhine, that the wines had absorbed its golden color, and that the only priceless treasure now remaining was the ancient epic poem, which has inspired many a modern bard.

The cathedral of Worms, one of the oldest along the mighty river, is richly decorated on the southern side by fourteenth century statues, representing the various characters of the Nibelungenlied, which is daily more admired by lovers of ancient literature.

As Worms was at times the residence of the emperor, many great tournaments have been held within its walls, and it was here that the Diet assembled before which Luther was forced to appear. In commemoration of the visit of the great reformer a Luther monument has recently been erected on the square bearing his name, where he stands aloft, Bible in hand, while Huss, Savonarola, Wyclif and Waldus, Philip of Hesse, Frederick of Saxony, Melanchthon and Reuchlin, his predecessors and supporters, are grouped at his feet.

The Unknown Knight.

ONCE when Maximilian was holding a great tournament at Worms, a gigantic French knight rode through the town challenging any man to come forth and fight him, and proposing that the conquered should serve the conqueror all the rest of his life.

WORMS CATHEDRAL.

Owing to the stranger's gigantic stature, and especially to this singular condition, none of the knights assembled at Worms dared accept his challenge. It was only on the tenth day that an unknown knight, with blank shield and lowered vizor, offered to meet him in the lists.

The people, assembled to view the jousting, were very glad indeed to think that a champion had at last appeared to pick up the Frenchman's gage, but owing to his much slighter build feared lest he should not prove very successful in fight. At the very first onslaught both combatants were dismounted, but manfully continued the battle on foot, and, thanks to his dexterity, the unknown finally disarmed the boastful Frenchman.

The assembled people cheered their champion uproariously, and insisted upon his revealing his name and station, that they might remember him forever. Slowly the stranger then removed his plumed helmet, and revealed to all the well-known and beloved features of the Emperor Maximilian, who declared he had been forced to defend the national honor, and that he claimed the Frenchman's loyal service for the rest of his life.

The Greatest Wealth.

THE Emperor Maximilian once sat over his wine at Worms on the Rhine, gayly challenging the nobles, his guests, to reveal the source of their wealth, promising a prize to the one who proved that he had the most inexhaustible supply on hand.

The elector of the Rhine, speaking first, declared he prided himself most upon his sunny vineyards, which, year after year, produced many a barrel of priceless wine.

The Prince of Saxony declared the ores from his mines were his greatest treasures, and described how the miners daily brought them out of the bowel of the earth, where they lay in immeasurable stores.

Then the ruler of Bavaria proudly extolled the beauty of his palaces and art collections, which contained the choicest gems of ancient painting and sculpture.

One after another vaunted his wealth, and when all but the prince of Würtemberg had spoken, the emperor suddenly turned to him and inquired of what he was most proud.

"Of my people's affection, most gracious majesty, for well I know they would give me their houses, children, and even their own lives, should I require such a sacrifice at their hands."

Touched by this reply, the emperor sprang to his feet and exclaimed: "Eberhart, the prize is yours, for there is certainly nothing more precious to a ruler than the genuine love and devotion of his subjects."

RODENSTEIN.

The Raging Host.

THE ruined castle of Rodenstein, which is one of the reputed haunts of the traditional Wild Huntsman, is surrounded by wild forests, and stands in the midst of grim mountains. This castle was once inhabited by a knight of Rodenstein who declared himself the champion of the German fatherland, swore to fight for it against any foe, and vowed to love it forever.

To serve his country more entirely, this knight refused to marry, so no one mourned him greatly when he vanished from the castle one day and did not reappear. The peasantry, however, aver that he did not die in war, as was commonly reported, but withdrew into the vaults of his castle, whence he issues when any special danger threatens his beloved fatherland. In corroboration of this belief, they

WORMS.
Cathedral Choir.

declare that whenever a war has broken out, the tramp of mailed steeds is heard in the ruins, and that at nightfall a shadowy army, led by the lord of Rodenstein, sweeps across the sky in the direction where the danger is greatest. Just before peace is proclaimed the shadowy host returns to Rodenstein, and re-enters the castle with a glad song of triumph, to linger there unheard and unseen until its services are again required to free the beloved fatherland from a hated yoke.

Some German writers further declare that Frederick Barbarossa is slumbering in the castle vaults. He awakens from time to time to hold grand underground receptions, at which the gnomes and dead knights appear. Here he has amassed great treasures for future use, for like Arthur the people expect he will return to rule over his kingdom once more and raise it to higher glory.*

OGGERSHEIM.

The Deserted City.

THE little town of Oggersheim, besieged by the Spaniards during the Thirty Years' War, held out bravely as long as provisions lasted. But when the inhabitants saw they must either surrender to the enemy, whom they had incensed by their resistance, or perish of hunger, they were sorely dismayed.

One of the oldest councilors offered to save them, and revealed the existence of a secret passage which would enable them to escape in the enemy's rear. He now proposed to lead them all out during the night and to leave the enemy the doubtful glory of taking a deserted city. This plan was hailed with enthusiasm, and all the people left the town by the secret passage, one man only remaining to care for his wife and child, the latter being but a few hours old.

* See "Legends of the Middle Ages," in press.

The Spaniards hearing no noise on the morrow, and seeing no sentinels on the ramparts, fancied the inhabitants were planning a sortie, but after waiting three whole days for an attack they were surprised to see a man appear upon the ramparts with a flag of truce. He promised to open the gates, providing the inhabitants were allowed to escape with their lives. The condition was accepted, the gates opened, and the Spanish army, riding in, was surprised to find streets and houses deserted.

"Where are the inhabitants," demanded the general of the man who had opened the gate.

"Here," he simply replied, pointing to his wife and babe, and then he recounted how the people of Oggersheim had escaped, and how he had remained alone with his wife, who was only now fit to travel. The Spanish general was so surprised at the unexpected termination of the siege that he forbade his men to pillage or destroy the city, and when the inhabitants returned shortly after, they found all their possessions quite unharmed and their houses undisturbed.

HEIDELBERG.

Legends of the Castle.

THE castle of Heidelberg was founded by Count Otto of Wittelsbach, who moved thither from his ancestral seat of Stahleck near Bacharach on the Rhine. The castle, perched up on the wooded heights near the junction of the Neckar and Rhine, soon became the central point of the lands of the elector of the Rhine, and it was only in 1802 that it was incorporated into the State of Baden.

From the river, through the picturesque little town of the same name, the road winds upward to the great castle, whose beautiful site and fabled ruins are the admiration of all travelers. They are attracted thither also by the well-known

University, which, founded in 1386, has since been frequented by students from all parts of the world. This university was the bulwark of Protestantism during the wars of religion, and in its library are preserved many curious and interesting manuscripts in Luther's own handwriting. The castle itself has been so often besieged, that, in spite of much repairing, many parts of the building are in ruins. Still the whole construction is one of remarkable beauty and of peculiar interest, as its various component parts are of different styles of architecture, and were added according to the whim or taste of the princes by whose order they were erected.

The castle suffered particularly during the wars of Louis XIV., as did most of the feudal strongholds along the Rhine, and it was set on fire by order of the French general when he evacuated Heidelberg in 1689. Rebuilt in 1742, the castle was again burned, this fire being caused by a thunderbolt. Since then many parts have remained in ruins, which, half covered with ivy, are picturesque in the extreme.

The beautiful gate of the castle was erected by the elector Frederick V. in honor of his wife Elizabeth, daughter of James I. of England, and in another part of the edifice can be seen two columns which once formed part of Charlemagne's famous palace at Ingelheim.

Frederick, surnamed the Victorious, one of the owners of this mighty pile, was once attacked by the allied knights and bishops of the Rhine. Undaunted by the superior number of his foes, he made a bold sally with his men. They were all armed with sharp daggers instead of the usual weapons, and first attacked the horses instead of the riders. Thus brought to the ground, the knights, unable to move in their ponderous armor, were soon made prisoners and marched into the castle, where Frederick invited them all to partake of a sumptuous banquet.

As he sat at the richly spread board with his enemies, Frederick served them bountifully. There was meat and wine in abundance, but the guests gazed at each other in surprise, for there was no bread. This strange omission on the bill of fare was not an oversight, however, for when one of the guests ventured to ask for a piece of bread, the elector, turning to the steward, bade him bring some. The man, who had received private instructions, respectfully informed his master that he was very sorry but that there was none.

"Go and bake some!" commanded Frederick.

"Master, I can't. We have no flour."

"Have some ground."

"Master, I can't. We have no grain."

"Have some thrashed."

"Master, I can't. The harvests have all been burned."

"Then, go and sow grain that we may soon have bread in plenty."

"Master, I can't, for the enemy have also burned down all the peasants' barns and dwellings with the grain set aside for seed time."

Frederick then dryly remarked as he turned to his guests: "Gentlemen, you'll have to eat your meat without bread. Moreover, you must give me the necessary funds to rebuild the houses and barns you have burned down, and to buy the seed for sowing. Henceforth, I advise you to remember that it is not right to make war against the poor and defenseless, and to rob the peasant of his tools and seed, his only means of subsistence. If you do so, you will invariably find, as to-day, that you too must suffer some discomfort in return for all the harm you have done."

This selfsame count of Heidelberg once made a rash vow that he would never marry a noblewoman, yet soon after he fell deeply in love with Princess Elizabeth. She returned his affection, and would gladly have become his wife, had he not felt that he could not ask for her hand in marriage owing to his foolish oath. Frederick felt so miserable to think he had thus forfeited his own happiness,

ELIZABETH GATE.

Heidelberg Castle.

and that of his beloved, that he joined the army, hoping soon to find an honorable death.

Elizabeth, discovering shortly after that nothing but her rank and his unfortunate vow prevented their being happy, left her princely home and title, and under the common name of Clara, and in the garb of a strolling singer, courageously followed him. They met face to face one beautiful evening when Frederick was wandering disconsolately about, and the princess told her lover, in answer to his eager inquiries, how she had renounced name and rank for his sake.

The nominal barrier thus broken down between them, the count was not slow in wooing the beautiful bride who had forsaken home and station for him, and soon conducted her to the castle of Heidelberg, where they lived together for many years the happiest couple along all the Rhine.

The Dwarf and the Tun.

THE dwarf Perkeo, who was once court-fool of the count of Heidelberg, was, although so tiny of stature, a veritable giant as far as drinking was concerned. All the castle and his master's wealth seemed as nothing to him compared with the mighty Heidelberg tun, which he admired beyond measure. He was so in love with this wine-barrel that he finally refused to leave the vault where it was kept, and spent all his time beside it, drawing beaker after beaker of wine, and gazing upon it with anxious eyes.

During fifteen years he sat beside the tun, turning the faucet, emptying his cup, and jealously guarding the wine which he alone was entitled to drink. To his surprise and dismay, however, he finally discovered that there was not a drop of wine left within its mighty, bulging sides. When he realized that he, the dwarf Perkeo, had drained such an immense caskful of wine, he proudly compared himself to David, and declared that he too had conquered a Goliath.

Then, feeling that life was no longer worth living now that the tun was empty, he lay down beside it and quietly passed away, requesting that he might be buried directly under the faucet he had so diligently turned, and that a statue representing him might be placed where he was wont to sit.

These recommendations were duly observed, and the traveler visiting the Heidelberg tun, which has stood empty for many a year, will see Perkeo's statue very near it, on the spot which he occupied during his fifteen years carousal.

KAISERSLAUTERN.

Barbarossa's Sleep.

On the spot where the prison now stands, at Kaiserslautern, the emperor Frederick Barbarossa once erected a palace, which was destroyed during the war of the Spanish succession. While history reports that this popular ruler perished in the waves of a swollen torrent on his way to Palestine, tradition declares that the emperor is not dead, but fast asleep in the vaults of the old palace at Kaiserslautern, patiently awaiting the time when his country will have need of him.

According to the other versions of this same tradition, Barbarossa is sleeping under the Kyffhäuser mountain, or in the castle of Rodenstein; all, however, agree in declaring that he sits motionless in front of a marble table, through which his fiery red beard has grown nearly to the floor, or around which it has coiled itself nearly three times.

The emperor's enchanted slumbers are broken only every hundred years, when he bids the page beside him go up on

FREDERICK I., Barbarossa. *Hader.*

the mountain and see whether the ravens are still circling overhead.

"O dwarf, go up this hour
And see if still the ravens
Are flying round the tower.
And if the ancient ravens
Still wheel above me here,
Then must I sleep enchanted
For many a hundred year."

—*Rückert. Translated by Taylor.*

The page obeys, and returning, reports that the ravens are still flying, and his master, sighing because the auspicious time has not yet come, sinks back into a slumber which lasts another century. When the fiery beard has completed its third circle round the marble table, however, the ravens will have ceased to flutter round the ruins, the battle trumpet will sound, and the emperor will rise from his enchanted sleep, and hang his shield on a withered pear tree, which will blossom at his touch, while the Germans rally once more around him to free their country from oppression.

"In some dark day when Germany
Hath need of warriors such as he,
A voice to tell of her distress
Shall pierce the mountain's deep recess—
Shall ring through the dim vaults, and scare
The spectral ravens round his chair,
And from his trance the sleeper wake.
The solid mountain shall dispart,
The granite slab in splinters start
(Responsive to those accents weird)
And loose the Kaiser's shaggy beard.
Through all the startled air shall rise
The old Teutonic battle cries ;
The horns of war, that once could stir
The wild blood of the Berserker,
Shall fling their blare abroad, and then
The champion of his own Almain,
Shall Barbarossa come again !"

—*Appleton's Magazine, November* 4, 1871.

The legends of Kaiserslautern further relate that the emperor's servants are constantly heaping up treasures and weapons in the vaults of the castle, where these vast stores for future use have been seen by peasants fortunate enough to pluck the mystic herb, which alone acts as "Open Sesame."

But the man who has once visited the spot is never allowed to enter it again, and vainly seeks an entrance to those underground regions, where he would fain gaze again upon the majestic sleeping figure in martial array with its long red gold beard.

SPEYER.

The Battle of Leipsic.

In 1813, when Napoleon was concentrating all his forces at Leipsic to overwhelm the allied armies, the town of Spires or Speyer was almost deserted for none but women, children, and old men were left. The ferryman, weary of his labors, for he had conveyed many passengers across during the past few days, was nodding over his oars, when he was suddenly roused by a loud call from the other side of the river, where the city lay.

In the dim starlight he quickly rowed across, and as he touched the landing, a tall shadowy form, closely enveloped in a military cloak, silently entered the skiff. This person was immediately joined by a number of others, who, emerging from the cathedral shadows, came rapidly and noiselessly down the street.

When the last passenger had embarked and taken his place in silence, the ferryman pushed his boat from the shore, but before he could bend to his oars he noticed that it was speeding forward without aid, as if propelled by invisible hands.

Not a word was spoken, and the poor ferryman shivered

with fear when the tall figures silently stepped ashore as soon as they reached the opposite landing place, and vanished one by one in the gloom beyond. Under the great cloaks he had caught a glitter of armor and gold lace, and saw murderous-looking weapons gleam. The passenger who first entered the vessel left it last, and, pausing a moment, bade the ferryman watch for their return, when they would pay him double fare.

Three whole days passed by, and in spite of the anxious lookout of the ferryman, no trace of the mysterious passengers was seen. The man was just beginning to wonder whether he had been the victim of a hoax or of a hallucination, when at midnight on the third day, while he was fastening his boat to the landing at Spires, he suddenly heard a loud halloo from the opposite shore. Rowing rapidly across, he soon descried the same stalwart figures, which again crossed in silence and vanished in the cathedral shadow, each dropping a coin in his outstretched palm as they stepped out of the ferry.

The boatman, who knew everyone in town, wondered more than ever who these passengers might be, and when morning dawned gazed with wonder upon the coins he had received, for, instead of the usual penny, the mysterious travelers had given him golden coins, each bearing a different effigy and date.

The priest to whom he showed this gold, after examining it carefully, declared that the effigies were those of the emperors buried in the cathedral of Spires, and silently wondered why they had left their tombs.

On the morrow he heard of the terrible three days' battle at Leipsic, and of the defeat of the French. He saw their routed army wildly beating a retreat across the Rhine, and then he knew that the old legends were true, and that the German emperors had risen from the tomb, and had gone forth to battle to deliver the beloved fatherland when it was in imminent danger.

The Two Bells.

THE city of Speyer, which was founded by the Romans, was very important indeed in early historical times in Germany, and was often selected as capital by the rulers of the land. In this city were once two bells, which were never rung by human hands, but were said to toll of their own accord. One, made of pure silver, was called the emperor's bell, for it softly tolled when an imperial soul was called away; the other, of iron, was the sinner's bell, and rang whenever a notoriously wicked person breathed his last.

On one occasion, a poor old man lay dying on the damp straw in a hovel at Spires, and as his spirit passed away, the emperor's bell began to ring a mournful knell. The people all rushed out in surprise, for Henry V. was perfectly well, and they loudly wondered how the generally discriminating bell could make such a mistake, when they heard that it was only a poor old beggar who had just died.

That selfsame night, however, in spite of the sentinel watching at the palace gate, the angel of death stole in and called the emperor away. Henry V., who recognized no superior on earth and only followed his own sweet will, was forced to obey the summons. And, as his soul reluctantly went forth to meet his Maker, the sinner's bell began to toll, and the people, turning over sleepily in their beds, declared it was evident some very wicked person had passed away. When they discovered the true state of affairs on the morrow, they crossed themselves in awe, and whispered that "The last shall be first and the first last." Then they added that the bells had proved to all that a virtuous death amid poverty was more worthy of honor than the death of an unrepentant sinner at court, and that the souls of the good were imperial in God's sight.

PHILIPPSBURG.

The Raw Recruit.

A RAW recruit was once stationed upon the walls of Philippsburg, which was then besieged by the French, and told to mount guard there, an unimportant point being assigned him, as the captain fancied he was none too quick-witted.

The Frenchmen, however, who were weary of the siege, had just decided to attempt a midnight surprise, and selecting this point as the most likely to further their enterprise, they noiselessly brought their scaling ladder and placed it against the wall. Nimble as a cat, a Frenchman climbed up the ladder, reached the top, and peered over the wall just as the sentinel reached that point, which was at the end of the place he had been told to guard.

The raw recruit calmly raised his bayonet and thrust the Frenchman back so suddenly that he lost his balance and fell over, but without uttering a single cry. The sentinel resumed his walk as if no interruption had occurred, but when he came back to this spot, he again saw a black, pointed mustache appear above the wall.

"Ah," thought the raw recruit, "you want a second dose, do you?" and he again thrust back the foe, and resumed his walk. Twelve times in succession the same pale face, with beady black eyes and pointed mustache, peered over the wall, and twelve times the raw recruit thrust it back, ere the captain came on his usual rounds, and, for form's sake, carelessly inquired whether the sentinel had anything to report.

"No, captain," answered the man, "nothing, except that a black-mustached Frenchman tried to climb over the wall, and I had to run my bayonet through him and push him over twelve times before he would stop."

The captain first gazed at the sentinel in surprise, and then contemptuously bade him point out the exact spot in the wall over which the black mustache had appeared. As he glanced carelessly over the wall, he suddenly started back in amazement, for at the foot of a great scaling ladder, which the assaulting party had left there in their panic-stricken flight, he saw twelve black-mustached Frenchmen, their pale faces turned upward and a bright red spot in their coats.

The captain reported the whole affair to the general, and concluded by inquiring what reward should be given, for, while the man only claimed that he had slain one enemy, twelve dead men lay in the trench.

"Oh," cried the general, "give him twelve times the amount promised for the death of one enemy, and Heaven grant that I may have plenty more such raw recruits!"

KARLSRUHE.

The Count's Vision.

Count Karl, hunting alone in the forest one day, once came to a delightful spot near the edge of the great Black Forest, about one league from the Rhine, from whence he could obtain a wonderful view. He flung himself down upon the grass to rest, listened to the song of the birds, the hum of the insects, and finally fancied that he heard an angel voice bidding him admire the beauty of the scene and compare its peaceful quiet with the restless bustle of his court.

Seated on the soft green sward, Count Karl lent an attentive ear to that admonishing voice, and when in conclusion it bade him build a dwelling there, that he might occasionally forget the cares of state and renew his youth by gazing upon the imperishable beauty of nature, he solemnly vowed to obey.

When the gathering shades of night finally roused him

from his peaceful day dreams, he rose and wended his way back to the haunts of men, but soon gave orders for the construction of a beautiful little hunting lodge, to which he gave the suggestive name of Karlsruhe, or Karl's resting place.

In the course of time this hunting lodge was transformed into a palace, the primeval forest became a park, and many broad alleys, branching out like the sticks of a fan from the palace, have been lined with the fine houses which now form the town of Karlsruhe.

BRETTEN.

The Tailless Dog.

OVER the city gate of the little town of Bretten is the image of a tailless dog, with a crown above its head. This effigy was placed there in honor of a dog belonging to a cruel and hard-hearted man in the city, who had trained the intelligent animal to do a good part of his work.

After a watchful night the poor dog of Bretten was daily dispatched on various errands, and had to go to the butcher's and baker's, carrying a basket containing a slip of paper on which his master had written his orders. After waiting patiently for the butcher's and baker's good pleasure, the faithful creature wended its way home, carrying the heavy basket, receiving only the most scanty meals and many a blow in return for its manifold services.

This master was also an atheist, and wishing to show his contempt for the church he sent the dog to the butcher's on a solemn fast day, with an order for several pounds of nice fresh sausages. Of course the poor dog carried the message, but the butcher, who was a good Catholic, was so angry at the man's sacrilegious conduct that to punish him he chopped off the poor dog's tail, flung it in the basket, and bade him carry it home.

The poor animal, after uttering a few pitiful howls, took up his burden and returned home, leaving a bloody trail behind him. Arrived in his master's presence he laid the basket at his feet as usual, then, weakened by loss of blood, he fell down beside it, dead. The people of Bretten, touched by the dog's fidelity, placed his effigy over their gateway, with the martyr's crown above it, and thus the dog, like many a hero, received the honors due him only after death.

ALT-EBERSTEIN.

The Court Ball.

THE castle of Alt-Eberstein, from which a magnificent view can be obtained, not only of the Rhine but also of the Vosges and the Black Forest, belonged for many years to the family whose name it still bears.

It seems that one of the castle owners once fell deeply in love with the daughter of the emperor Otto I., and, although he and his imperial master were not on the best of terms, he was invited to be present at one of the court balls at Spires. As he hoped to tread a measure with his beloved, Eberstein hastened joyfully thither, and was warmly welcomed by the princess. She, having overheard her father give orders to surprise the castle of Eberstein and take its lord prisoner on his return from the ball, was very anxious indeed to warn her lover of the threatening danger. While they were dancing together, she managed to whisper ere the waltz was ended: "Love, take care; your castle is to be surprised and you will be made prisoner."

For a moment Eberstein gazed at her in amazement, then, suddenly understanding the warning, he made his way unseen out of the ballroom, vaulted upon his horse, reached home before the attacking party, and cleverly disposing an ambush, he made them all prisoners without any bloodshed. Early the next morning Otto rode into Eberstein castle, which he expected to find occupied by his own men, and found himself face to face with its owner! Whether the latter made use of this opportunity to force the emperor to grant his consent to his suit, or whether Otto, admiring his courage, consented to the marriage of his own free will, remains to this day a matter of conjecture.

What is certain, however, is that a merry wedding took place shortly after, and that as Lord Eberstein danced with his bride he softly whispered: "Love, take care; you will be made prisoner!" The princess, in spite of this warning, made no attempt to escape, but blushing rosy red, declared she felt no fear of a jailor whose only bonds were love.

NEU-EBERSTEIN.

The Count's Leap.

The castle of Neu-Eberstein, which towers above the Murg, a tributary of the Rhine, was once closely surrounded by the Würtemburgers, who, in anger, had solemnly vowed to remain there until they had starved Wolf von Eberstein to death. Aware that nothing would induce them to rescind this vow, and anxious to save his garrison from slow death by famine and to effect his escape, the daring lord of Eberstein mounted his favorite steed, and galloping wildly along the ramparts suddenly made it leap down into the swollen river below.

The enemy, who had viewed this rash leap, rushed to the steep banks of the river, and saw master and steed rise safely, breast the tide, and vanish in the forest on the opposite side. The prisoner having flown, the Würtemburgers raised the siege, but the account of this prowess reaching the emperor, so excited his admiration that he pardoned the count of Neu-Eberstein and permitted him to return to his fortress, where tourists can still see the famous spot, known as "the Count's Leap," from which he sprang into the river.

BADEN.

The Devil's Pulpit.

NOT very far from the ruins of Alt-Eberstein, and on the road to the castle of Neu-Eberstein, are two great rocks, popularly designated as the angel's and the devil's pulpits. The legend concerning them relates that the devil once left the red-hot regions of the nether world, and came up on the surface of the earth through the springs of Baden, which have since retained a peculiar sulphurous taste.

His Satanic Majesty was in search of new victims to roast in his everlasting fires, and as there were then no gaming tables at Baden, and the place offered less scope for the exercise of his talents than it has done since, he posted himself on the edge of the highway, and began to preach with great eloquence.

Either because they wished to judge of the devil's theology, or because they were anxious to obtain a near view of the preacher, priest, knight, and peasant turned aside to hear what he had to say, and, fascinated by his eloquence, allowed him to prove in the most plausible way that black was white, and white was black, and that wickedness and virtue were synonymous terms.

Just as the devil fancied he had fully convinced his hearers, the heavens suddenly opened, and a radiant angel, palm in hand, floated down upon snowy pinions, and taking up his station on a rock directly opposite him began to preach also, but in a far different strain.

The devil raised his voice louder and louder to drown the

sound of the angel's gentle admonitions, and preached faster and faster, redoubling his proofs and arguments, but one by one his hearers left him to gather around the angelic preacher, and listen to every word from his lips. Before long, therefore, Satan found himself entirely deserted. In a fit of ungovernable rage the devil then tore up grass, trees, and shrubs by the roots, stamped his red-hot feet on the rock until he left their imprint there, and finally vanished in an abominable atmosphere of curses, sulphur, and brimstone. The traveler passing by can still see the two pulpits, but the diabolical and angelic preachers, instead of remaining there, are both wandering incessantly around the world still trying to win proselytes.

OBERACHERN.

The Petrified Church.

A WILD troop of Huns once came to Oberachern, where they knew they would find a convent and seven lovely nuns, whom they had determined to torture in every way to compel them to renounce their vows. The poor nuns, hearing of the barbarians' invasion and unable to defend themselves, took refuge in the church, bolted the heavy oaken doors, and, kneeling before the altar, began singing with all their might, "Good Lord deliver us!"

The Huns soon came up and tried to force open the doors, which resisted their first onslaught, but the pious nuns continued their fervent prayer, singing as loud as they could. Then, seeing their hands were not strong enough to break in the oaken doors, the barbarians rushed into the neighboring forest to cut down trees to serve as battering rams.

But, when they would fain have made use of them, they found the church had been changed into an impenetrable rock, and although they could still hear the pious nuns chanting loudly "Good Lord deliver us!" they were not able to get at them, and were obliged to withdraw entirely baffled. The nuns are said to inhabit this rock still, and to be occupied in praising God forever, and many a peasant, passing near the stone church at nightfall, avers he has caught the sound of their pious hymns.

MÜMMELSEE.

The Water Sprites.

THE almost circular sheet of water known as the Mümmelsee, surrounded by rocky, pine-covered slopes, is said to be haunted by a water god, called Mümmel, and by his numerous daughters, the beautiful nymphs, named Mümmelchen. No fish are found in these waters, which generally lie smooth and unruffled in their dark bed.

The legends relate that a desperate poacher once slew the gamekeeper of the neighboring forest, and flung the body into the Mümmelsee, thinking it would keep the secret of his crime. Before he could extricate his garments from the thorn bush near the water brink, however, and escape up the hillside, the irascible water god, who would not even allow a pebble to be cast into his domain, rose up out of the waters, caught him by the ankles, and drew him irresistibly down to the bottom of the lake, where he was drowned in punishment for his crime.

The daughters of old Mümmel are said to rise up out of the lake on moonlight nights, to dance on the green sward, clad all in white, with glistening pearls and diamonds in their long golden hair. During the daytime these maidens, in the form of water lilies, rock gently upon the smooth waters, and, as they are weary with the night's exertions, they fall sound asleep soon after the rising of the sun. Their grim old father, Mümmel, is said to keep close watch over them, and when the first glimmer of dawn appears, he slowly rises out of the flood, beckons sternly to his dancing daughters, and imperiously commands them to return to their native element, and resume the flower-like form which serves to delude mortals and conceals their true nature.

TRIFELS.

The Faithful Minstrel.

BATTERED walls and a ruined tower are all that now remain of the castle of Trifels, famous in history and legend as the prison of Richard, the lion-hearted king. During the third crusade Richard and Leopold of Austria were engaged in besieging the stronghold of Acre. As both were noted for their courage, they vied with one another in performing many valiant deeds of arms, and little by little became rivals.

Leopold of Austria, jealous of Richard's superior glory, finally gave up the siege and returned home, vowing in his heart that should the opportunity ever present itself he would make the king of England rue the day when he had outdone him. This chance occurred only too soon, for Richard on his way home shortly after suffered shipwreck on the coast of Illyria, and found himself obliged to work his way back to England alone and on foot.

Disposing of his garments, the only thing he had saved, for a pilgrim's robe and scrip, Richard proceeded on his way, passing safely through the greater part of Austria. Finally he found himself obliged to pawn his signet ring at an inn to obtain food. This ring, being shown to Leopold, revealed the pilgrim's identity. Richard was therefore seized by his enemy, who imprisoned him in the Fortress of Durrenstein, where he detained him prisoner until Henry IV. of Germany took him into custody, and transferred him to the castle of Trifels on the Rhine.

While Richard was languishing thus in prison, wondering why his faithful subjects made no attempt to find him, his brother, John Lackland, usurped the throne and was reigning in England according to his own sweet will. The English hated his rule and longed for Richard's return, but only one of them, Blondel, the king's minstrel, ventured to set out in search of him.

Shrewdly conjecturing that his master must be detained prisoner by the emperor of Germany, in one of his many strongholds, Blondel wandered from place to place, questioning all he met, and playing a peculiar air known to him and the king only at the foot of every dungeon where he fancied Richard might be detained.

After many weary months of wandering, Blondel came at last to Trifels, where he as usual played his lay. Imagine his delight when he suddenly heard a voice within take up the strain and sing the second verse. Richard, his long lost master, was found, and his weary search was ended at last.

Of course the poor minstrel could not deliver the king; but he hastened back to England, told the English noblemen the result of his journey, and soon prevailed upon them to negotiate for his master's release. Richard came home in triumph as soon as the required ransom had been paid, ousted the traitor, John Lackland, and ruled over England until 1199, when he died and was buried in the principal church of Rouen, where his tomb can still be seen.

ZABERN.

The Jealous Husband.

THE haughty Lord of Zabern, or Saverne, was proud of his castle, proud of his wealth, and particularly proud of his beautiful young wife, who was as virtuous as she was pretty. Unfortunately for her, the Lord of Saverne was of a jealous, suspicious disposition, and listened only too often to the advice of Robert, his huntsman, who by skillful flattery had won great influence over him.

Robert having discovered the count's jealousy, and wishing to get rid of the fair countess' young page, Fridolin, whose position he envied, gradually managed to convey to his master, by sly innuendo, that his mistress took more interest in the page than was seemly, as he was deeply in love with her. The count of Saverne flew into a terrible passion when he heard this, and vowed he would take a terrible revenge if the tidings were true. As they came home from the hunt one day, Robert maliciously directed his master's attention to Fridolin, who was gratefully kissing the countess' hand as was then customary when a favor had been received. The count, willfully misconstruing this simple action, rode off in hot haste to his foundry, where he bade his men kindle a great fire and roast alive the first person who came to inquire whether his orders had been fulfilled.

This done, he returned home, summoned Fridolin, and bade him hasten off to the foundry and ask whether his orders had been carried out. The young page, remembering that he was specially in the countess' service, sought her presence ere he departed to inquire whether she had any commands for him. He found her anxiously bending over her sick child, and she told him to enter the church on his way and pray for her babe's recovery, adding that God would surely grant the prayers of one as innocent and dutiful as he.

Fridolin immediately set out, entered the village church, and finding the priest embarrassed because his acolyte was not there to serve the mass, the page offered his services. He rang the little bell, made the responses; and carefully set aside the holy vessels, hastening on to the foundry only when all his pious duties had been accomplished, and the prayer for the child's recovery duly said. In the meanwhile Robert, to whom the count had confided his plan, anxious to make sure that Fridolin was dead, had hurried secretly to the foundry. As he did not enter the church he reached the goal first, and inquired whether the count's orders had been fulfilled.

"Not yet," answered the grim founders, "but they soon will be," and before he could utter a protest they seized and flung him into the furnace, where he was soon burned to a crisp. Fridolin, coming up a few minutes later with his question, was gleefully told to look into the flames, where he saw a blackened corpse, and he hurried back to his master, who was greatly amazed when he saw him appear.

In the course of a few minutes, however, the count of Saverne had learned the whole story, and realizing now how foolish had been his jealousy, he declared that God had taken the judgment into his own hands and punished the real criminal. Then, leading Fridolin to the countess, whose child was now peacefully asleep, he commended him to her good graces, telling her how greatly he had misjudged them both, and how happy he was to find he had been needlessly jealous.

STRASBURG.

Cathedral Legends.

THE first cathedral of Strasburg, founded by Clovis in 510, almost immediately after the conversion at Zülpich, was almost entirely destroyed by fire a few centuries later, and replaced by the present building, which, although begun in the twelfth century, rose very slowly and still remains unfinished.

Various architects have had a share in erecting this magnificent building, but the chief legendary interest is concentrated around the name of Edwin of Steinbach, who, after laboring at it for many a year, left the continuation of his task to his children.

STRASBURG CATHEDRAL.

Side Portal.

This architect, wandering abcut in search of stone suitable for the construction of the cathedral tower, once found a quarry near the banks of the Rhine, where the stone was enriched by tiny veins of gold. He decided to use this material, and then began to think about the plan which the bishop, Werner of Hapsburg, had bidden him design.

On his way home from the quarry, Steinbach lost his way and accidentally came to a little chapel in the woods, built on the plan of the manger. It was the first rudely-fashioned sanctuary which the pious missionaries had erected on the banks of the Rhine. While kneeling at the altar there, the architect was suddenly inspired with the general design of the cathedral he was to build. He hastened home and informed the bishop that he was ready to begin the construction. A day was appointed for the laying of the corner stone, and as the bishop had promised full absolution instead of money to all those who labored diligently at the erection of the cathedral, he soon found plenty of workmen.

Werner of Hapsburg, in full pontifical array, lowered the great corner stone, and blessed it, while the people all eagerly pressed forward to touch it. Two brothers, standing in the first rank, accidentally jostled each other. The elder, who was irascible, resented being pushed. In anger, he then and there slew his junior, whose blood defaced the purity of the priestly garments and of the corner stone.

The murderer was immediately seized and condemned to die, but ere he was led away to be hung, he fell at the bishop's feet and repentantly exclaimed:

"My lord, I acknowledge that I deserve to die, but let not my death be entirely in vain. Directly under the corner stone, which you have just lowered, are living springs which will in time undermine the foundations and prevent their enduring for ages as you hope. But, if you bury me, a murderer, beneath that stone, the waters, pure and undefiled, shrinking from contact with my polluted bones, will work their way to the surface elsewhere, and my body will serve as a protection to the cathedral."

Strange to relate, the murderer's suggestion was adopted, the ponderous stone again raised, and the man of his own free will stepped down into the hollow prepared for it, and gave the signal for its descent. The stone thus lowered upon a living man forms the corner of the Strasburg cathedral tower, and as it still stands firm, popular superstition avers that the murderer's bones had the desired effect.

Edwin of Steinbach, as already stated, dying before the cathedral was finished, implored his son and daughter, Jean and Sabine, to continue his work, and bitterly regretted that he had never committed to paper the complete design. When he had been duly laid to rest in the unfinished cathedral, where his monument can still be seen, the magistrates of Strasburg decreed they would intrust the completion of the work to the artist who furnished the best design, and soon all the architects in town were drawing diligently.

Jean of Steinbach, in his feverish eagerness to fulfill his father's last request, overworked himself and fell seriously ill before his plan was finished. In his delirium he constantly murmured that another would wear his father's laurels. These ravings greatly troubled his sister Sabine, especially when Polydore, a young architect who had long sued for her hand in vain, proudly exhibited his plan, which was very beautiful indeed.

The maiden could not restrain her tears at the thought of her brother's bitter disappointment, so Polydore offered to suppress his plan, and finish Jean's, providing Sabine would promise to marry him. But the girl, who had plighted her troth to another young architect, called Bernard, virtuously refused to break faith, even to save her brother's life and secure the fulfillment of her father's last wish.

That selfsame night, as she sat before her brother's drawing table, upon which a great sheet of parchment was spread, she idly seized a pencil, and, overcome by the weariness produced by several night's watching, fell asleep still holding it in her hand. When she awoke she gazed at the sheet in wonder, for it was no longer blank, but covered with a wonderful design. She appended her brother's name to this plan and hastened to carry it to the city hall, where she arrived a few minutes only before the contest was closed. When the judges had seen it, they all decided that Jean of Steinbach should finish the work and gave him the prize.

This news proved far better than any medicine to the sick man, who was soon cured, and took up his abode with Sabine in a little house very near the cathedral, that they might both be near their work, for the girl, who was a skillful sculptor, was busy carving the statues for the cathedral portal.

To her great surprise, however, the work planned in the evening was already far advanced when morning dawned. Bernard, her lover, soon noticed that the people began to look askance at her, and to whisper about magic and witchcraft, evil insinuations made by Polydore in his jealous anger at having failed to secure either the girl or the prize.

One morning on reaching her work, however, Sabine was greatly dismayed to find that one statue had been sadly disfigured during the night, and she tearfully showed it to her brother and lover, who also lived in full view of the rapidly advancing cathedral tower.

That night Bernard stood at his window, thinking of his beloved, and wondering how he could silence the evil reports, when the sound of hammer and chisel suddenly fell upon his ear. He glanced hastily up at the cathedral tower, whence the sound seemed to proceed, and saw, by the silvery light of the moon, his betrothed, Sabine, clad all in white, with flowing hair, carving as busily as if it were broad noonday.

A moment later he heard another sound, and looking on

the other side of the tower he beheld Polydore, rapidly defacing the delicate carving finished the day before. Trembling with fear for his beloved, Bernard hastened across the square and up the tower, and emerged noiselessly on the scaffold beside Sabine, who, to his utter amazement, was sound asleep. The mystery was now explained, the fragile girl, haunted by the thought of her work, had become a somnambulist, and continued to labor even in her sleep. As he feared to startle her, Bernard stood motionless behind her. All at once she paused in her work, and then, as if disturbed by the louder hammering on the other side of the tower, glided suddenly round the corner.

Polydore, terrified by this apparition in white, stepped back into space, and with a blood-curdling cry fell to the foot of the tower, a mangled corpse. This cry awakened Sabine, and she would have fallen too had she not been caught by Bernard. He clasped her close, and gently revealed to her the secret of her somnambulism and the death of Polydore, and prevailed upon her to consent to a marriage on the following day, that he might be privileged to watch over her even in sleep.

The cathedral tower, which is entirely finished, is adorned by many a statue from the fair Sabine's hand, and the only part of the edifice which now remains to be finished is the second spire.

In the south transept of the cathedral is the world-renowned astronomical clock, which has replaced a somewhat similar construction of great antiquity.

This clock, which boasts of a complete calendar and planetary, regulates itself at midnight on the 31st of December, and is calculated to run on for an indefinite space of time. The quarter hours are marked by the successive appearance of a boy, youth, man, and old man, and the days of the week by their symbolical gods: Apollo, Diana, Mars, Mercury, Jupiter, Venus, and Saturn.

At twelve o'clock Christ and his disciples appear, the

latter marching gravely around their Lord, and a cock, perched aloft, stretches out its neck, flaps its wings, and lustily crows. A man who turns an hourglass every sixty minutes, and an angel who strikes the quarter hour bell, complete the number of movable figures, whose constant performance is a source of never-failing wonder and delight to the spectators crowding around it.

The first clock is said to have been the work of one Isaac Habrecht. While he was engaged in its construction, a little old man continually haunted the spot, leaning against the wall near by, and deriding all his efforts to make it go. Isaac, however, paid but little heed to the mocker, but when the clock began to run and the little old man vanished, he set up an effigy of him on the very spot where he had been wont to stand. Angry at this, the devil, for it was he, now slyly whispered to the councilors that Isaac was about to construct similar clocks for all the other cathedral cities, and so excited their jealousy that they determined to blind the poor clockmaker, so as to hinder him most effectually from ever duplicating his masterpiece.

In vain poor Isaac protested his innocence, and promised to bind himself by solemn oath to work for them alone. They would not listen to aught he said, and only allowed him a few hours reprieve because he declared there was a little piece of mechanism in the clock which still required a finishing touch.

This last thing being finished, they led Isaac away and put out his eyes ; but just as the barbarous deed had been committed, the sexton of the cathedral rushed into the council hall to announce that the wonderful clock had stopped. The councilors angrily demanded of Isaac what he had done ; but after answering that he had cursed it, and that they would never again succeed in making it go, the poor man breathed his last.

The cathedral annals declare, however, that the clock ran on until 1789, when it stopped because the wooden works were worn out, although the legends report that it stopped when the light was quenched in Isaac's eyes, and that no watchmaker ever succeeded in making it go after he had cursed it.

The present timepiece, which is deservedly considered a masterpiece of the clockmaker's art, was finished and began running in 1842, since when it has excited the admiration of visitors from every clime.

The Vow of Obedience.

BEFORE the present cathedral was erected in Strasburg, Henry of Bavaria, surnamed the Holy, once entered the church which occupied this site, and falling on his knees before the bishop, confessed that he was weary and would fain be made a priest also, that he might spend all his time in serving the Lord.

His courtiers and attendants, hearing this request, began to wail and protest, imploring him on bended knee to continue to govern them, and reminding him that the country needed him. The only reply which the emperor made to these remonstrances and prayers, however, was to lay his crown and scepter on the altar, and to fling his purple and ermine robes at the bishop's feet, renewing his request to be accepted as a priest.

The bishop, seeing he was in earnest, immediately signified his consent, and without further ado, began the ceremony of ordination. He made the emperor take all the vows, and paid no heed to the tears and groans of the assembly, who regretfully witnessed the sacrament which was to rob them forever of a beloved master.

When all was ended, the bishop said: "My son, you have now taken the solemn vows of the church, and have promised to obey me, your ecclesiastical superior. It is therefore incumbent upon you to accept, without murmur, the charge which I am about to give you. Be a priest of the Lord Almighty, serve him in word and deed, but erect your altar near the throne, and by your wise administration of the government constantly show forth the glory of God. Resume your crown, which I trust is only the perishing symbol of the immortal diadem awaiting you in heaven, and serve God so faithfully that you will one day hear the grateful words, 'Well done, thou good and faithful servant; enter thou into the joy of thy Lord.'"

Seldom has a charge been received with more humility by the recipient, and with more enthusiasm by the bystanders, overjoyed to find that they would not lose their beloved master, who courageously took up the burden he had thought to lay aside forever, and ruled faithfully unto the end.

Conflicting Customs.

In the days when Strasburg still belonged to the French, a German once came there to pay a visit, and gladly accepted a Frenchman's invitation to enter an inn and take a drink.

"Why should not the French and Germans agree and be good friends?" argued these two men. "It is high time that the long feud between our nations should come to an end."

"Let us drink to future good fellowship!" exclaimed the Frenchman, courteously filling his guest's glass.

The German, who had been carefully trained in his country's etiquette, immediately emptied his glass, which the Frenchman wonderingly refilled ere he touched his own wine. The German promptly emptied it again, only to see it refilled before he could catch his breath.

Prevented from quenching his own thirst by the rapidity with which the German emptied the contents of his glass, the Frenchman began to get wrathy, and poured faster and faster, while the German rapidly became apoplectic in hue, and finally exclaimed:

"Donner Wetter, mine freund, what do you mean by taxing my politeness so sorely?"

"Tonnerre de mille bombes!" sputtered the Frenchman, "it is you who are taxing my politeness."

"Bah!" answered the German, "every beardless lad in Germany knows that a guest is in common courtesy bound to drink immediately, and without flinching, any stuff his host chooses to set before him, but no human being could be expected to drain glass after glass as fast as a man can pour."

"Ah!" said the Frenchman, "every schoolboy in France knows that a guest's glass should never remain empty, even for a moment."

From argument to dispute, the Frenchman and German soon came to blows, and only when weary did they part, exclaiming that people who could not even agree in such a simple matter as drinking could never be good friends, and that it was quite evident that the two nations would never long remain at peace.

The Hot Porridge.

THE little town of Zürich, in Switzerland, once sought the alliance of Strasburg, but the magistrates of the larger city, thinking so small an ally of no importance, rudely declared that Zürich was too far away to lend them any assistance in case of need and bluntly refused the honor.

When the councilors of Zürich read the Strasburgers' answer they were very indignant indeed, and talked of challenging them, but the youngest among them declared he would make them eat their words, and pledged his honor to bring a different answer ere long.

The other councilors agreed to let him arrange the matter as he pleased, and leisurely returned to their dwellings, while this man went home in a great hurry, selected the biggest pot in his kitchen, and calling his wife, bade her cook as much oatmeal as it would contain. Wondering greatly at this command, the woman quickly bade her servants build a roaring fire, and stirred and cooked the oatmeal while her husband rushed down to the quay, prepared his swiftest vessel, collected a number of the best oarsmen, and when all was ready, bade two of them accompany him home. He sprang breathless into the kitchen, and learned that the oatmeal was ready. So he bade the youths lift the pot from the fire, and run down to the boat with it. He followed them quickly, saw it placed in the stern, and turning to his men, exclaimed:

"Now lads, row with all your might, for we are bound to prove to those stupid old Strasburgers that we are near enough to serve them a hot supper in case of need."

Inspired by these words the youths bent to their oars, and the vessel shot down the Limmat, Aar, and Rhine, leaving town, village, and farm in its wake, and only stopping when it reached the quay at Strasburg. The councilor sprang ashore, bade the two youths follow with the huge pot, and striding into the council hall, had it set before the assembled magistrates, and exclaimed:

"Gentleman, Zürich sends a warm answer to your cold refusal."

With gaping mouths the Strasburgers gazed at the still steaming pot, and when the young Züricher explained how it got there, they were so amused by the wit and promptitude which their would-be allies had displayed, that they unanimously voted for the alliance. It was duly signed and sealed ere they called for spoons, and laughing heartily, ate every bit of the oatmeal, which was declared excellent, and proved hot enough to burn more than one councilor's mouth.

Ever since then this huge iron pot, which is known as

the "pot of alliance," has been carefully preserved in the town hall of Strasburg, where it can still be seen.

HASLACH.

A Giantess' Playthings.

In mythical ages there dwelt at Nideck, in Alsace, a mighty and gigantic race. The daughter of the Nideck giant, a damsel of colossal size, in spite of her tender years, once started out for a walk. As her mode of locomotion consisted in clearing with a bound all intervening valleys, she soon arrived at Haslach, where for the first time in her life she suddenly beheld a peasant plowing his field.

Delighted with the marvelous activity of these, to her, wonderful and tiny beings, she clasped her hands in rapture, then snatched up peasant, plow, and team, and bundling them into her apron, ran home as fast as her legs could carry her.

"Father, see the pretty playthings I found yonder in the valley," and she opened her apron to let him see the new found treasure.

"My daughter," said the giant gravely, "these are no playthings, but living creatures as well as we. Carry them quickly back to the place where you found them, and henceforth forbear to lay a finger upon them, for those tiny creatures are destined to be our supplanters."

Sorrowfully the giant maiden carried peasant, plow, and team back to the field, set them down in the unfinished furrow, and returned home, mourning the loss of the cunning playthings which she had not been permitted to retain.

ECKHARDTSBERG.

Tannhäuser.

THE eminence known as the Eckhardtsberg is one of the favorite haunts of the faithful German mentor, Eckhardt, who is supposed still to linger near there. His object is to prevent rash mortals from listening to the alluring strains of Venus, who has taken refuge within this mountain, in order to entice travelers thither to enjoy all manner of sensual pleasures in her company.

Tannhäuser, the master-singer, wandering near there, once heard her alluring song, and wending his way into the mountain, forgot the lovely maiden to whom he had been betrothed, and yielding to Venus' witching spells, spent some time in her company. After a while, however, the carnal pleasures offered him palled upon his taste, the longing for the pure, disinterested love of his betrothed returned to him, and forcibly wrenching himself out of Venus' detaining arms, he hastened out of the mountain and into the neighboring valley.

He would fain have returned into the presence of his betrothed, but the recollection of the time he had spent in the Venus mountain filled him with such loathing, and the sense of his sin was so oppressive, that he hastened off to Rome to confess all to the Pope, and implore him to grant him absolution for his sins.

When Pope Urban had heard his confession he recoiled with horror, and told the heartbroken Tannhäuser that since he had visited the heathen goddess, he could no more hope for forgiveness of his sins than he could expect the papal staff to become green again and bear leaves.

Sadly now Tannhäuser wended his way home once more, and, disowned by all, a moral outcast, he finally resolved to return to Venus, and taste, to the dregs, the only joys now allowed him. In vain the faithful Eckhardt sought to detain him, Tannhäuser vanished in the Venus hill, whence he never again emerged. A few moments after he had vanished, a messenger of the Pope came in search of him, for the papal staff had budded and borne leaves, thus proving to Urban that the minstrel's sin was not as unpardonable as he had declared, and that absolution should be granted to all truly repentant sinners.

The news had come too late, however, for Tannhäuser had returned to Venus, with whom, tradition declares, he will remain until the judgment day.

This legend, which is also told of the Hörselberg in Thuringia, has further been connected with the Wartburg and the fair mistress thereof, who, loving Tannhäuser, is said to have died of grief when he returned unforgiven from Rome. Wagner has made use of this beautiful tradition, and has founded upon it his immortal opera of "Tannhäuser," which is always heard with new delight.*

The Dumb Plaintiff.

THE story of "The Bell of Atri," which Longfellow has so charmingly told in his "Tales of a Wayside Inn," is said to have originated in Eckhardtsberg near Breisach.

In early days, when the ruins now crowning the hill were part of a strong fortress, the lord of Eckhardtsberg, wishing to render justice to all men, placed a bell in his tower. He fastened to it a long piece of rope which hung outside the gate, within easy reach of every hand, and bade all those who wished redress to ring it loudly, promising to grant them an immediate hearing.

One day the bell pealed loudly, and when in answer to its call the lord of Eckhardtsberg, followed by all his retainers, came out to hear the complaint, he was surprised to find a poor old horse, which, urged by hunger, was trying to chew the end of the hempen rope. One of the bystanders im-

* See "Stories of the Wagner Operas," by the author.

mediately recognized the horse as belonging to a neighboring knight. For many a year the horse had been his favorite steed, had borne him safely through many a fight, but now that it was old and useless the cruel master had turned it out to seek pasture along the highway, where it found but scant subsistence.

The lord of Eckhardtsberg, seeing the animal's sorry plight, and hearing how faithfully it had served its master in the days of its youth, declared that in return for its former services it should now be treated with respect, and condemned the unfeeling, avaricious owner to give it a place in his stable and plenty of food as long as it lived. Longfellow closes his version of this legend thus:

"And thereupon the Syndic gravely read
The proclamation of the king; then said:
'Pride goeth forth on horseback, grand and gay,
But cometh back on foot, and begs its way;
Fame is the fragrance of heroic deeds,
Of flowers of chivalry and not of weeds!
These are familiar proverbs; but I fear
They never yet have reached your knightly ear.
What fair renown, what honor, what repute
Can come to you from starving this poor brute?
He who serves well and speaks not, merits more
Than they who clamor loudest at the door.
Therefore the law decrees that as this steed
Served you in youth, henceforth you shall take heed
To comfort his old age, and to provide
Shelter in stall, and food and field beside.'
The knight withdrew abashed, the people all
Led home the steed in triumph to his stall.
The King heard and approved, and laughed in glee,
And cried aloud: 'Right well it pleaseth me!
Church-bells at best but ring us to the door;
They go not in to mass; my bell doth more:
It cometh into court and pleads the cause
Of creatures dumb and unknown to the laws;
And this shall make in every Christian clime,
The Bell of Atri famous for all time."

—*Tales of a Wayside Inn*.—*Longfellow.*

BASEL.

The Change of Time.

THE people of Basel, however antiquated and behind the times they may be in other matters, are nevertheless an hour ahead of all the other Swiss cities. The legends account for this fact by reporting that once, during the Middle Ages, some traitors within the city walls promised to open the gates and deliver the town into the hands of the enemy as soon as the clock struck the midnight hour.

This plan, discussed and agreed upon in secret, was detected by the warder of the gate. It was too late to give the alarm or warn the magistrates, for he knew that he was closely watched and would be murdered if he attempted to slip away and reveal the treacherous design. As the old man was also bell ringer, he quickly devised a way to outwit the enemy, and creeping noiselessly up to the tower, he carefully manipulated the clock, which, instead of striking twelve, slowly and solemnly tolled out one.

The conspirators within awakened at this sound, for they had fallen into a doze while waiting for the agreed signal. They immediately concluded that they had either missed the time or been discovered, and stole cautiously away, while the enemy without, equally surprised at hearing but one stroke, vainly waited for the gates to be opened, and were obliged to steal away angry and crestfallen in the gray dawn.

When the mayor inquired on the morrow why the clock was an hour ahead of time, the warder revealed the conspiracy, and the means which he had used to save the town. The city council, quickly convened, disposed of the traitors, praised the warder, and decreed that the clock should ever after remain an hour ahead of time, to remind the inhabitants of Basel of their narrow escape.

To mock their would-be assailants, the Baslers also placed upon the tower a mechanical figure called the "Lällenkönig,"

BASLE.
Old City Gate.

which derisively stuck out its tongue every few seconds. In time this curious statue was transferred to the bridge, and from thence to the city museum, where it can still be seen, although the mechanism is now out of order and it no longer protrudes its tongue.

Basel, which is situated at the great bend in the Rhine where it suddenly turns northward, was founded by the Romans, but soon became a free city and entered the Swiss confederacy in 1501. Its most remarkable building is the cathedral, built by Henry II. in 1010, on the site of a former church erected by Charlemagne and almost destroyed by a terrible earthquake in 1336. In this cathedral lie buried the learned Erasmus and the empress Anna, wife of Rudolf of Hapsburg. In the Basel museum are fragments of Holbein's famous "Dance of Death," curious articles of ancient household furniture, a collection of musical instruments, and the armor of Charles the Bold, duke of Burgundy.

From Castle to Cot.

NOT far from Basel rose the castle of Christopher of Ramstein, who, having inherited it from spendthrift ancestors, soon found that he would be obliged to sell it in order to satisfy the claims of old creditors. Honorable in all things, Christopher sold all, reserving nothing for himself, and when the bargain was concluded, he divided the money among the assembled creditors, paying every debt in full.

Although not a penny was over when he had ended, and although he and his lovely young wife were homeless and destitute, Christopher of Ramstein stood proudly in their midst, thankful to know that no stain rested upon his name. The creditors, touched by his brave bearing, now crowded around him, offering him aid. But he refused it, saying he had hired a little dwelling, was about to till the soil for a rich farmer, and was sure that by the sweat of his brow he would be able to secure daily bread for himself and his wife, who had nobly encouraged him to do his duty.

The creditors insisted upon giving him something, however, so he begged them to procure for his wife a silken dress, as he could not bear to see her attired in the rough garments they had assumed, for they had even sold their clothes to clear their debts. The silken garment was immediately ordered, and the Basel merchants furnished such good material that the dress lasted for many a year. Christopher, returning home from his work in the fields had the satisfaction of seeing his lovely wife, clad as richly as of old, standing in the doorway of their humble cottage to welcome him home with the loving kiss which made him forget toil and privation, and their mutual love enabled them to remain happy, though poor, as long as they lived.

The Dance of Death.

Some fragments of the celebrated fresco painted in the fifteenth century, and generally known as "The Dance of Death," are still to be seen in the cathedral of Basel, in the St. Nicholas chapel. These peculiar figures inspired Goethe to write a poem upon them which has been translated into English and is added here :

"The warder looks down at the mid hour of night
On the tombs that lie scattered below ;
The moon fills the place with her silvery light,
And the churchyard like day seems to glow.
When see ! first one grave, then another opes wide,
And women and men stepping forth are descried,
In cerements snow-white and trailing.

"In haste for the sport soon their ankles they twitch,
And whirl round in dances so gay ;
The young and the old, and the poor, and the rich,

BASLE.

But the cerements stands in their way ;
And as modesty cannot avail them aught here
They shake themselves all, and the shrouds soon appear,
Scattered over the tombs in confusion.

" Now waggles the leg and wiggles the thigh,
As the troop with strange gestures advance,
And a rattle and clatter anon rises high,
As of one beating time to the dance.
The sight of the warder seems monstrously queer,
When the villainous tempter speaks thus in his ear :
'Seize one of the shrouds that lie yonder ! '

" Quick as thought it was done ! and for safety he fled
Behind the church door with all speed ;
The moon still continues her dear light to shed
On the dance that they fearfully lead.
But the dancers at length disappear one by one,
And their shrouds, ere they vanish, they carefully don,
And under the turf all is quiet.

" But one of them stumbles and shuffles there still,
And gropes at the graves in despair,
Yet 'tis by no comrade he's treated so ill ;—
The shroud he soon scents in the air.
So he rattles the door—for the warder 'tis well
That 'tis blessed, and so able the foe to repel,
All cover'd with crosses in metal.

" The shroud he must have, and no rest will allow,
There remains for reflection no time ;
On the ornaments Gothic the wight seizes now,
And from point on to point hastes to climb,
Alas for the warder ! his doom is decreed.
Like a long-legged spider, with ne'er changing speed,
Advances the dreaded pursuer.

" The warder he quakes, and the warder turns pale,
The shroud to restore fain had sought ;
When the end—now can nothing to save him avail—
In a tooth formed of iron is caught,
With vanishing luster the moon's race is run
When the bell thunders loudly a powerful One,
And the skeleton falls, crush'd to atoms."

—*Goethe.*

AUGST.

The Snake Lady.

At a short distance from Basel is the picturesque little town of Augst, and near here, according to the legend, is a hollow mountain, in which a mysterious creature has taken up her abode. This creature, half woman and half snake, is detained there by a horrible spell, from which she can be released only if a pure youth voluntarily kisses her thrice. As the legend declares she will reward her deliverer by giving him a great treasure, which she is guarding with the help of two baying hell hounds, several youths have been anxious to find her.*

A youth of Augst, named Leonard, who was somewhat of a simpleton, being told of this wonderful creature, was desirous to see her. He therefore armed himself with a taper, which had been duly blessed by the priest, and, venturing alone into the legendary valley, soon discovered an iron door in the mountain side. He quickly passed through it, along a corridor, and came at last to a beautiful cave, where he saw a lovely woman beckoning to him to draw near.

Beside her was a great chest, on either side of which sat two fierce hounds, whose wild barking the lady stilled with a gentle wave of her hand. Then, taking a key from the bunch at her belt, she unlocked the chest, and the dazzled youth saw gold, silver, and precious stones in untold profusion.

"All these treasures will be yours, good youth, if you will only thrice kiss my lips," replied the lady, advancing toward him, and then Leonard noticed, for the first time, that although the upper part of her body was lovely indeed, the lower was formed of the repulsive coils of a snake. After a moment's hesitation, however, he drew near and twice kissed the snake lady's lips, but, frightened by the

* See Note 16 in Appendix.

swishing of her tail, he fled ere the last kiss had been given.

In his terror he rushed out of the cave and into the town, where some youths, under pretext of helping him recover his senses, made him drunk, while extracting the particulars of his tale.

On the morrow, sober once more and longing to release the lady from the loathesome spell which bound her, and to secure his reward, Leonard again set out, but, as he was no longer perfectly pure, he could not find the entrance to the cave. Since then many a youth has tried to find it and win the treasure, but as these young men had some time in their life, lied or stolen, drunk or sworn, they were not allowed to find the mysterious door, and the snake lady is still waiting for her deliverer.

SÄKINGEN.

St. Fridolin.

St. Fridolin, the holy hermit who had taken up his abode near Säkingen on the Rhine, that he might preach the gospel and at the same time save the people from a watery grave, was present at the death of Count Urso, who promised him all his lands and wealth for the newly-founded monastery.

But, when Count Urso had duly been laid to rest in his grave at Glaris, his only brother Landolf seized all his inheritance, utterly refusing to give it up to Fridolin when he came to claim it. To end the saint's importunities, he finally declared that if his statement were true, he need only summon his dead brother to appear in Rankwyl, where he was about to dispense justice, and there personally declare that he wished the property to go to the monastery, or he would never relinquish it.

Without wasting another word, Fridolin, though old and feeble, wended his way over the mountains to Glaris, summoned Urso to rise from the tomb, and leading the dead man to Rankwyl, and into the courtroom, bade him speak aloud and declare his last wishes.

In sepulchral tones Urso now addressed his brother, stated he had willed all his wealth to the monastery, and, still led by Fridolin, retraced his steps to Glaris, when he resumed his place in the tomb. As for Landolf, convinced by this miracle of the truth of Fridolin's words, he not only relinquished all claims to his brother's wealth but also willed his own property to the monastery, dying peacefully a few days later, and being laid to rest beside his brother.

The Trumpeter of Säkingen.

THE little town of Säkingen, with its picturesque castle, is famous principally on account of Scheffel's delightful poem "The Trumpeter of Säkingen," which forms also the basis of a pretty modern opera by Nessler. The outline of the poem, which is one of the German classics, and which has inspired several artists, is as follows:

Late in March, when the snow still lay thick upon the wooded paths of the Black Forest, a handsome young man rode briskly along, peering right and left in search of a village or farm where he might take shelter during the rapidly approaching night. The wind, blowing his wide cavalry cloak aside from time to time, revealed a bright bugle, which the young man tried to guard from the fine snow which came powdering down from the fir branches on either side of the narrow path. Ere long the youth emerged from the dark pine forest, and drawing rein at the top of a hill saw the Rhine at his feet, a little town on the opposite shore, in the midst of sheltered meadows, where the grass was already growing green, and in the background the long range of snowy mountain tops, illumined by the setting sun and flashing beneath its last rays. Standing there, he watched the light glow and disappear, saw the gray shadows slowly creep upward until they reached the topmost peaks, then, seizing his bugle, he played a merry tune which roused all the neighboring echoes.

This gay music attracted the attention of a village priest, slowly climbing the hill. As he turned the bend in the road he came face to face with the trumpeter, entered into conversation with him, and hospitably invited him to accompany him to the parsonage, where he promised him a hearty welcome. The trumpeter gladly accepted the priest's cordial invitation, accompanied him home, and after supper began to tell the good old man his story.

Young Werner, for such was the trumpeter's name, came from Heidelberg, where he had paid but scanty attention to the learned discourses of his professors, but had diligently taken music lessons from an old army trumpeter, who was troubled by chronic thirst, which could only be quenched by many a glass of beer. When Werner was eighteen his guardian strongly advised him to study law, but after vainly trying to concentrate his attention upon the various codes, the youth pawned his books, and, joining a noisy band of students, led a merry life. He serenaded the pretty Heidelberg girls by moonlight, fought countless harmless duels, and led such a generally reckless life that he was finally expelled by the college faculty.

After paying his debts—for in spite of all his high spirits, the young man was honorable to a fault—Werner enlisted in a cavalry corps, and after the end of the Thirty Years' War found himself the owner of a fine young steed and of his beloved bugle, with the whole world open to him so that he could range about it at will.

The village priest, in answer to his inquiries, told him

that the neighboring town, which he had seen from the heights, was Säkingen, where the holy missionary St. Fridolin had once established his hermitage, set up a cross, and daily tolled a bell for morning and evening prayers, which at first he alone attended.

Little by little, however, the good saint had preached to the Alemans, converted them, and so won their good graces that he was soon able to build and endow the monastery of Säkingen—thanks to their gifts. Dying at last in the odor of sanctity, St. Fridolin was buried in the church he had founded, and, as he was considered the patron saint of the town, all the inhabitants were wont to celebrate his festival by a solemn yearly procession, which was to take place on the morrow.

Werner, attending this festival, saw and fell in love with a beautiful young lady who headed the detachment of girls, and, feeling sentimentally inclined, he entered a boat at nightfall and rowed slowly down the Rhine. Suddenly the young god of the Rhine—the same who further down the stream is called old Father Rhine—slowly rose up out of the water, told him how many lovers he had seen since he had taken up his abode in that stream, and how clearly he could recognize all the symptoms of dawning passion.

Then, pointing slyly to a neighboring castle, he told Werner that the lady of his dreams dwelt there, and hinted that if he could not devise some way of attracting her attention, he was not worthy of being called a lover. Thus encouraged, Werner rowed down to the castle landing, sprang ashore, and, seeing a light up at the window, put his bugle to his lips and breathed forth the sweetest and tenderest of love songs.

These liquid, eloquent notes fell not only upon the ear of the young lady, but also attracted the attention of her gouty old father, who was just then telling her how, when young, and prisoner of war in France, he had fallen in love with and won the affections of her sainted mother. Leaning upon his daughter's arm, the old man limped to the window, hoping to catch a glimpse of the musician, who, standing in the shadow of the trees, could not be seen from above.

The old lord then summoned a servant, bidding him hasten down, present his compliments to the musician, and invite him to enter the castle, unless perchance the music was produced by the ghost of the old trumpeter of Säkingen who, after repeated potations, had been drowned in the Rhine the year before. The old servant's movements were in no wise accelerated by these last words, and Werner had re-embarked and rowed out into midstream ere he reached the garden. Forced to pursue his search for the musician in the streets of Säkingen on the morrow, old Anton found him in the city inn, and invited him to the castle, where Werner hastened with joyful alacrity. There he gladly accepted the post of cornetist in the old lord's band, as well as of music teacher to the lady of his dreams.

A new life now began for Werner, who, admitted in the bosom of the gouty old lord's family, daily saw the fair Margaretha, listened to the old man's tales, took his place in the village band, and spent all his spare moments in composing charming love songs, which he played and sang to his pupil to cultivate her musical taste.

Week after week passed by all too swiftly, and on the 1st of May the old lord organized a grand picnic in the Black Forest, inviting the ladies of a neighboring sisterhood, the chief dignitaries of Säkingen, and all the members of his band, who, enticed by the prospect of fishing and of partaking of the celebrated Mai Trank, hastened thither joyfully.

The *al fresco* feast ended, the schoolmaster sang a song of his own composition to the accompaniment of Werner's bugle, and the performance won such rapturous applause that Margaretha laughingly proposed to crown the poet with the dainty wreath she had just been weaving. Her old father approved of the idea; still, knowing the old schoolmaster would prefer a more substantial prize, bestowed upon him the largest fish they had secured, and bade Margaretha crown Werner instead, as his performance also deserved a reward. The lovely maiden blushingly complied with her father's request, and crowned the proud young head which bowed so humbly before her alone.

The poem then goes on to relate how Werner and Margaretha organized a birthday party for the old man, the former training the village band to play a grand symphony, while the latter hired an artist to decorate the walls of a garden pavilion. When the birthday came, Margaretha triumphantly led her old father thither, and while his ears were delighted with the music of his band, his eyes rested admiringly upon the scantily attired Loves and goddesses which he admired greatly, although he acknowledged that in times to come it might prove necessary to paint a little extra drapery over the walls to satisfy the prudish demands of modern taste.

Of course all these plans only drew the young people closer together, and Margaretha, wandering aimlessly in the garden on the morrow, entered the arbor, and, seeing Werner's trumpet on the table, could not resist the temptation to try whether she too could draw sweet tones from it. She was quite unskilled, however, and only blew such harsh, discordant sounds, that her cat began to howl, and Werner, roused from a day dream, stole noiselessly up to the arbor intending to chastise the impudent lad who had dared to touch his favorite instrument.

But when he saw Margaretha with cheeks distended like a musical cherub, his raised hand fell, his anger vanished, and he then and there taught her a simple bugle call, which she readily learned to execute properly. Needless to add, that after that the enamoured youth guarded the trumpet her rosy lips had pressed with the most jealous care, considering it his choicest treasure.

A few weeks after this occurrence the Säkingen magistrates promulgated a new law, whereby the peasants were taxed a little more heavily than usual, and this decree so enraged the people that a riot ensued. The old lord, hearing the town was in danger, immediately set out to defend it, intrusting the care of his castle and daughter to Werner, who, discovering a midnight attempt to seize and burn the castle, routed the foe with much bravery but received a wound in the fray.

Margaretha, seeing him fall and fearing lest he should be slain, caught up his trumpet and blew a shrill call, which made her father hasten home in time to drive away the few remaining foes, gather up the wounded, and secure a physician's service for Werner's wound.

The young hero, duly taken care of, soon sank into a profound sleep, during which Margaretha softly tip-toed into his room with the physician's permission, to assure herself that the youth was still alive and that she need have no further fears for his safety. Two days later Werner was so far recovered that he could sun himself upon the castle terrace, where Margaretha, coming accidentally upon him, showed so much joy at his recovery that he forgot he was only a musician and she a lady of noble birth, caught her in his arms, and rapturously kissed her.

After a delightful hour spent together, exchanging vows and confessions of love, Werner returned to his chamber, and only on the morrow sought the old lord's presence to make known his love. Before he could open his lips, however, the baron informed him that he had just received a letter from an old army friend, who proposed to send his only son to visit him in hopes that their children might fall in love with each other, and eventually marry. This letter the baron asked Werner to answer, giving a full description of Margaretha's charms, and extending a cordial invitation to the young man, but this Werner refused to do, manfully confessing that he would fain claim the young lady's hand for himself.

The old baron, who had vowed his child should never

marry any except a nobleman, now sadly dismissed Werner, who, without daring to see his beloved again, mounted his steed and rode away, pausing only on the opposite side of the river to breathe a last farewell upon his bugle, while gazing mournfully at the tower where dwelt the maiden whom he loved so dearly and could never forget.

Several years now passed by, during which Werner roamed from place to place, ever faithful to Margaretha, who, mourning his departure, gazed across the Rhine in the direction in which he had vanished, dismissed her suitors without vouchsafing them a glance, and finally grew so pale and thin that her father sent her to Italy in charge of his sister, an abbess, thinking a change of air would do her good.

One Easter Sunday in St. Peter's Church at Rome, Margaretha fainted at the sight of Werner, who, somber and melancholy, headed the papal choir, for his musical talent had won for him the post of chapel master and the favor of the Pope. Noticing the confusion of the young musician and the sudden swoon of the beautiful stranger, the Pope suspected the existence of an unhappy love affair, and having cleverly learned the whole story, benevolently took upon himself to make the young people happy.

He summoned Margaretha and Werner into his presence, made the latter Marquis of Campo Santo, and then, averring that he knew nothing but the lack of a title had hindered their union, he proposed to marry them right away, a plan which the young people hailed with rapture.

Their wedding journey back to Säkingen was a dream of bliss, and the old baron, delighted to see them both, welcomed them so heartily that their measure of happiness was full. Werner now breathed only the gayest tunes in his trumpet, which seemed incapable of producing the heart-rending tones which he had played during the past years while he was separated from his beloved, with whom he now lived blissfully all the rest of his life.

Assmus.

FAREWELL TO SACKINGEN.

KÖNIGSFELDEN.

The Murder.

Not far from Hapsburg castle are the remains of the ancient Roman settlement of Vindonissa, the rapids of Höllenhaken, the Rhine salt works, and the town and abbey of Königsfelden. The latter was founded in 1310 by the Empress Elizabeth and her daughter Queen Agnes of Hungary, on the spot where Albert of Austria, husband of the former, had been murdered two years before.

The Emperor of Germany and Duke of Austria, Albert, or Albrecht, after long fighting against the Pope, Holland, Zealand, Friesland, Hungary, Bohemia, and Thuringia, heard in 1308 that a rebellion had broken out among the Swiss in the Cantons of Unterwalden, Schweitz, and Uri, and hastened thither to suppress it. Before he could do so, however, his nephew, John of Suabia, whom he had defrauded of his rights, finding there was no hope of redress, formed a conspiracy against him.

Albert, having embarked with John and three of his accomplices in a little bark which was to carry him to Rheinfelden, was murdered by these conspirators in the boat.

His wound, although mortal, did not immediately prove fatal, and the emperor, forsaken by the murderers, who pushed ashore and hastened to seek a place of safety, breathed his last in the arms of a passing beggar woman who alone took pity upon him.

This death, magnificently rendered in Schiller's "William Tell," where it forms an effective scene of the play, was fearfully avenged by Agnes of Hungary, whose history is depicted on the stained glass windows in the choir of the old Königsfelden Abbey Church. Here are also the portraits of various of the heroes who fell at Sempach, but as the church is in ruins these works of art are sadly damaged.

HAPSBURG.

The Best Defense.

THE ancient castle of Hapsburg, which overlooks the Rhine in the Canton of Aargau, is the cradle of the imperial dynasty bearing the same name, and was founded in 1020. According to the legend the founder built no ramparts around it. A neighboring bishop, coming to visit him, so loudly deplored the absence of all the usual defenses that the owner, somewhat piqued, boldly declared that ere sunrise on the morrow he would have surrounded his castle with impregnable walls.

Of course the bishop smiled incredulously at this statement, but he was awakened on the morrow by the count's voice at his bedside, bidding him look forth and satisfy himself that his promise had been duly kept. The bishop ran hastily to the window, and saw, to his utter surprise, that the castle was completely surrounded by the count's followers, all in martial array. The men looked so strong and faithful that he could not but recognize, what has ever since been the family's proudest boast, that the arms and hearts of their devoted subjects are their principal defense in all times of imminent danger.

SCHAFFHAUSEN.

Falls of the Rhine.

THE falls of the Rhine, very near Schaffhausen, are in point of volume the grandest in Europe, for the river, after passing through the Lake of Constance, descends here over a mighty ledge of rock about one hundred feet high.

In June and July, when the river is greatly swollen by the

melting of the snow on the Alps, the volume of water is very great indeed, and early in the morning and late in the afternoon the position of the sun is such that countless rainbow reflections can be seen, formed by the sunlight and the silvery spray. The scene is particularly impressive by moonlight, and the feeling of awe is increased by the roaring sound of the waters; whose force continually causes the rocks to tremble.

The earliest recorded mention made of these falls is in the year 960, and since then the channel has apparently been gradually deepened by erosion. Immediately above the cataract rise the tall rocks upon which is perched the picturesque little castle of Laufen, now used as a hotel, from which a beautiful view of falls and river can be obtained. On an island in the middle of the stream, directly opposite the falls, is another little castle called Wörth, which is a favorite place of resort for travelers, as they can from there gain the best idea of the volume of water and of the height of the rocky ledge, down which they plunge with their continuous deafening roar.

MAINAU.

The Templar's Home.

HUGO OF LANGENSTEIN, forced to leave home to redeem a vow made by his father and go and fight the Saracens, came to the island of Mainau, in the Lake of Constance, where his betrothed dwelt. He sadly took leave of her, promising to return when the war was over and to live on the island with her, eat the fruit of the trees they had planted and drink the wine pressed from the grapes of the vine forming a lovely bower over their heads. The lovers' plans were brought to nought, however, for Hugo soon fell into the hands of the Saracens, who detained him prisoner many a year. Although he prayed for deliverance and his betrothed longed for his return, month after month passed by without bringing any answer to their petition.

One night Hugo of Langenstein was favored by a vision, in which an angel of the Lord bade him dedicate the remainder of his life to God if he would be free. In obedience to this command, the knight, although sorely troubled at having to renounce the hope of eventually marrying the fair maid of Mainau, solemnly vowed to dedicate his life to the service of God, and enter the Teutonic order of knights, if he were only allowed to see his native land once more. Two days later he was miraculously set free, steered his course by the stars across the burning Syrian plains, made his way home, and, sending a friend to Mainau to explain the nature of his vow, he sadly sought the headquarters of the Teutonic order and enlisted in their band.

The fair maid of Mainau, hearing that her lover would never return to her, yet anxious to have him know every comfort, also journeyed to the same place. She gave her lovely island to the knights upon condition that her lover should be stationed upon it as head of that branch of the order, and would thus be able to eat the fruit of her trees and taste the juice of her vines.

When this was arranged to her satisfaction, and all her rights over Mainau had been transferred to the Teutonic order, the maiden vanished and was seen no more. Some say she built a hermitage, others that she entered a convent, but, however that may be, Hugo of Langenstein was soon sent to Mainau, where he spent many a year, but never ceased to mourn for his beloved.

BUCHHORN.

The Pilgrim's Return.

COUNT ULRICH of Buchhorn had gone away from home to fight in Hungary, and soon the sad tidings of his death reached his wife. She assumed a widow's garb, and spent all her time in doing good to the poor, distributing special largesses on the anniversary of her dear husband's death, when she implored all the recipients of her bounty to pray for the rest of his soul.

Four years had passed thus, and when the fourth anniversary came around a pilgrim presented himself among the beggars, imploring her to give him a new garment to replace his tattered robe. The gentle lady immediately bestowed the coveted raiment, but, instead of the usual thanks, the pilgrim caught her in his arms, and passionately embraced her.

The terrified lady called for her servants to protect her, sobbing that if her husband were only living none would dare thus insult her. But, when the pilgrim threw back his cowl, she clung closely to him, for she now recognized her beloved husband, who was not dead, but had come home to part from her no more.

BISCHOFSZELL.

The Bridge.

THE small town of Bischofszell, at the confluence of the Thur and Sitter, boasts of an arched stone bridge about which the following tale is told:

Many years ago a castle stood on one side of the river Thur, which was then spanned by no bridge and could only be crossed by means of a small boat. The lady of the castle, standing at the window to watch for her sons' return from the chase, one fine spring day, saw them jump merrily into the skiff on the opposite side and begin to row across.

Before they had reached the middle of the stream, however, a sudden freshet overturned the boat, and both youths, after a momentary struggle, sank forever beneath the flood under their distracted mother's eyes. Fearing lest some other mother should suffer as sorely as she, the poor lady knew no rest until she had built this solid bridge, and saw little children skipping merrily to and fro over it, no matter how rapidly the waters rushed beneath it.

ST. GALL.

The Emperor's Riddles.

THE emperor once rode past the monastery of St. Gall. As he was sorely oppressed with the cares of state he was so vexed to see the plump and well-fed abbot taking his ease, that he maliciously resolved to try and disturb his equanimity.

"Abbot," cried he, "I am going to give you three nuts to crack! You must have the answers all ready three months hence, under penalty of losing your place and of riding through the town, mounted upon a donkey, with your face turned toward its tail, and holding that appendage instead of a bridle. The first question I wish you to answer is this: How much time, within a second, would I require to journey all around the world on horseback? The second is: How much am I worth, within a penny, when I have my imperial crown on my head, my scepter in my hand, and am attired in all my court robes? And as third riddle you will have to guess my thought, but remember you must prove that thought is not true!"

Laughing immoderately at the abbot's comical look of

blank dismay, the emperor galloped off, delighted at having so cleverly attained his purpose, and so effectually troubled the poor man's peace of mind.

In vain the abbot questioned all the brethren, wrote to all the universities and learned men, in vain he burned the midnight oil and turned over his long-neglected books. He could not find the least clew to the answers of those three tantalizing questions, which haunted him day and night, deprived him of his natural rest, and utterly spoiled his once so flourishing appetite.

The three months were nearly over, and the abbot, thin and careworn, wandered pensively through the monastery meadows, thinking how soon he would be forced to leave them forever, to be exposed to the hooting and jeering of the populace. His reverie was suddenly interrupted by an exclamation of dismay on the part of one of his herdsmen, who anxiously inquired whether he had been ill.

Full of his grievance, and touched by the man's evident sympathy, the abbot confided the whole story to him, glibly repeating the three perplexing questions over which he had pondered so long, and ending with a sigh of utter despair. The herdsman, who had listened attentively to all his master had to say, then slowly remarked that if the abbot would only lend him his gown, miter, and crozier, he would willingly go to court and answer the questions in his stead.

Rapidly reasoning that in case of failure the man would have to endure the public disgrace from which he shrank, the abbot gladly gave him the articles he asked for and dismissed him with a fervent blessing and a great sigh of relief. The pretended abbot reached the imperial court at the appointed time, and duly presented himself before his sovereign, who exclaimed with mock sympathy:

"Why, my dear abbot, how you have changed! You are no longer as ruddy and plump as you were three months ago. Have my nuts disagreed with you? Pay strict attention now, and remember that upon your answers depend your weal or woe. How much time would I require to journey all around the world on horseback?"

"If your majesty were to mount your steed at the very second when the sun appears above the horizon, and to travel just as fast as that luminary, it is certain your majesty would ride all around the world in exactly twenty-four hours, neither one second more or less," replied the false abbot.

A murmur of amusement was heard in the assembly, and the emperor, somewhat taken aback by the unexpected answer, continued:

"Although I might refuse to accept an answer depending upon an *if*, I will waive my right to do so, providing you answer the next question correctly: How much am I worth when I have my imperial crown upon my head, my scepter in my hand, and am attired in all my court robes?"

"Your majesty," replied the shepherd in disguise, "cannot surely pretend to be worth more than the Saviour of the world, in spite of all your jewels. *He* was sold for thirty pieces of silver, so the very highest figure which I can set upon you is twenty-nine pieces of silver."

"Well," exclaimed the emperor abashed, yet not daring to claim he was worth more than Christ. "I am sure I never rated myself as low as that. But now, abbot, comes the last question of all, and if you fail to answer it, remember, you must straddle that donkey. What is my present thought, and why is it not true?"

"Your majesty thinks I am the abbot of St. Gall," answered the man slowly.

"Why, of course I do," interposed the emperor triumphantly.

"But your majesty is greatly mistaken, however," continued the man, unmoved, "for I am only his shepherd."

The emperor was so amused by the man's shrewdness and ready wit, that he swore he would grant him any favor he cared to ask, and even proposed to make him abbot in his master's place.

But the herdsman simply said that, since the emperor kindly allowed him to choose his own reward, he would prefer to see his master remain unmolested, while he received an increase of wages sufficient to enable him to have meat for dinner every day. This unselfish request was duly granted, but the abbot never again relapsed into the slothfulness which had once so sorely irritated his imperial master.*

TOGGENBURG.

The Countess Itha.

An old Toggenburg legend relates that a jealous knight of that name once married a fair wife by the name of Itha, to whom he gave a magnificent diamond ring. The lady, having laid it on her table one day, left the apartment, and when she returned could find no trace of it, and all search proved vain.

A few weeks later, however, the knight of Toggenburg met a handsome young huntsman, and seeing his wife's diamond ring upon his hand immediately concluded she was faithless. He dashed home, and in an ungovernable fit of rage flung her out of the window, without even waiting to hear whether she could clear herself of the accusation he hurled against her.

The countess of Toggenburg was not slain, however, as everybody supposed, but had fallen over the precipice, where her fall had been broken by angelic power or by the slender fir branches by which she lowered herself to the ground. Fearing her husband's further violence she thereupon fled into the woods, where she lived for many a year the life of a recluse.

The knight of Toggenburg having disposed forever, as he thought, of his guilty wife, now sought the young huntsman, who was dragged to death by wild horses, his master learn-

* See Note 17 in Appendix.

ing only after his death that the youth had found the glittering ring in a magpie's nest, where it had been carried by the thievish birds.

Full of remorse, the knight of Toggenburg now sought for his wife's remains to bury them properly, at least, but could find no trace of them. Years passed by and every day his sorrow for her loss became deeper. Hoping to find some relief from torturing thought in active exercise, he finally set out for the chase, and, penetrating deep into the forest, came upon the hermitage of his pious wife, whom he immediately recognized and would fain have carried home.

But Itha had taken a solemn vow to serve God only, and prevailed upon her husband to build the convent of St. Mary of the Angels, in honor of her rescue from certain death. There she spent the remainder of her life in prayer, and her husband, having given all his wealth to the poor, followed her example, and withdrew into a neighboring monastery to pray for the forgiveness of his sins.

The Faithful Lover.

THE knight of Toggenburg, having fallen in love with a fair lady who could not return his affections, sadly bade her farewell and went to fight in the Holy Land, whence he returned only after many a year. He had not forgotten the lady he loved, however, and hearing she had taken the veil and was now a nun in the convent of St. Mary of the Angels, he disposed of all his wealth, assumed a pilgrim's garb, and, building a little hermitage in the valley, spent his days in penance and prayer. Early every morning he sat in the door of his hut, gazing fixedly up at the convent, and never moving until a certain lattice window flew open and a lovely face looked down into the valley.

Day after day the knight of Toggenburg waited thus, but when many years had gone, and he was old and feeble, he glanced up for the last time, caught a last glimpse of the face of his beloved, and peacefully breathed his last.

Schiller has given us a beautiful poetical version of this legend which has been translated and concludes with these words:

> " 'Till her lovely looks entrancing
> All his sense the while,
> Calm, adown the vale were glancing,
> Sweet as angel's smile.
> And so sate he, there, one morning
> Lifeless—without fail,
> To that lattice loved still turning
> His cold face so pale."
>
> —*Schiller.*

NIDBERG.

The Knight Betrayed.

THE knight of Nidberg, whose castle was perched up on one of the picturesque rocks near Sargans, defended himself so bravely against his enemy that the latter was about ready to give up the attempt to secure him. As the besiegers were preparing to steal silently away, a pale-faced woman suddenly appeared before the leader, and, declaring she hated the knight, offered to show him how he might slay him.

The enemy immediately signified his pleasure at the proposal and silently followed the woman, who led him up a rocky path and brought him to a cliff directly opposite the castle, whence he could look straight down into the room where the weary knight lay fast asleep near the open window.

The woman pointed to the sleeping foe, and motioned to him to shoot. A moment later an arrow whizzed through the air and struck the sleeping knight, who never woke again. But, while his enemy departed in triumph, the pale-faced woman stood there gazing fixedly at the lifeless body, and she was never known to smile again.

PFÄFERS.

The Stolen Sacrament.

THE devil once took up his abode in the narrow ravine whence the hot springs of Pfäfers rise, and lying in wait there, soon saw Anna Vögtli pass by. He knew that she was a witch, and that she delighted in seeking herbs at midnight on the mountain side, so he promised her all manner of luck in her search if she would only steal into the neighboring church and throw away the holy wafer resting on the altar.

The girl, who had long ago given up going to mass, and who had already sold her soul to Satan, immediately obeyed. But, no sooner had she laid her hand upon the sacred host than the ground shook, the lightning played, the thunder rolled, and the mountain echoes began to awaken. Terrified at the sudden commotion, Anna Vögtli threw away the wafer, which fell on a thorn bush, whence sprang a silvery rose, which curled its petals all around it to protect it from all harm.

Some sheep passing by there reverently bent the knee, and a wolf, springing out of the thicket to devour them, lay down like a lamb among them. The people, attracted by these miracles, plucked the silvery rose, and laid it upon the altar of the church of Ettes Wyl, where it can still be seen, and is said to have very blessed and miraculous properties.

ST. GOTTHARD.
Cascade of Wyler.

COIRE.

The Prophecy.

A KNIGHT was once riding through the fields accompanied by his page. All at once he noticed a babe lying alone by the roadside, and charitably bade his attendant pick it up and carry it home. The page stooped to raise the infant, but, in spite of all his efforts, it was too heavy for him to lift.

The knight dismounted to help him, but all his strength could not suffice to raise the child. In vain he called squire and peasant to help him, in vain they strained every muscle, the babe still lay smiling on the grass. All at once the babe opened its mouth and predicted that they would have a very fruitful and prosperous year, and then it vanished.

The babe's prediction was verified, for the grain fields bore a hundredfold, the barns and granaries were full, all the poor had plenty to eat that year, and none knew want.

There are many picturesque and interesting spots along the Rhine below Coire. Many of them are easy of access, for the railroad follows the river for some distance further. Among the many more or less direct tributaries which come down from the mountains to swell the tide of this river, there is the Reuss, which takes its source in the St. Gotthard Mountain and forms a beautiful cascade at Wasen.

Farewell to the Rhine.

ADIEU to thee, fair Rhine! How long delighted
The stranger fain would linger on his way!
Thine is a scene alike where souls united,
Or lonely contemplation thus might stray,
And could the ceaseless vultures cease to prey
On self-condemning bosoms, it were here
Where nature, nor too somber, nor too gay,
Wild, but not rude, awful, yet not austere,
Is to the mellow earth as autumn to the year.

Adieu to thee again! a vain adieu!
There can be no farewell to scene like thine,
The mind is colored by thy every hue;
And, if reluctantly the eyes resign
Their cherished gaze upon thee, lovely Rhine!
'Tis with the thankful glance of parting praise.
More mighty spots may rise—more glaring shine,
But none unite in one attaching maze
The brilliant, fair, and soft—the glory of old days.

The negligently grand, the fruitful bloom
Of coming ripeness, the white city's sheen,
The rolling stream, the precipice's gloom,
The forest's growth, and Gothic walls between,
The wild rocks, shaped as they had turrets been,
In mockery of man's art; and there withal
A race of faces, happy as the scene
Whose fertile bounties here extend to all,
Still springing o'er thy banks, though empires near thee fall.

—*Byron.*

APPENDIX.

NOTE I. The fish-and-ring episode in this legend has many counterparts in the ancient annals of sundry nations. In the Indian drama of Sakuntala the heroine loses her ring on her way to join her husband. As the ring possesses magic powers, he fails to recognize her without it; it is only when the mystic circlet has been found in a fish that the memory of his marriage returns to him. In the Jewish legends, Solomon owes all his power to a magic ring. In punishment for worshiping idols during forty days, the Evil Spirit takes possession of his ring for an equal space of time, assumes his form, and reigns in his stead. The forty days ended, the Evil One is forced to relinquish his power, and casts the ring into the sea of Galilee, where it is immediately swallowed by a fish. Solomon, wandering disconsolate along the beach, begs food of a fisherman, who gives him the fish he has just caught. In its stomach Solomon finds the ring, which enables him to remount the throne.

In ancient history, Polycrates, king of Samos, boasts of his wealth and prosperity to Amasis, king of Egypt. The latter advises him voluntarily to sacrifice his dearest treasure, lest he should incur the wrath of the gods. In compliance with this advice, Polycrates casts his signet ring into the sea. Shortly after, a remarkably fine fish is brought to him as a gift, and in it he finds the magic ring.

There are numerous examples of magic rings not only in ancient literature, where Gyges is mentioned, but also in mediæval literature, where the Nibelungen ring in the great German epic, and the ring of Titania, which Oberon gives to Rezia, in the romance of Huon of Bordeaux, are the most famous specimens.

NOTE 2. The northern people were wont to drink certain toasts in honor of their gods on all solemn occasions. This custom was so popular that the Christian missionaries deemed it wisest not to attempt to suppress it entirely. Instead of drinking to the twelve principal Asas, the people were therefore taught to pledge Christ and his disciples.

Saint Gertrude, or the Virgin, was at the same time substituted for Freya, in whose honor a cup of mead was drained at marriage festivals and all great national feast days.

As for magic potions, they are very common in the folk-lore of all nations. Circe and Gudrun (Kriemhild) both detain their lovers by their means, but while they are generally supposed to induce love, as is seen in the story of Tristan and Isolde, they are also often intended to preserve the drinker from harm, as in this case.

NOTE 3. The dénouement of this story recalls the classic tale of Cleobis and Biton, related at length in the author's "Myths of Greece and Rome," p. 54.

NOTE 4. The story of Lohengrin, which is a part of the great mediæval cycle of the Holy Grail, is also a northern version of the well-known tale of Cupid and Psyche. The myth probably arose from some peculiar marriage custom. Psyche's faith is tested by not being allowed to see her beloved, under penalty of losing him; Elsa's by refraining from asking a momentous question.

The story of Parsifal, which is intimately connected with that of Lohengrin, is given in the author's work on the "Legends of the Middle Ages."

NOTE 5. There are countless variations of this beautiful myth in Northern literature. The oldest now extant is that contained in the heroic poems of the Elder Edda. This version was enlarged in the well-known Volsunga saga, where the principal characters are Sigurd, Gudrun, Grimhild, Gunnar, Högni, and Atli. An outline of this famous saga is given in the author's "Myths of Northern Lands," and it forms the basis of William Morris' epic poem, "Sigurd the Volsung." The Nibelungenlied, the great German epic, is a later version of the same tale, and according to Lachmann is made up from five different cycles of northern myths. The third version is the most popular one, and is given here in full.

NOTE 6. The old northern belief in Liosalfar, or Light Elves is here embodied. These beneficent creatures were supposed to aid mankind. With the introduction of Christianity, these helpful beings were called angels, and the worship previously given to them was transferred to the heavenly host. As in the myth of Lohengrin, any question concerning their origin entailed their departure; and, as their services were voluntary, the mention of a reward was an insult.

NOTE 7. The story of St. Ursula, which has prompted many noted works of art, especially in the Italian and German schools, has been identified by some folk-lorists with that of Diana, the moon maiden. Ursula is supposed to represent the orb of night, while her eleven thousand virgins are emblems of the manifold stars, which seem to follow in her train. This story, however, has given rise to much speculation, and noted writers have declared that Ursula really existed, and that she and eleven virgins were martyred by the Huns at Cologne. They claim that "eleven thousand" is a mistaken reading of an old inscription. For further details concerning this legend, see Mrs. Jameson's "Sacred and Legendary Art."

NOTE 8. The Heinzelmännchen, like the Brownies in Scotland, were supposed to be helpful beings, who continued their ministrations as long as they remained unseen. This is a remains of the old Northern belief in dwarfs and elves. There are countless similar tales told all along the Rhine, for the Heinzelmännchen play a prominent part in German folk-lore.

NOTE 9. The blooming of a withered staff is a feature which often reappears in sacred and mediæval literature. The first instance is, of course, the rod of Aaron, long preserved in the holy ark. In the legends of the Virgin we are told that the high priest was warned in a dream to give Mary in marriage to one of the widowers in Israel. Summoned by the High Priest, the widowers all laid their rods or staffs upon the altar. Joseph's bloomed, and, according to some authorities, a dove came and perched upon it. In paintings depicting the marriage of the Virgin, Joseph is, therefore, always represented with a blooming rod, on which a dove is sometimes perched. In mediæval literature the most noted example of this miracle is related in the story of Tannhäuser, which is given in this volume.

NOTE 10. The way in which Arnold obtained a large grant of land from the emperor is a parallel to the story of St. Lüfthilde. Stratagems in such matters were considered praiseworthy, and are not without their counterparts in more ancient literature. In the Greek myths we find Dido resorting to the stratagem of the oxhide to obtain a grant of land from the Carthaginians. Gefjon also avails herself of a ruse to secure land from Gylfi, the northern king, and Ragnar Lodbrog's sons thus obtain the spot where they founded London.

NOTE 11. Charlemagne's miraculous ride from the far East to Aix-la-Chapelle, in the space of a few hours, has its counterpart in many fairy tales. One of the favorite modes of transportation in mediæval literature was by means of an enchanted steed, and most mediæval heroes have one at their disposal, like Renaud of Montauban.

NOTE 12. The monk of Heisterbach is the German version of the old myth, which, as the Seven Sleepers of Ephesus, Epimenides (the Sleeper of Athens), Brunhild, and the Sleeping Beauty, is always reappearing in literature. It has found one of its latest, and certainly its most beautiful setting at the hands of Washington Irving, in his legend of Rip Van Winkle.

NOTE 13. Roland is the principal hero of the great cycle of Carolingian myths. He is also the most famous warrior in the great French epic, "La Chanson de Roland." A full account of this cycle will be found in the author's "Legends of the Middle Ages." The story of the Drachenfels is merely a later version of the episode of Lady Alda. Ariosto and Boiardo, the Italian poets, have written long and beautiful works about this hero, who is admirably depicted in James Baldwin's "Story of Roland."

NOTE 14. Early in the Middle Ages it was popularly believed that the blood would flow from the wounds of a murdered man at the touch of his assassin. This belief is exemplified in the Nibelungenlied, where Siegfried's body is laid in state in the Worms Cathedral, and the huntsmen are all summoned by Kriemhild to submit to the test. The blood flows at Hagen's touch, and Kriemhild vehemently denounces him. After she has thus discovered his guilt she knows no rest until she has avenged her hushand, although this revenge entails the death of all the Burgundian knights.

The episode related in this legend forms the basis also of Chaucer's charming "Prioress' Tale."

NOTE 15. In the "Heimskringla," or Chronicle of the ancient kings of Norway, where the historical Odin is described, we are told that his soul often left his body in the shape of a mouse. This superstition was a common one in the north. In the tale of the Pied Piper of Hamelin, the mice are the souls of the dead, and the Piper is Odin, the northern Psychopompus. In the tale of the Mäusethurm the rats and mice are also human souls animated by a burning spirit of revenge.

NOTE 16. This is the German version of the myth which reappears in all works on demonology. The Snake Lady is a counterpart of the Greek Lamia, and of the Hebrew Lilith, the first wife of Adam.

NOTE 17. The story here related is told with many variations. There is one version of it in Percy's "Reliques," where King John and the Abbot of Canterbury play the principal parts. The story is, in all other points, the same. The love of riddles is common to all nations, and many early specimens have been preserved. Besides the riddle propounded by the Sphinx to Œdipus, the riddle which Samson asked the Philistines, the one concerning Odin and his steed, there are such as the one on the wind, "What flies forever and rests never?" which are of great antiquity.

INDEX.

A

B

THE END.

www.ingramcontent.com/pod-product-compliance
Lightning Source LLC
Chambersburg PA
CBHW032259280326
41932CB00009B/620